GREAT BLACK MEN OF MASONRY

Joseph Mason Andrew Cox

AN AUTHORS GUILD BACKINPRINT.COM EDITION

Great Black Men of Masonry
All Rights Reserved © 1982, 2002 by Joseph Mason Andrew Cox

No part of this book may be reproduced or transmitted in any form or by any means, graphic, electronic, or mechanical, including photocopying, recording, taping, or by any information storage or retrieval system, without the permission in writing from the publisher.

AN AUTHORS GUILD BACKINPRINT.COM EDITION
Published by iUniverse, Inc.

For information address:
iUniverse, Inc.
5220 S. 16th St., Suite 200
Lincoln, NE 68512
www.iuniverse.com

Originally published by Blue Diamond Press

ISBN: 0-595-22729-5

Printed in the United States of America

This volume is dedicated to
Joseph Mason Andrew Cox
Poet,
Author,
Lecturer,
Television Producer,
Educator,
Psychologist,
Historian
whose resourcefulness, tireless energy
and commitment made this enlarged and
revised edition of GREAT BLACK MEN OF
MASONRY an accomplished fact.

GREAT BLACK MEN OF MASONRY 1723-1987

By
Joseph Mason Andrew Cox, Ph.D.
Historian
Antioch Lodge #66
Under Charter

Most Worshipful Prince Hall Grand Lodge of New York State
and Member of
The Prince Hall Grand Lodge Historical Committee
of New York State

Dedicated to
Great Black Brothers Who Illuminated Freemasonry

John Pine
Distinguished Engraver of The Globe Travner Lodge
of Mooregate, England—1723

Samuel Fraunces
Chief White House Steward to President George Washington
and Patriot Member of the Holland Lodge Number Eight
of New York City—1762

Prince Hall
Founder and Worshipful Master of the African Lodge #459,
Boston, Massachusetts
Worshipful Grand Master of
the African Masonic Lodges—1775

Pinckney Benton Stewart Pinchback
United States Senator of Louisiana
Governor of the State of Louisiana (1872–1873)
Member of Berry Lodge Number 2, New Orleans, Louisiana

Fred D. Patterson
Manufacturer of the Patterson-Greenfield Automobile
Worshipful Master of Cedar Lodge #17, Greenfield, Ohio

Leon M'Ba
First President of the Republic of Gabon
Premier of the Republic of Gabon
Master Mason Lodge Loyaute-Fidelite, Paris, France

Thurgood Marshall, 33°
Associate Justice of the United States Supreme Court
Member of Coal Creek Lodge #88, Under the Jurisdiction
of the Prince Hall Grand Lodge of the State of New York

Alexander Pushkin
(1799–1837)
Poet, Novelist, Playwright
Member of the Czarist Russian Grand Masonic Lodge

Alexander Dumas
Writer, Dramatist, Novelist
Member, Grand Masonic Grand Lodge of France

Egbert Austin Bert Williams
(Bert Williams)
Actor and Comedian
Member of Waverly Lodge #597, of Scotland
and the Grand Lodge of Scotland

Albert Bernard Bongo
President, the Republic of Gabon
Past Master Under the Grand Orient of France
Member of the Masonic Lodge #209, at Libreville
(Le Dialogue #209)

James Herbert Blake
(Eubie Blake)
Composer, Musician, Producer
Member, Medina Lodge #19, Prince Hall
Free and Accepted Masons

Anthony Williams Amo, Ph.D.
Scholar and Lecturer, University of Wittenberg
Hebrew, Greek, Latin, German, French, Dutch
Counsellor of State by Court of Berlin, Germany
Member of the Masonic Grand Lodge of Germany

Errol Walton Barrow
Barrister
Minister of External Affairs of Barbados
Prime Minister of Barbados
Thirty-Third Degree, Ancient and Accepted Scottish Rite
of Freemasonry, Prince Hall Affiliation,
Northern Jurisdiction, United States of America

Jack Arthur Johnson
World Heavyweight Boxing Champion
Waverly Masonic Lodge #597, Glasgow, Scotland
and the Grand Lodge of Scotland

William R. Tolbert, Jr.
Past Worshipful Grand Master of
the Prince Hall Grand Lodge of Liberia
Former President of the Republic of Liberia
Former Chairman of the Organization of African Unity

Joseph A. Walkes, Jr.
Editor, Author, Writer, Masonic Leader
President of the Phylaxis Society
The Society of Prince Hall Masons Who Seek Light
and Have Light to Confer
Reporter, United Supreme Council,
Northern and Southern Jurisdiction,
Thirty-Third Degree, Ancient and Accepted Scottish Rite
of Freemasonry, Prince Hall Affiliation,
United States of America

John H. Johnson
Publisher
Quality Trade Books
and
Ebony, Jet, Ebony, Jr.
and Associate Editor,
The Bulletin, Official Organ, the United Supreme Council,
Ancient and Accepted Scottish Rite of Freemasonry,
Prince Hall Affiliation, Northern Jurisdiction,
United States of America, Inc.

Francois (Papa Doc) Duvalier
Physician and Surgeon
(M.D. and Ph.D.)
President of the Republic of Haiti, Minister of Health
Masonic Membership, Grand Lodge of France

Martin Robinson Delany
(1812–1885)
Medical Doctor, Author, Editor, Major, United States Army
Man of Letters
Lieutenant Governor of South Carolina
Masonic Scholar, Lecturer and Leader

Lynden Oscar Pindling
Barrister
Prime Minister of the Commonwealth of the Bahamas
Thirty-Third Degree, Ancient and Accepted Scottish Rite
of Freemasonry, Prince Hall Affiliation,
Northern Jurisdiction, United States of America

Joseph Jenkins Roberts
(1809–1876)
First President of the Republic of Liberia
Father of Prince Hall Freemasonry in the Republic of Liberia
Second Grand Master of Liberia's Prince Hall Freemasonry
(1869–1872)

Harry A. Williamson
Author, Lecturer, Researcher, Historian
Founder of the Harry A. Williamson Collection on Black
Masonry at the Schomburg Library of Black History and
Culture, New York Public Library
Grand Historian and Deputy Grand Master of the
Most Worshipful Prince Hall Grand Lodge of New York State

Linden Forbes Sampson Burnham
President, The Cooperative Republic of Guyana
Former Prime Minister of Independent Guyana
Member, English Mechanics Lodge of Freemasonry of
Guyana
President, Scholar, Lawyer
Former Premier of British Guyana
President of Guyana Bar Association

Hope Stevens
Lawyer
Senior Law Partner—Stevens, Hinds, Jackson & White
President, United Mutual Life Insurance Company (1956–1960)
Former Chairman, Board of Directors, The Carver Federal Savings and Loan Association
Co-Founder, Allied Federal Savings and Loan Association
Former President, The Uptown Chamber of Commerce of New York City
(Presently, The General Counsel)
Founding Member, The World Association of Lawyers
Member, Allied Lodge #1170, New York State Free and Accepted Masons
Alpha Lodge #116, Free and Accepted Masons, New Jersey

Samuel Wilcox Clark
(1846–1903)
Most Worshipful Grandmaster of The Prince Hall Grand Lodge of Ohio and Jurisdiction
(1879–1902)
Author, Lecturer, Scholar
Author: *Negro Mason in Equity*

W. E. B. DuBois
(1868–1963)
Educator, Professor, Poet, Writer, Editor, Leader, Lecturer
Harvard University, Ph.D.
University of Berlin, Post-Doctoral Studies
Professor of Latin and Greek at Wilberforce University in Ohio
Made a Prince Hall Freemason on sight by the Most Worshipful Grandmaster
Founder of The Council on African Affairs
Founder of The Pan African Congress
A Founder of the National Association for the Advancement of Colored People and served as a member of the Board of Directors

Founder and Editor-in-Chief, *The Crisis* Magazine, Official Organ
Director of Research of the N.A.A.C.P.
Spingarn Medalist, N.A.A.C.P.
Editor-in-Chief, *Encyclopedia Africana*
Headquarters: Accra, Ghana
Thirty-Third Degree, Ancient and Accepted Scottish Rite of Freemasonry, Prince Hall Affiliation, Southern Jurisdiction, United States of America
Documentation: The Schomburg Library, Williamson Masonic Collection

Benjamin Hooks
Lawyer, Judge, Minister, Federal Commissioner
Most Worshipful Grand Secretary of the Most Worshipful Prince Hall Grand Lodge of Tennessee and Jurisdiction
Former Commissioner, the Federal Communication Commission
Executive Director, the National Association for the Advancement of Colored People

Edward Kennedy Ellington
(1899–1974)
Duke Ellington
Musician, Composer, Orchestra Conductor
Thirty-Second Degree, Ancient and Accepted Scottish Rite of Freemasonry, Prince Hall Affiliation, Southern Jurisdiction, Acatia Grand Lodge, Washington, District of Columbia, United States of America
Duke's Autobiography: *Music is My Mistress*
Honors: Emperor's Star, Government of Ethiopia; Legion of Honor, Government of France; Gold Medal, President Johnson, United States
Duke Ellington Center at St. Peter's Lutheran Church in New York City
Documentation: *A Portrait of Duke Ellington,* by Jewell, Norton Publishers

Paul Robeson
Actor, Singer, Lawyer, Editor, Writer, Freemason
Education: Rutgers University, B.A., Phi Beta Kappa
Columbia University Law School, LL.B., Order of Coit
Member of the Bar of New York State
Sixteen letter man at Rutgers University—Walter Kemp All-American Football Selection
Editor of *Freedom,* weekly newspaper
Made a Prince Hall Freemason by the Most Worshipful Grandmaster of the Prince Hall Grand Lodge
Springarn Medalist, N.A.A.C.P.

Richard (Dick) Gidron
Member, Boyer Lodge, Number One, Prince Hall Affiliation
President, Richard Gidron Cadillac Dealership, Bronx, New York
President, Gun Hill Real Estate Venture Corporation
President, Bronx Chamber of Commerce

Arthur A. Schomburg
Educator, Librarian, Scholar, Masonic Official, Researcher, Book Collector
Grand Secretary of the Prince Hall Grand Lodge of the State of New York and Jurisdictions
Librarian at Fisk University and Creator of the Schomburg Collection
Author of Masonic Historical Works
The Schomburg Library of Black History and Culture is named as a monument in his memory and honor

Thomas Bradley
Lawyer
Mayor, the City of Los Angeles, California.
Democratic candidate for the Governor of the State of California.
Thirty-third Degree, Ancient and Accepted Scottish Rite of Freemasonry, Prince Hall Affiliation, Southern Jurisdiction, United States of America.

Robert Brown Elliot
United States Congressman from South Carolina
Speaker U.S. House of Representatives
(1875–1876)
Second Grandmaster of Prince Hall Freemasons
of South Carolina.

Benjamin E. Mays, Ph.D.
Educator
President, Morehouse College, Atlanta, Georgia. (Retired)
President, The Board of Education of Atlanta, Georgia. (Retired)
Thirty-Third Degree, Ancient and Accepted Scottish Rite
of Freemasonry, Prince Hall Affiliation, Southern Jurisdiction,
United States of America.
Awarded the sixty-seventh (67) Spingarn Medal (N.A.A.C.P.) at
the National Convention in Boston, Massachusetts (July 1982).

John Peterson
Educator, Minister, Masonic Leader.
The first black schoolmaster in New York City, New York,
and was assigned to the Public School for Colored Children,
Number One, located on Mulberry Street.
Member of Goyer Lodge, Number One.
Grand Chaplain, Grand Lodge, State of New York (1855-58).
Grand Secretary, Grand Lodge, State of New York (1859).
Grand Treasurer, Grand Lodge, State of New York (1860–1869).

Harold Washington
Mayor
Former U.S. Congressman of Chicago
Member of Harmony Lodge #88, Chicago, Illinois
Ancient Accepted Scottish Rite, Western Consistory #28
Shrine, Arabic Temple #44

The extensive list of dedication biographical sketches represent some of the numerous Great Black Men of Freemasonry who have increased light, enlarged minds, and enriched lives worldwide. Their unshakable monument of illumination is additional evidence of man's remarkable mind, unshakable spirit and immortal soul, focusing and ennobling in uninterrupted succession from here and now to tomorrow and eternity.

Brothers and Friends:

It is with immense pride and profound respect that I welcome *Great Black Men of Masonry—Qualitative Black Achievers Who Were Freemasons*. This inspirational series of worldwide biographical sketches date from the Fifteenth Century to the present. The book documents that the history of black people, and their leadership is interwoven with the history of Freemasonry.

On these pages we meet Presidents of Nations, Builders of States, Discoverers and Inventors, Leaders in Governments, Arts, Sciences and Letters. Men of sterling qualities and ennobling leadership, in war, crisis and peace. This book offers a key to racial understanding and harmony.

Dr. and Brother Joseph Mason Andrew Cox has written a monumental book, seemingly to create greater awareness of Great Black Men of Masonry—Qualitative Black Achievers Who Were Freemasons who transmitted, unimpaired, a priceless heritage to America and the World.

>Most sincerely,
>
>Eli J. Allen, III, 33°
>Grand Master
>
>ATTEST
>
>Harry Stevens, Jr.
>Grand Secretary

QUALITATIVE BLACK ACHIEVERS WHO WERE FREEMASONS: GREAT BLACK MEN OF MASONRY

By Joseph Mason Andrew Cox, MPS (N.Y.)

GREAT BLACK MEN OF MASONRY is a series of biographical sketches of an endless procession of great black men who were freemasons and doesn't treat or deal with masonic secrets. Here we bear witness to great men and their contributions, down through the ages, that have, and continue to enrich humankind immeasureably, in terms of relieving human suffering, the struggle to make the nation's constitutional concepts a reality, and the creation and preservation of the nation, and assisting the nation in advancing its worldwide freedom proclamation.

The history of great black men of masonry, provides fundamental emphasis for the declaration that history deals not only with dead past, but also directly and indirectly with the life-giving spirit of the present, and the promise of the future. Let light be focused on the most luminous achievement of black reconstruction, to see and witness the advent of free public education for poor white people, as well as poor black people.

History is made by great men. Therefore, it is necessary that we know of and about the great men who have, and are making history. In the study of the past, we seek to know the motives, that have inspired great men who have made history, and who are continuing the history-making process. Authorities have repeatedly proclaimed that the history of black people, is closely related to the history of freemasonry. Perhaps, these biographies will cause future historians, poets, writers and playwrights to appreciate what has been accomplished. Hereafter, future generations will have a fair basis for the evaluation of our times. The major concern of mankind in history, in general is related to the degree that it exhibits a steady gain in right and truth. Truth and right, even an infinitesimal amount will begin freedom's procession. ·

Freemasonry, the most worthy brotherhood of humanity; its sacred purpose exudes with the sublime spirit of inner freedom, truth and spiritual realism, and depicts the most exalted hope of mankind. Yet, too long the names, the roles, and the biographies, of "Great Black Men of Masonry" were known to relatively few masons, and comparatively fewer nonmasons. Therefore, this book is a concerted attempt to illuminate the magnificent contributions of black brethren for the world to see, know, understand and evaluate. This is another exemplary-role-model for youth, regardless of race, creed or color, or national origin.

Freemasonry, for "The Most Worshipful, Prince Hall, Grandmaster," was synonymous with human service. And he was a loud, and clear voice for social change. Prince Hall saw the need to save America, and tried to awaken the Nation's conscience, when it was denerved by unspoken things. Therefore, let's share the sense of partial fulfillment, and arresting gratitude, for the permanent footprints, "Great Black Men of Masonry," have left solidified in marble, during our transfigured night.

"Great Black Men of Masonry," through words and deeds, have prevailed under Herculean difficulties, to illustrate graphically that the history of America, and the history of black men in America, was made in a large measure by Freemasons, who were also black men. Case after case is cited to support and sustain this point of contention. Black Freemasons were leaders and key figures in helping runaway slaves through the underground railroad, and also in avoiding the effects of the Fugitive Slave Act. Black Freemasons have been active historically in aiding cities and towns during epidemics, and also in furnishing the leadership for preventing race riots and lynchings, and in racist court hearings and proceedings. Black masons have joined and supported others in the struggle for racial equality, equal opportunities and universal freedom.

We must never forget, as Pauline E. Hopkins wrote: "In Puritan Massachusetts, a traffic in human beings was carried on far over a century. Thousands were sold; and the profits accruing from the sale of black slaves, in all parts of the country, laid the foundation of the wealth of many old Massachusett's families." Nevertheless, I must quote Brother W. E. B. DuBois, "Throughout history the powers of single black men flash, here and there, like a falling star, and die, sometimes before the world has rightly gauged their brilliance."

Let this volume stand on its merits as a memorial for objective criticism and future evaluation. What other group of men have accomplished as much, considering the circumstances? The record documents that for more than two hundred years, black masons have produced men of leadership, vision and moral fibre, men of knowledge, men of leadership and skill in science, arts and letters. Men who fought against human slavery, of both body, mind, and spirit. Men determined to secure liberty, regardless of cost. And if, and when, the cost was life itself, the cost was willingly paid. Now, before letting the record speak for itself, the question remains . . . what yardstick must be used to measure the accomplishments of "Great Black Men of Masonry?"

However, I must agree with the late Dr. Martin Luther King, Jr., when he said, "I refuse to accept the view that Mankind is so tragically bound to the starless night of racism and war, that the bright light of peace and brotherhood can never become a reality."

PRINCE HALL'S LETTER

"Brother Prince Hall, Master of African Lodge, working under dispensation by authority of the Most Worshipful Grand Lodge Free and Accepted Masons of England, wrote the following letter, June 30th, 1784:

"William M. Moody, Most W. Master"

"Permit me to return you my hearty thanks for your brotherly courtesy to my Brothers Reed and Mene, when in a strange land and in a time of need, you were so good to receive them as brothers, and to treat them so cordially as they informed me you did. What you have done to them I look upon as done to me and the whole of us, for which I give you many thanks and likewise to all the lodges. I hope they behave themselves as men and as Masons with you; if not I would beglad if you would be so good as to let me know of it and they shall be dealt with accordingly. Dear Brother I would inform you that this Lodge hath been founded almost this Eight years and had no Warrant yet, but only a permit from Grand Master Row to work on St. John's Days and bury our dead in form, which we would enjoy. We have had no opportunity until now of applying for a warrant though we were pressed upon to send to France for one, but we refused for reasons best known to ourselves. We now apply to the Fountain from whom we received light for this favor, and Dear Sir I must beg of you to be our advocate for us by sending this our request to his Royal Highness, the Duke of Cumberland, Grand Master, and to the Right Honorable Earl of Effingham, acting Grand Master, the Deputy Grand Master and Grand Wardens, and the rest of the Brethren of the Grand Lodge that they would graciously be pleased to grant us a Charter to hold this Lodge as long as we behave up to the spirit of the Constitution.

"This, our humble petition, we hope His Highness and the rest of the Grand Lodge will graciously be pleased to grant us there.

"Though poor, yet, sincere brethren of the craft, and therefor in duty bound, ever to pray. I beg leave to subscribe myself.

"Your loving Friend and Brother,
"Prince Hall,
"Master of the African Lodge No. 1.

"June 30th, 1784; in the year of Masonry 5784
In the name of the Holy Lodge.

C. Underwood, Secretary.

ORIGINAL CHARTER GRANTED BY THE GRAND LODGE OF ENGLAND
(Modern) in the Year of 1784
"Warrant of AFRICAN LODGE No. 459"
WARRANT OF CONSTITUTION: A.G.F.

To All and Every:
Our right worshipful and loving brethren:—We, Thomas Howard, Earl of Effingham Lord Howard; etc.; Acting Grand Master, under the authority of his Royal Highnes, Henry Frederick, Duke of Cumberland, etc.; Grand Master of the Most Ancient and Honorable Society of Free and Accepted Masons, send greeting:
Know ye that we at the humble petition of our Right Trusty and well beloved brethren, Prince Hall, Boston Smith; Thomas Sanderson, and several other brethren residing in Boston, New England, and North America do hereby constitute the said brethren into a regular Lodge of Free and Accepted Masons, under the title or denomination for the African Lodge, to be opened in Boston, aforesaid; and do further; as their said petition and of the great trust and confidence reposed in every one of the said above named brethren hereby appoint the said Prince Hall to be Master; Boston Smith, Senior Warden; and Thomas Sanderson' Junior Warden for the opening of said Lodge, and for such further time only as shall be thought by the brethren thereof, it being our will that this our appointment of the above officers, shall in no wise effect any further election of officers of said Lodge, but that such election shall be regulated, agreeable to such By-Laws of the said Lodge, but that such election shall be regulated, agreeable to such By-Laws of the said Lodge as shall be consistent with the Grand Laws of the Society, contained in the Book of Constitutions; and we hereby will' and require of you, the said Prince Hall; to take special care that all and every, the said brethren are to have been regularly made Masons and that they do observe, perform, and keep all the rules and orders contained in the Book of Constitutions; and, further, that you do from time to time cause to be entered in a book kept for that purpose, an account of your proceedings in the Lodge, together with all such Rules, Orders and Regulations as shall be made for the good government of the same that in no wise you omit once

in every year to send to us for our predecessors, Grand Masters' or Royland Holt, Esq., our Deputy Grand Master for the time being an account of your said proceedings and copies of all such Rules Orders and Regulations as shall be made as aforesaid, together with the list of the members of the Lodge, and such sum of money as may suit the circumstances of the Lodge and reasonably be expected toward the Grand Charity.

Moreover, we will, and require of you; the said Prince Hall, as soon as conveniently may be, to send an account in writing of what may be done by virtue of these presents.

Given at London under our hand and seal of Masonry, (SEAL) this 29th day of September A.L. 5784, A.D. 1784; by the Grand Master's command.

R. HOLT, Deputy Grand Master

Attes:—WILLIAM WHITE, Grand Secretary.

ROBERT SENGSTACKLE ABBOTT
Publisher

ROBERT SENGSTACKLE ABBOTT, Publisher and Founder of The Chicago Defender. (1870-1940) Born at Saint Simon Island, Georgia.

Education
Beach Institute, Savannah, Georgia.
Claflin College, Orangeburg, South Carolina.
Hampton Institute, Hampton, Virginia.
Kent Law School, Chicago, Illinois.

On May 5, 1905, Abbott started "The Chicago Defender" with three hundred copies of a four page handbill-size newspaper. And selling this newspaper from door to door. The circulation grew and grew until The Chicago Defender reached more than a quarter of a million according to the Audit Bureau of Circulation.

Robert Sengstackle Abbott was a crusader for economic, political and social justice.

Member of the Prince Hall Grand Lodge of Illinois. Thirty-third degree, of the Ancient and Accepted Scottish Rite of Freemasonry, for the Northern Jurisdiction, Prince Hall affiliation, of the United States of America.

Masonic Documentation: Harry A. Williamson Collection on Black Masonry The Schomburg Center of Black History and Culture.

RALPH DAVID ABERNATHY
Minister and Civil Rights Leader

Thirty-Third Degree, Ancient and Accepted Scottish Rite of Freemasonry, Prince Hall Affiliation, Southern Jurisdiction of the United States of America.

Reverend Abernathy, Minister and Civil Rights Leader, was born in Linden, Alabama on March 11, 1926, and after graduating from Linden Academy, he served in the U.S. Army during World War Two.

Education
Alabama College. B.A.
Atlanta University. M.A. 1951.

Reverend Abernathy was a close friend of Dr. Martin Luther King, Jr., and also closely associated with the "Movement for Social Change," in Montgomery. He was appointed Minister of The First Baptist Church of Montgomery, and became an Officer of the Southern Christian Leadership Conference, and after the assassination of Dr. King, Rev. Abernathy was elected President of the conscious awakening organization. The conference took on new militancy without abandoning the philosophy of non-violence, to which Dr. King, had dedicated it.

In 1968, Rev. Abernathy led the "Poor People's March on Washington," from Nationwide departure points. The underlying philosophy being, "You can kill the dreamer, but you can't kill the dream."

Masonic documentation: Southern Masonic Jurisdiction Report.

DAVID ABNER, JR
Editor—Lecturer—College Professor
District Master of the Masonic Order
of the State of Texas.

DAVID ABNER, JR., was born November 25, 1860, in Upshur County Texas. His parents sought early to give him a good education.

Wiley University—Marshall, Texas.
Straight University—New Orleans, Louisiana.
Fisk University—Nashville, Tennessee

David not only stood high in all of the branches of discipline, but he exerted a noble influence on all the schools and universities that he attended and graduated from.

The Baptist State Convention of Texas, representing a membership of seventy-thousand in 1884, chose David Abner, Jr., as Corresponding Secretary.

As District Master of the Masonic Order, David spoke with both command and ease, and he seldom, if ever left an assembly unmoved. He accepted nothing without thought, and with positive thinking, he succeeded in the most difficult undertakings.

He was both contributor and editor of some of the leading newspapers in the State of Texas. During the Summers, he traveled delivering speeches and lecturers.

Masonic Documentation: Harry A. Williamson Collection on Black Masonry.

FLOYD ADAMS, JR.
Editor/General Manager
First District Alderman
City of Savannah

FLOYD ADAMS, JR., editor/general manager of the Savannah Herald Newspaper, was born May 11, 1945, at Savannah, Georgia.

Education
Public Schools of Savannah
Armstrong State College

Serves on the Board of Directors of the Savannah NAACP, Mutual Benevolence Society, and Rape Crisis.

Vice Chairman, Private Industry Council.

Member, National Newspaper Publishers Association.

Thirty-Second Degree member, Pythagoras Lodge #11, Ezra Consistory #27 AASR, Omar Temple #21.

Documentation: Georgia Masonic Research Center.

◊ ◊ ◊

CARNOT ADRIEN
Attorney and Certified Public Accountant
Grand Master of the Grand Orient of the Republic of Haiti

Positions
Counsel and Legal Advisor to The President of Haiti
President of the Accountants Association of Haiti
Professor of Law, the University of Haiti
Professor of Accounting, the University of Haiti

Documentation: Personal interview at the Grand Orient of the Republic of Haiti.

◊ ◊ ◊

IRA ALDRIDGE
(1805–1867)
Actor
Member of the Masonic Grand Lodge of Scotland

IRA ALDRIDGE, born in Bel-Air, Maryland, in the year 1805.

Education
African Free School, in New York, N.Y.
Schenectady College, in Schenectady, N.Y.
University of Glasgow, Glasgow, Scotland.
(Academic Honors)

Ira Aldridge discovered his acting potential while in college, but realizing there was little or no opportunity for him in the United States, at the time. Therefore, he went to Scotland and continued his education.

In the year, 1833, Actor Aldridge became the toast of the European Continent with his Shakespearian roles. He successfully appeared as Othello, at Covent Garden, in London, England. He also played the same role in Ireland, along with the lead in "Macbeth," "King Lear", and "Shylock", as well. The first medal of arts and science was awarded to Actor Aldridge, by the King of Prussia.

Today, at Stratford-on-Avon, an Ira Aldridge Chair is designated for him in the Shakespearan Memorial Theater. Nevertheless, Actor Ira Aldridge died in Lodz, Poland, in 1867, without having performed on the American Stage, as an actor, although he had received the highest awards that Europe could bestow.

Masonic Documentation: Philatelic Freemasons.

**BOOKER T. ALEXANDER, 33°, Active
Grand Commander
United Supreme Council, AASR, N.J.
M. W. Grand Master
M. W. Prince Hall Grand Lodge of Michigan
1963–1965
14th Imperial Potentate, AEANOMS
1955–1962
Imperial Recorder, AEANOMS**

BOOKER T. ALEXANDER was born November 25, 1904, in Cairo, Illinois, and reared in Champaign, Illinois.

Education
Attended Detroit College (now Wayne State University), and is a member of Phi Beta Sigma fraternity.
Honorary Fellow: The Phylaxis Society.

He has worked for Ford Motor Company, dabbled in real estate, and owned a laundry and dry cleaning shop. Past Grand Master Alexander was the first director of the Imperial Council's Talent and Scholarship Pageant.

1983 Recipient: Jno G. Lewis FPS, Medal of Excellence.

Masonic membership: Hiram Lodge #1, F. & A. M., Detroit Chapter #1, RAM, Eureka Commandery #1, KT, Wolverine Consistory #6, AASR, Marracci Temple #13, AEANOMS.

Masonic Documentation: Georgia Masonic Research Center.

LINCOLN M. ALEXANDER
Queen's Counsel
And
Member of Parliment
And
Shriner and Thirty-Third Degree
Ancient and Accepted Scottish Rite of Freemasonry
Prince Hall Affiliate, Dominion of Canada.

LINCOLN M. ALEXANDER, was born in Toronto, Ontario, Canada, on January 21, 1922.

Education
McMaster University—1949.
Osgood Hall Law School—1953.

Attorney Alexander was elected to the House of Commons, in 1968, and re-elected in 1972 as a Member of Parliament for Hamilton, West.

Masonic Documentation: "Masonic News Quarterly."

◊ ◊ ◊

RAYMOND PACE ALEXANDER
Judge
Judge of the Common Pleas Court of the State of Pennsylvania
and
Distinguished Constitutional Attorney
Alexander and Alexander Law Firm

Thirty-Third Degree, Ancient and Accepted Scottish Rite of Freemasonry, Northern Jurisdiction, Prince Hall Affiliation, U.S.A.

Documentation: The United Supreme Council, Northern Jurisdiction, Prince Hall Affiliation, U.S.A., Philadelphia, Penn.

ELI J. ALLEN
Most Worshipful Grandmaster of the Prince Hall Grand Lodge of New York State
Charter Member of Nimrod Lodge #96
The First Junior Warden of Nimrod Lodge #96

Grandmaster is employed as a Solid State Electronics Technician by International Business Machine.

Masonic Documentation: Victor O. Morris, Prince Hall of New York State.

◊ ◊ ◊

FRANK G. ALLEN
Grand Chancellor

United Supreme Council, Thirty-Third Degree, Ancient and Accepted Scottish Rite of Freemasonry, Southern Jurisdiction, Prince Hall Affiliation, United States of America.

And

Thirty-Third Degree, Ancient and Accepted Scottish Rite of Freemasonry, Southern Jurisdiction, Prince Hall Affiliation, United States of America.

◊ ◊ ◊

JOHNNY ALLEN
Most Worshipful Prince Hall Grand Master of The State of Washington, and Jurisdiction

Thirty-Third Degree, Ancient and Accepted Scottish Rite of Freemasonry, Northern Jurisdiction, Prince Hall Affiliations, United States of America.

Documentation: The United Supreme Council, Northern Jurisdiction, Prince Hall Affiliation, United States of America, Inc.

◊ ◊ ◊

RICHARD ALLEN
Minister—Religious Leader
Prince Hall Masonic Leader.
African Lodge #459—Philadelphia, Pa.

RICHARD ALLEN, Minister and Founder of The African Methodist Church in America His church the "Mother Bethel African Methodist Episcopal Church" in Philadelphia, Pennsylvania. He was born a slave in Philadelphia, in 1760. His master was a Quacker lawyer named Benjamin Chew, Chief Justice of Pennsylvania during the American Revolution. Slavemaster Chew sold Allen, his Mother and Father to Slaveowner Stokly, in Dover, Delaware. In his youth Allen converted to Methodism and began attending class meetings in the forest.

Later, while praying on his knees, Richard Allen was dragged from his knees and treated worse than an escaped slave. Then came the dawn of a radical vision to seek and find a free church and African organization, which he organized and named the "Free African Society," with assistance from his friend and associate Absalom Jones.

Benjamin Franklin and Benjamin Rush encouraged Allen to work on the problems arising from black people being barred from the white church. Nevertheless, it was one thing to erect an African Church, but another to agree upon what separate doctrine it should be founded upon. This was resolved through numerous conferences.

Bethel African Methodist Episcopal Church, was much more than a House of Worship, it was a school and a community meeting place. It became to be known as "The Society of Free People of Color For Promoting the Instructions and School Education of Children and Adults of African Descent."

Masonic Documentation: Harry A. Williamson Collection on Black Masonry.

◊ ◊ ◊

THOMAS G. ALLEN
Pastor
Certificate of Merit, United Supreme Council, Ancient and Accepted Scottish Rite Consistory—Thirty-Second Degree
Prince Hall Affiliate

THOMAS G. ALLEN, was born in Pine Bluff, Arkansas, on July 28, 1945.

Education
Shorter Junior College. Associate Degree 1971.
Philander Smith College. B.A. 1973
Jackson Theological Seminary. B.D. 1976.

Positions
Former Field Secretary, Student Non-violent Coordinating Committee.
Vice-President, Jackson County Association of Ministers.

Certificate of Merit Award—United Supreme Council—Scottish Rites—Thirty-second degree—Prince Hall Affiliation.

Masonic Documentation: Masonic News Quarterly—Prince Hall Freemasons Southern Jurisdiction.

◇ ◇ ◇

WILLIAM ALLEN, JR.
Medical Doctor and Radiologist

DR. ALLEN is the first black radiologist in the world to receive a Gold Medal from the American College of Radiology, and he has been recommended to receive the Scottish Rite Medal.

Thirty-Third Degree, Ancient and Accepted Scottish Rite of Freemasonry, Southern Jurisdiction, Prince Hall Affiliation, the United States of America.

Member, The Square Deal Lodge of Saint Louis Missouri.
Chairman, of the Prince Hall Grand Lodge Library Committee of Missouri.
Grand Medical Examiner of Missouri.

Masonic Documentation: Masonic News Quarterly—Southern Jurisdiction.

◇ ◇ ◇

ANTHONY WILLIAM AMO
Doctorate from the University of Witteberg
Philosophical Lecturer
Scholar in Latin, Greek, Hebrew, German, French, Dutch.
Member of the German Masonic Grand Lodge
Counsellor of State by the Court of Berlin.

ANTHONY WILLIAM AMO, was born in Guinea, West Africa, and brought to Europe, when very young, and thereafter the Princess of Brunswick, took charge of his education.

Amo, pursued his studies at Halle, in Saxony, and at Wittenberg University, and distinguished himself with and by his talents, and good conduct. The Rector and the Council of the University, gave him a public testimony, and a letter of congratulations. This being a reward for having mastered Latin, Greek, Hebrew, German, French and Dutch. Also for being well versed in Astronomy.

He was a member of the "German Masonic Grand Lodge." During this historical period, the University of Wittenberg, and Germany in general, considered skin-color-prejudice absurb.

This is the essence of, "A Tribute For The Negro," published in 1848, by Armistead.

Lodge Documentation: Mille Volti Di Massoni di Giordano Gamberini—Roma—1975.

◊ ◊ ◊

CHARLES W. ANDERSON, JR.
(1907–1960)
Representative of Kentucky General Legislature
and
Alternate Delegate to the United Nations General Assembly.

CHARLES W. ANDERSON, was born in Louisville, Kentucky in 1907.

Education
Kentucky State College.
Wilberforce University.
Howard University Law School.

After being admitted to practice law, Attorney Anderson opened his law office in Louisville, Kentucky. Thereafter, he entered politics, and was elected to the Kentucky House of Representatives, term after term, until he had served six terms.

Anderson's outstanding legislation included laws to admit blacks to white Universities, and to increase facilities for rural black schools. He also obtained a repeal of the public hanging law of Kentucky.

He was the first black, Assistant Commonwealth Attorney for the State of Kentucky.

President Dwight D. Eisenhower appointed Attorney Anderson to the post of Alternate Delegate to the United Nations General Assembly.

Masonic Documentation: Masonic News Quarterly—Prince Hall Masons.

◊ ◊ ◊

JOHN C. ANDERSON, JR.
Probation Officer (Ret.)

Education
B.A., University of Toledo (Ohio)
LL.B., Golden State Law School (California)
Ph.D., University of California
Post-Doctoral Study, University of California
Positions
Senior Probation Officer,
Alameda County Department of Probation
Past President, Beth Eden Housing, Inc.

Member of Monarch Lodge #73, Prince Hall Masons.

Documentation: Who's Who Among Black Americans, 1980–81.

JAMES F. ANDREWS
Educator

Positions
Principal, Plain View Elementary School, North Carolina
President, Bladen County Teachers Association
Secretary, Kappa Rho Chapter of Omega Psi Phi Fraternity
Member, The Young Democrats of North Carolina

Member of Lodge #374, Prince Hall Masons (F. & A.M.).

Documentation: Who's Who Among Black Americans, 1977-78.

◊ ◊ ◊

C.C. ANTOINE
State Senator
And
Lieutenant Governor of the State of Louisiana.

Louisiana's Lieutenant Governor, C.C. Antonie, was a great black man, who attributed his greatness to his Grandmother, the Daughter of an African Chief. It was from her that he inherited intellect, industry and discretion.

And from his Father, a valiant soldier in the battles about New Orleans, in 1812, he attributed his upright character and fearless advocacy of human rights. This made him a leader of the people.

When the Louisiana Constitutional Convention was called, Antoine was an elected delegate, and was elected State Senator by the Convention. He served with distinction until 1872, when the State Nominating Convention was held in Baton Rouge, Louisiana, in August, and Senator C.C. Antoine, was Nominated unaminously for Lieutenant Governor, a position he filled with credit to the people, and satisfaction to his political party.

C.C. Antoine's private and public life was exceptional and above reproach. So great was the enthusiasm manifested by his nomination that he was carried bodily to the rostrum. Whereas in his usual unaffected manners he delivered a profound and spellbinding address.

Masonic Documentation: Masonic News Quarterly—Prince Hall Freemasons. Williamson Collection on Black Freemasonry.

◊ ◊ ◊

BENJAMIN WILLIAM ARNETT
(1838–1906)
Bishop

Positions
Bishop of The African Methodist Episcopal Church
Representative of the Ohio State Legislature (1886)
(Assisted in drafting a bill to abolish the black laws)
Trustee of Wilberforce University (Ohio)
Secretary of The Bishops Council, A.M.E.
Director, Payne Theological Seminary, Wilberforce, Ohio

Masonic: Corinthian Lodge of Free and Accepted Masons of Cincinnati, Ohio. Grand Orator of the Ohio Grand Lodge, 1879.

Documentation: New York State Grand Lodge (F. & A.M.) Library and Museum.

◊ ◊ ◊

CARL VERNON ARTHUR, SR.

Past Grand Master of the Most Worshipful Grand Lodge of the State of New Jersey and Jurisdictions.

Past Master of Sanford Lodge #26, of Vineland, New Jersey.

Grand Lodge Trustee of the Most Worshipful Prince Hall Grand Lodge of New Jersey and Jurisdictions.

The "Carl Vernon Arthur, Sr.," building located in the City of Vineland, is the only public building in the State of New Jersey, to bear the name of a "Prince Hall Freemason."

◊ ◊ ◊

W. Q. ATWOOD
Realestate Dealer—Lumber Merchant—Orator

W. Q. ATWOOD, was born in Prairie Bluff, Alabama., 1 January 1839, under the yoke of slavery. His father was his master. The only thing that he was denied being an education. Nevertheless, the desire to know burned deep, both in his mind and heart. After his father's death, Atwood, went North to Ripley, Ohio, arriving on May 15, 1853, and entered a twelve month year school. In this all year school, he learned, mastered and applied his knowledge.

In 1863, Atwood went to East Saginaw, Michigan with Compass and Maps. He bought and sold land, and also City Realestate. In the same year he purchased sixteen-hundred acres of land and sold it, making four thousand dollars profit. He was considered by friends and foes alike to be a shrewd businessman, and a careful newspaper reader, one who was familiar with all details of business.

In 1864, he sold pine lumber and made a profit of six thousand dollars. W. Q. Atwood, was also a spellbinding orator, and also the leading spirit in political, social and commercial matters, in the City of Cleveland, Ohio. His career was highlighted and marked with worthy examples, and noteworthy accomplishments.

Masonic Documentation: Harry A. Williamson Collection on Black Masonry. The Schomburg Collection on Black Culture & History.

◊ ◊ ◊

ALEXANDER T. AUGUSTA

ALEXANDER T. AUGUSTA, born in 1825. He was a physician and Surgeon, and Soldier and Commissioned Officer.

Dr. Augusta, was the first black American to head a hospital in the United States. He was also one of the relatively few black Commissioned Officers, during the Civil War. When he became a Surgeon with the Union Army, he was the first black man to hold that title and position.

When peace was declared, Dr. Alexander T. Augusta, went to practice as a physician and surgeon, in Washington, D.C.

Masonic Documentation: Masonic News Quarterly—Prince Hall Freemasons. Southern Jurisdiction. Williamson Collection on Black Freemasonry.

◊ ◊ ◊

LEON M' BA
(1902–1967)
First President of the Republic of Gabon.
Mayor of the City of Librevelle.
Premier of The Republic of Gabon.

MASTER MASON LODGE "LOYAUTE-FIDELITE" in Paris, France under the Grand Orient de France. He affiliated December, 11, 1961, in the Lodge Akademos, and June 20, 1966, in the Lodge Condorcet.

Initiated April 15, 1958.
Master Mason March 3, 1959.

Masonic Documentation: Philatelic Freemason.

◊ ◊ ◊

CHRISTIAN E. BAKER, SR.
First Worshipful Master of Gbarnga Lodge, of Bong County,
Republic of Liberia.
Officer of the Grand Committee of
Bong County Masonic Association
Republic of Liberia.

Master Baker encouraged, fitted and furnished the new Gbarnage Lodge, and also conferred the Title of Worshipful Master Emeritus, on the Late President Dr. William R. Tolbert, Jr., in view of his great service to Freemasonry in Liberia and West Africa.

Masonic Documentation: Presidential Papers. President William R. Tolbert, Jr. Republic of Liberia (1971–1972).

◊ ◊ ◊

WILLIAM HENRY BALLARD, SR.
Grand Historian

Education
Doctorate in Pharmacology, Northwestern University

Author: *History of Prince Hall Feemasonry in Kentucky.*

President of The Blue Grass Medical Society.

Grand Historian of the Prince Hall Grand Lodge of the State of Kentucky.

Thirty-Third Degree, Ancient and Accepted Scottish Rite of Masonry, Prince Hall Affiliation, Southern Jurisdiction, United States of America.

◊ ◊ ◊

WALDO R. BANKS, SR.

WALDO R. BANKS, SR. Educator, Consultant, Corporate Director.

Born: Beaumont, Texas—March 30, 1928.

Education
Bishop College. B.A. 1951.
Prairie View University M.A. 1952.
Indiana University. Ph.D. 1964.

Administrative Assistant—Knoxville, College.
Researcher—Indiana University.
Assistant Professor—University of California.
Member of Board of Education—Los Angeles, California.
Consultant—Department of Housing, Education and Welfare.
Speaker—United Nations Speaker's Bureau
President—Global Oil Company, Inc.

Member: Prince Hall Masons. National Urban League N.A.A.C.P.
Listed: Who's Who in Black America.

Masonic Documentation: "Masonic News Quarterly." "The Crisis."

◊ ◊ ◊

E. M. BANNISTER
Artist—Photographer—Painter.

E.M. BANNISTER, was born in the Town of Saint Andrews, New Brunswick, Canada, was educated and spent his youth there. At the age of eighteen, Bannister came to Boston, Massachusetts, where he learned and worked by day at the photographic trade, for a number of years, using his nights to study drawing and art.

Training
Lowell Institute, in Boston, Massachusetts. And under the careful artistic eye of Dr. Rimmer, he learned the anatomy of art, and art anatomy. He later said the reminder was accomplished through, "God's help."

Bannister artistic sketches appeared
The Boston Globe.
The Boston Traveller.
The Boston Transcript.
The New York Herald Tribune.
Artwork appeared
The American Artist Museum.
Artist of the nineteenth century Museum.

Centenial Exhibition 1876. E. M. Bannister's pictures were awarded a "Place of Honor."

Masonic Documentation: "Williamson Prince Hall Masonic Collection."

ERNEST MARK BARKLEY
Business Executive

Positions
Cartographer (1962–64)
Supervisor, Defense Mapping,
Aerospace Center, St. Louis, Missouri (1964–69)
Operation Research Analyst,
United States Army Aviation System Command,
Mathematician (1969–70)
Chairman of the Board, Program Innovators, Inc., 1972

Prince Hall Free and Accepted Mason, Lodge and Consistory, Birmingham, Alabama

Recipient: Department of Army Sustained Super Performance Award, 1967.

Listed: (Biography) Marquis Who's Who, Inc.

◊ ◊ ◊

EARNEST O. BARKLEY, JR.
Mayor

Positions
Mayor of the City of Gretna, Florida
System Analyst of the State of Florida
Professor of Mathematics at Florida A. & M. University

Secretary of John G. Riley Consistory #207.

Thirty-Third Degree, Ancient and Accepted Scottish Rite of Freemasonry, Prince Hall Affiliation, Southern Jurisdiction, United States of America.

Documentation: Who's Who Among Black Americans, 1980–81.

RIGHT HONORABLE. ERROL WALTON BARROW
Minister of External Affairs.
(1966–1972)
Prime Minister of Barbados, 1966–78

ERROL WALTON BARROW was born in Barbados, on January 21, 1920.

Education
Combermere School, Harrison College.
Lincoln's Inn, London, England.
London University, London, England.
Former Member: Royal Airforce.
Founder and Member: Democratic Labour Party
Minister of External Affairs—Barbados. 1966–1972.
Prime Minister of Barbados—1966–1976
Member of Prince Hall Grand Lodge—New York,
New York 10032
Marquis
WHO'S WHO IN THE WORLD (1978–1979)

◊ ◊ ◊

MARION S. BARRY, JR.
Mayor
Mayor of the City of Washington, District of Columbia
(1983)

Education
LeMoyne College, B.A. 1958
Fisk University, M.S. 1960
University of Kansas and University of Tennessee,
Post Graduate Study

President of Washington, D.C., Board of Education (1972).

Councilman at Large, City Council, Washington, D.C.

Member: Third World Coalition Against War.

Chairman of the Board, and Founder, Pride Economy Enterprises.

First National Chairman, Student Non-Violent Coordination Committee.

Thirty-Second Degree, Acatic Grand Lodge, Prince Hall, A.A.S.R.

Documentation: Who's Who Among Black Americans, 1980–81.

◊ ◊ ◊

WILLIAM "COUNT" BASIE

WILLIAM "COUNT" BASIE, Orchestra Leader and Composer. He is one of the great jazz orchestra leaders in the United States. After learning to play the organ from the great "Fats" Waller, in the early 1920's, he toured the vaudeville circuit.

In 1935, he formed his own orchestra at the Reno Club, in Kansas City. After hearing him perform a local radio announcer nicknamed his "Count."

Count Basie and his orchestra played a royal command performance in 1957 for the Queen of England. And his orchestra was the first black orchestra to play at the Waldorf Astoria, in New York City.

The Count Basie Orchestra is the recipient of numerous awards, including the "Most Popular Band" by the Musicians of America. All American Band Award, by Esquire Magazine. Downbeat International Critics poll winner from 1952 to 1956.

Masonic Documentation: Member of Medina Lodge #19, F.A.M. Prince Hall Masonry.

EBENEZER DON CARLOS BASSETT
(1833-1908)
Educator and Government Official.

EBENEZER DON CARLOS BASSETT, Educator and Government Official was born in Litchfield, Conn., on October 15, 1833.

Education
Wesleyan Academy.
Connecticut State Normal School.
Yale University

Bassett was Principal of the Institute for Colored Youth in Philadelphia, Pennsylvania. He served the Institute with dedication and extraodinary ability. On April 6, 1869, President Ulysses S. Grant, appointed him Resident and General Consul or Consul General to Haiti. Bassett was the first black in the nation's history to hold this position. He again, proved his skill, as a successful Diplomat.

Masonic Documentation: Masonic Grand Lodge of New York State.

◊ ◊ ◊

VINCENT AGUILAR BENNETT
Industrial and Analytic Chemist
Pioneer Drug Manufacturer in Jamaica.

Director of Bennett National Laboratory Limited of Jamaica.
(Director of Central Pharmacy.)

Chairman, Colonial Insurance Company, Limited.
Director, City Printery Limited.
Past President, Pharmaceutical Society of Jamaica.

Member of the Minimum Wage Board of Jamaica. (Drug Trade.)
Freemason—Grand Lodge of England.

Masonic Documentation: International Guide To Who's Who In The West Indies. (Personalities In The Carribean.)

◊ ◊ ◊

LEONIDAS H. BERRY, M.D.
**Medical Doctor and Author
Senior Attending Physician at Micheal Reese and Provident Hospitals in Chicago, Illinois.
Thirty-Third Degree, Ancient and Accepted Scottish Rite of Freemasonary
Prince Hall Affiliations, Northern Jurisdiction
United States of America.**

Education
Wilberforce University B.S. 1924
University of Chicago S.B. 1925
Rush Medical College M.D. 1929
University of Illinois M.S. 1933

Fellow In The Academy—New York Academy of Medicine.
Past President—Cook County Medical Association.
Past President—National Medical Association.

His monumental and Best Selling Book:

"I Wouldn't Take Nothing For My Journey"

In his narrative biography Dr. Berry writes of his family across six generations, and documents the impact of The African Methodist Episcopal Church and other black Churches upon the cultural development of the Black Family.

Masonic Documentation: Ebony Success Library—One Thousand Successful Blacks.

PAUL V. BEST
Executive Secretary of The Phylaxis Society

Life member and Fellow of The Phylaxis Society.

Thirty-Third Degree, Ancient and Accepted Freemasonry, Scottish Rite, Prince Hall, Northern Jurisdiction, United States of America.

Graduate: A.T. University and Lincoln University.

Publications:
Prince Hall Was A Man.
St. John's Day: Now is The Time.
From My Point of View.
A.F. & A.M., What? Why? Wherefore?
Solomon, And The King of Kings.
The Badge of A Mason, Research in depth, "The Apron."

Documentation: Tenth Anniversary Journal, The Phylaxis Society.

◊ ◊ ◊

VINCENT E. BEST
Civic Leader

Graduate: New York State College of Mechanical Dentistry.

President, The North Amityville Civic Association, New York State.

Vice-President, New York State Conference of National Association for the Advancement of Colored People.

Past Worshipful Grand Master of Prince Hall Freemasonry in the State of New York. Thirty-Third Degree Prince Hall Freemason, Northern Jurisdiction.

JAMES J. G. BIAS
Physician and Clergyman
Member of African Lodge #549
of Philadelphia, Pennsylvania.

JAMES J. G. BIAS, was a distinguished physician and Clergyman of Philadelphia, but he was also one of the key operators of the Underground Railroad, the escape route from slavery to freedom in the North. Bias' home and bed were always available to slaves directed to him by the abolitionist. He also gave his guest a check-up, and medical attention if it was needed, after being examined.

Dr. Bias was a member of the Pennsylvania Anti-Slavery Society, and a founder of the Philadelphia Vigilance Committee, established in 1838, which assisted more than three hundred slaves annually before passing out of existence in 1844.

Dr. James J. G. Bias, was an active member of the African Masonic Lodge, #549, of Philadelphia, Pennsylvania.

Masonic Documentation: *"Historical Society of Pennsylvania."*

◊ ◊ ◊

RONALD A. BLACKWOOD
Mayor
The City of Mount Vernon, New York

Member: Progressive Lodge #64, F. & A.M. (Prince Hall)

Past President, The City Council of Mount Vernon.

Mayor Blackwood is the first elected black Mayor in the history of New York State.

Director: Mount Vernon Hospital, Mount Vernon Y.M.C.A., and Community Action Group.

Recipient: Honeywell Corporate Community Service Award

Motto: Life is service, the one who progresses is the one who gives his fellow being a little more, a little better service.

Documentation: The Prince Hall Sentinal, Fall, 1985, Grand East, State of New York.

◊ ◊ ◊

HENRY BLAIR
The First Black Inventor to Receive a United States Patent.

HENRY BLAIR, inventor, was granted a patent for his corn planting machine, on October 14, 1834, and two years later, another patent for a somewhat similar machine to be used for planting cotton.

Blair was both a Freemason and a free man, and probably the first black inventor to receive a United States Patent, since slaves couldn't legally obtain patents. The only unresolved question seems to be whether he was a Prince Hall Freemason before receiving his patent, or if he became a Prince Hall Freemason, thereafter?

Masonic Documentation: Williamson Collection on Prince Hall Freemasonry.

◊ ◊ ◊

JAMES HERBERT BLAKE
(EUBIE BLAKE)
Composer—Pianist—Musical Artist

Member of Median Lodge #19, Prince Hall Freemasons. (F.& A.M.) Gold Medal for his contribution to the Arts and Music from President Ronald Reagan, at the "White House," in 1982, at the age of ninety-two.

James Herbert Blake (Eubie Blake) was born February 7, 1883, at Baltimore, Maryland, and he is without a doubt the most remarkable composer and musical artist of them all; indeed, his life from 1883, to the present spanned virtually the entire field of Rags and Jazz.

Education
Brooklyn College—1937 Doctorate of Hebrew Letters.
Dartmouth College—1974 Doctorate of Humanity.
New England Conservatory of Music—1974 Doctorate of Fine Arts.

Advance Study
Schellinger System of Composition—New York University.
Studied piano with Margaret Marshall—New York University.
Composer and Producer—Shuffle Along with
Llewelyn Wilson

Hit and Campaign song, "I am just wild about Harry." Dedicated to President and Brother Harry S. Truman. (Re-election Theme.) Eubie Blake also composed some music that was unique, often sophisticated; but with roots in America, and in African tribal rhythms, and calls.

Honored by
The American Society of Composers, Authors and Publishers.
The Thirty-Sixth Annual Chicago Music Land Festival.

Witnessed the showing of "EUBIE" based on the legend around his life.

CONWELL BLANTON
Secretary General, United Supreme Council

Past Grand Master of The State of Delaware and Jurisdiction. (PHA.)

Thirty-third Degree, Ancient and Accepted Scottish Rite of Freemasonry, Northern Jurisdiction, Prince Hall Affiliation, United States of America.

Documentation: New York Prince Hall Lodge for Research.

◊ ◊ ◊

McHENRY RUTHERFORD BOATWRIGHT
(Singer)
Concert Artist
Member: Medina Lodge #19, F. & A.M.,
Prince Hall Affiliation.

MCHENRY RUTHERFORD BOATWRIGHT, was born February 29, 1928, in Tennille, Georgia.

Education
New England Conservatory of Music.
Bachelor of Music, Degree 1950.

Musical Debut as a Concert Artist, 'Jordan Hall,' Boston, Massachusetts 1954.

Appeared as Guest Soloist
Boston Pops Orchestra
Boston Symphony Orchestra
New York Philharmonic
Chicago Philharmonic
New England Opera Theatre Orchestra

Awards
Marion Anderson Award, 1953.
National Federation of Music Clubs Award, 1954.

Concert Artist Boatwright has made concert tours in the United States, Canada, Japan, and Hong Kong, Crown Colony.

Masonic Documentation: The Schomburg Library on Black History and Culture.

◊ ◊ ◊

JULIAN BOND
Georgia State Senator (1974–)
Georgia State Representative (1967–74)
President, Atlanta Chapter-NAACP

Born January 14, 1940 in Nashville, Tennessee.

Education
Primary School, Lincoln University, Pennsylvania
The George Preparatory School, Bucks County, Pennsylvania
Morehouse College, B.A. 1971
Holds honorary degrees from 14 colleges and universities

Was elected in 1965 to the Georgia House of Representatives, he was barred from taking office in January 1966, by legislators who objected to his statements against the Vietnam War. He won a second election in February 1966, to fill his vacant post, but a special House committee again voted to deny him membership. Bond won a third election in November 1966, and in December 1966, the United States Supreme Court ruled unanimously that the legislators had erred in refusing to seat him. On January 9, 1967, he took the oath of office.

Helped found the Student Nonviolent Coordinating Committee (SNCC) in April 1960. That summer, he joined the staff of the *Atlanta Inquirer,* a new Black weekly newspaper. He served as reporter and feature writer, and later became managing editor.

Bond was recently named to *Time*'s 200 Leaders list.

Julian Bond's collected speeches have been published under the title *A Time to Speak, A Time to Act.* His poems and articles have appeared in *Negro Digest, Motive, Rights and Reviews, Life, Freedomways, Beyond the Blues, New Negro Poets, American Negro Poetry, The Book of Negro Humor,* et al.

Masonic membership: St. James Lodge #4 F. & A.M., Atlanta.

Masonic Documentation: Georgia Masonic Research Center.

◊ ◊ ◊

ALBERT BERNARD BONGO
President
The Republic of Gabon
Past Master under the Grand Orient of France. President and Brother Bongo, is now a member of The Lodge #209 at Librevelle. (Le Dialogue #209.)

ALBERT BERNARD BONGO, was elected President in 1967, after the death of the Republic's first President, Leon M. Ba, himself a Mason.

Bongo a mason, after having undertaken a pilgrimage to Mecca, he is known as, 'El Hadj.' Later he was initiated on May 13, 1965, in the lodge, "Les Hommes Libres," at Angouleme, France, under the Grand Orient de France. There was at that time some lodges in the Republic of Gabon, working under the jurisdiction of this French Grand Lodge.

Master Mason, September 26, 1976.
Libreville, Capitol of Gabon.
Past Master under the Grand Orient de France.

President and Brother Bongo, is now a member of the Lodge, Le Dialogue 209, at Librevelle, a lodge founded 12 June 1977.

Masonic Documentation: Philatelic Freemason.

◊ ◊ ◊

EDWARD BOUCHET
(1852–1918)
Black Genius

EDWARD BOUCHET was made a Freemason on sight by the Most Worshipful Grandmaster of the Most Worshipful Grand Lodge of Massachusetts, and Jurisdictions.

Edward Bouchet earned his Doctor of Philosophy degree at Yale University in 1876, and was the first black man to earn a Ph.D., in the United States of America.

Brother Bouchet was also the first black man in the United States of America to be elected to the "Phi-Beta-Kappa" Society.

Masonic Documentation: Williamson Masonic Collection—The Schomburg. Collection of Black History and Culture.

◊ ◊ ◊

HAROLD R. BOULWARE
Judge

Past Associate Judge of Columbia, South Carolina, Municipal Court.

Judge of Family Court of Richland County, South Carolina.

Former Special Hearing Officer, Department of Justice for Government Appeals.

Board Member of The State Appeals Board of Selective Service.

Master Mason, College Lodge #378, and C. C. Johnson Consistory #136.

Documentation: Who's Who Among Black Americans, 1980–81.

◊ ◊ ◊

JOHN H. BOWLES
Grand Historian

Grand Historian of the Prince Hall Grand Lodge of Ohio.
Deputy Grand Master of Prince Hall Grand Lodge of Ohio.
Chairman of the Grand Committee on Foreign Correspondence.
First Black Officer of the Fifty-fourth Regiment of Massachusetts Volunteer Infantry

The records of the fifty-fourth and fifty-fifth Regiment Massachusetts Volunteer Infantry and combined for Military purposes.

Masonic Documentation: Records of Service of Fifty-fifth Regiment of Massachusetts Volunteer Infantry which is combined with her sister Regiment.
Regimental Association-John Wilson & Sons.

RICHARD HENRY BOYD
Founder and President
The National Baptist Publishing House

RICHARD HENRY BOYD, was born a slave. He left home as a slave and followed his master into the Army, where he witnessed the Civil War, between the North and the South. That was to him the fight for freedom. And when his master was killed in action, he returned home to Texas, with the body, assuming a free man's task of disposing of the farm property, and making the necessary arrangements and purchases for the family of his former master.

Boyd, was a sterling example of a former slave endowed with the qualities necessary to raise money to establish, "The National Baptist Printing and Publishing House," and Institution that was, and remains a credit to the City of Nashville, the State of Tennessee, and to the United States of America.

Masonic Documentation: The Library of The Masonic Grand Lodge of New York State

◊ ◊ ◊

W. T. BOYD
Grand Master of The Most Worshipful Grand Lodge of The State of Ohio

Publications
"An Address to the Colored Masonic Fraternity of the United States." Masonic historians consider this the ablest and most illuminating historical review of this body to have been published. Grand Master Boyd was painstaking and also accurate in his investigations, and during his long and useful years in the masonic fraternity, he accumulated a vast amount of material that made him powerful, respected by many, and feared by others.

"The Grand Lodge Proceedings," was published by Grand Master Boyd in 1883. It is a document of major historical importance, written without bias or controversy.

◊ ◊ ◊

JEAN BOYER
President, General, Statesman
President of the Republic of Haiti, 1818

Officer in the Grand Masonic Orient of The Republic of Haiti.

PRESIDENT BOYER was greater in deed than he was in word. Vast was the influence which he acquired by the mere force of his silent example. His name became a tower of strength to his friends and terror to his foes. Hence his presence was so impressive that none approached him without fear, nor left him without emotion.

In 1824, The African Lodge of New York changed its name in Honor of Jean Boyer, President, General and Statesman, who in 1818, became The Chief Executive Officer of The Republic of Haiti.

The world has reason to thank the Creator for great men, and with special gratitude we should acknowledge the Divine goodness of Great Black Men of Masonry.

Masonic Documentation: The Schomburg Library of Black History and Culture. And Right Worshipful Leslie C. Norris, Jr., 33° Grand Trustee, Most Worshipful Prince Hall Grand Lodge of New York State and Jurisdiction.

◊ ◊ ◊

THOMAS BRADLEY
Lawyer
Mayor of Los Angeles, California

Democratic Candidate for Governor of the State of California (1982).

Councilman, Los Angeles City Council (1963–71).

Former member of the Law Department of Los Angeles Police Department.

Thirty-Third Degree, Ancient and Accepted Scottish Rite of Freemasonry, Prince Hall Affiliation, Southern Jurisdiction, United States of America.

Awards: "Sword of the Haganah of the State of Israel," presented by Israel Ambassador Simcha Dinitz (1974) and "David Ben Gurion Award for Oustanding Achievement" (1974). Thurgood Marshall Award, N.A.A.C.P., Legal and Educational Fund (1975).

◊ ◊ ◊

WALTER T. BRADLEY

Right Worshipful "Walter T. Bradley," Grand Secretary of The Most Worshipful Prince Hall Grand Lodge (Free and Accepted Masons) of the State of Kentucky.
and
EDITOR-IN-CHIEF—THE MASONIC HERALD,
Under the Masonic Leadership
of
Most Worshipful Frank Brown, Jr.
Grandmaster of Prince Hall Freemasons
of The State of Kentucky.

Masonic Documentation: The Masonic Herald.

WILLIAM STANLEY BRAITHWAITE
(1878-1962)
Poet—Writer—Educator
Critic and Book Reviewer.

WILLIAM STANLEY BRAITHWAITE, was a book reviewer and critic for The Boston Transcript. His first poems was published in 1904, and was titled, "Lyrics of Life And Love."

Other published books
1908 Titled—The House of Falling Leaves.
1909 Book of Elizabethan Verse.
1948 Selected Poems.

Braithwaite from 1913 to 1929, published an Annual Anthology of Magazine verse, in which he introduced, "Carl Sandburg, Edgar Lee Masters, and Vashel Lindsey."

He was for many years, Professor of Creative Literature, at Atlanta University. In 1918, Brother Braithwaite was awarded the Spingarn Medal, by The National Association for the Advancement of Colored People.

Masonic Documentation: Williamson Prince Hall Masonic Collection. The Crisis Magazine, Official Organ, N.A.A.C.P.

◊ ◊ ◊

WILEY A. BRANTON
Attorney

Dean of Howard Law School, of Howard University, Washington, D.C.

Vice-President, N.A.A.C.P., Legal Defense and Educational Fund, Inc.

Deputy Grand Master of Prince Hall Masonry of Arkansas, F. & A.M.

Chief Counsel for the Little Rock Nine, 1957–58.

Director, Voter Educational Project, Atlanta, Georgia, 1962–63.

Special Assistant to United States Attorney General, 1965–67. (Attorney Generals Nicholas Katzenbach and Ramsey Clark.)

Honorary Grand Master of Prince Hall Masonry of Arkansas, F. & A.M.

Documentation: Who's Who Among Black Americans, 1980–81.

◊ ◊ ◊

REVEREND E. M. BRAWLEY
A.B., A.M., D.D.

E.M. BRAWLEY, President of Selma University, Editor of the Baptist Trubune, Minister and Sunday School Agent in South Carolina.

Born: March 18, 1851, in Charleston, South Carolina, to James and Ann Brawley. He was always free.

Education
Howard University, Washington, D. C.
Bucknell University, Lewisburg, Pennsylvania.

Brawley was licensed to preach by the Baptist Church (White) when he graduated by a vote of the Church Council composed of thirty-five ministers, mainly college professors, and other eminent men. After being ordained he was commissioned by "The American Baptist Publishers or Publication Society as Missionary for South Carolina."

In January 1887, Brawley began publication of "The Baptist Tribune," a weekly denominational organ. It became one of the best papers in the South, and was a credit to his ability and earnest Christian labor.

Masonic Documentation: Member of the Prince Hall Grand Lodge of The State of South Carolina. Williamson's Prince Hall

Masonic Collection. The Schomburg Library of Research in Black History and Culture.

◊ ◊ ◊

HARPER BREWER, JR.
**Assistant Majority Leader, General Assembly
State of Tennessee
and
Vice-President—Brewer's Delivery Service.**

HARPER BREWER, JR., was born in Memphis, Tennessee, on December 22, 1937.

Education
Fisk University—A.B.
Fisk University—M.A.

Positions
President, Memphis Area Teachers Credit Union.
Assistant Majority Leader, Assembly of the State of Tennessee.
Vice-President—Brewer's Delivery Service.
Administrative Assistant, Memphis Board of Education.

Member
Prince Hall Freemasons—Urban Policy Institute.
National Business League.

IRVING L. BRIDDELL
Commissioner

Positions
Commissioner, New Jersey Selective Service Commission
Administrator, United States Department of Labor's Office of Federal Contract Compliance Program

Masonic membership: Tuscan Morning Star Lodge #48.

Past Regional President of Kappa Alpha Psi Fraternity.

Graduate of Temple University.

Documentation: The Winter Bulletin, Official Organ of The Supreme Council, Northern Jurisdiction, March 1983.

◊ ◊ ◊

RAMSEY M. BRIDGES
Clergyman

Education
Masters in Religious Theology,
Howard University, School of Theology

Director: Wesley Foundation at Howard University, Washington, D.C.

Trustee: West Virginia Wesleyan College.

Minister: First Black to be Senior Pastor to a significantly all white congregation in Charleston, West Virginia.

District Superintendent: First Black District Superintendent in the history of West Virginia Methodism.

Chaplin: Most Worshipful Prince Hall Grand Lodge of the State of West Virginia and Jurisdictions.

Documentation: Who's Who Among Black Americans, 1977–78.

◊ ◊ ◊

PAUL W. BRIGGS
Educator

Professor: Cleveland State University, Cleveland, Ohio.

Lecturer: Ohio State University, Columbus, Ohio.

Officer: Board of Managers, Cleveland Metropolitan Y.M.C.A.

Recipient: American Brotherhood Award, National Conference of Christians and Jews.

Thirty-Third Degree, Ancient and Accepted Scottish Rite of Freemasonry, Northern Jurisdiction, Prince Hall Affiliation, United States of America.

Documentation: Who's Who Among Black Americans, 1975–76.

◊ ◊ ◊

HARTFORD H. BROOKINS
Clergyman
Pastor, First A.M.E. Church of Los Angeles, California

Former Pastor, Saint Paul A.M.E. Church of Los Angeles, California.

President, Western Division, Southern Christian Leadership Conference.

Participant, Sixth Pan-African World Conference (1974), in Tanzania.

Member of the Board of Directors of Operation Push (People United To Save Humanity).

Thirty-Third Degree, Ancient and Accepted Scottish Rite of Freemasonry, Prince Hall Affiliation, Southern Jurisdiction, United States of America.

Documentation: Who's Who Among Black Americans, 1980–81.

◊ ◊ ◊

BOBBIE EUGENE BROOKS
Chemist and
Mayor Riviera Beach, Florida

BOBBIE EUGENE BROOKS, was born in West Palm Beach, Florida, on November 9, 1935.

Education
Bethune Cookman College—B.S. Chemistry

Positions
Senior Chemist—Pratt and Whitney Aircraft.
Chairman of the City Council 1971–1974.
Member of American Society of Planning Officials.
Mayor of Riviera Beach, Florida
Chairman of Florida's Black Mayors Association

Member: N.A.A.C.P., Masonic Lodge.

◊ ◊ ◊

L. SHERMAN BROOKS
Patent Draftsman, Calligrapher, Cost Estimator, Teacher

Teacher, Naval Drafting School, Roger Williams, Jr., College.

Fellow, The Phylaxis Society.

Secretary, Sylvan Lodge #303, New York.

Thirty-Second Degree of Scottish Rite of Freemasonry.

Award: Royal Arch Dedicated Service Citation.

Brother Brooks has exhibited his work in more than fifty art shows in Northeastern United States and was awarded more than twenty-five blue ribbons. He has exhibited in eight one-man shows in New York, London, and Toronto. His biography appears in *Who's Who In Freemasonry*.

Documentation: The Phylaxis, Vol. XI, No. 2, Second Quarter 1985.

◊ ◊ ◊

W. WEBSTER BROOKS
Educator

Principal: West Lee Primary School, Lee County (1958).

Educational Director: Head Start, Lee County (1968–70).

Chairman: Lee County Adult Educational League.

Chairman: Lee County Voter's League.

Member, National Educational Association.

Masonic membership: Sandy Bluff Lodge #44, Prince Hall Masons. Ashland Consistory #246. Crescent Temple #148.

Documentation: Who's Who In American Education.

◊ ◊ ◊

WILLIAM H. BROOKS
Attorney

Positions
Chairman, Civil Service Commission,
City of Columbus, Ohio (1950–60)
Director, Public Utilities Department,
City of Columbus, Ohio (1964–71)
Commissioner, Public Utilities Commission of Ohio (1983)

Graduated: Ohio State University, A.B., LL.B., J.D. (1965).

Former Judge, The Municipal Court of Columbus, Ohio.

Special Counsel for the Attorney General of the State of Ohio.

Thirty-Third Degree, Ancient and Accepted Scottish Rite of Freemasonry, Northern Jurisdiction, Prince Hall Affiliation, United States of America.

Documentation: The Winter Bulletin of The Supreme Council, March 1983.

◊ ◊ ◊

GORDON E. BROWN
Masonic Leader

The First Black Deputy Grand Master of The New York State Grand Lodge in its more than Two Hundred Year History.

Past Master of Allied Lodge #1170, F. & A.M.

Past Master of Alpha Lodge #116, of New Jersey.

Electronics Instructor, Thomas A. Edison High School of Jamaica, New York.

Brother Brown served in the Army Air Force from 1943 to 1946. He received his pilot training at Tuskegee Institute in Alabama and was thereafter assigned to the 20th Airforce Unit in the Philippines.

Masonic Documentation: The Most Worshipful Grand Lodge Library and Museum, F. & A.M., of New York State, and The New York State Grand Lodge, F. & A.M.

◊ ◊ ◊

JEREMIAL A. BROWN
and
WILLIAM H. PARHAM
Members of the Worshipful Grand Lodge of "F.A.M." of the State of Ohio.

These two brethren collaborated in the compilation and the publication of the, "History of the Grand Lodge, Free and Accepted Masons, of Ohio, in 1906." And for a long time Ohio, was the only Prince Hall Grand Jurisdiction, which had published its "Official History."

Masonic Documentation: "Prince Hall Lodge for Research of New York."

JEREMIAH A. BROWN
Carpenter—Joiner—Clerk—Deputy Sheriff Legislator

JERMIAH A. BROWN, Born in Pittsburgh, Pennsylvania in 1841.

Education
Avery College, Allegheny, Pennsylvania

Campaigning on the Republican ticket he was elected to the Ohio State Legislature, from Cuyahoga County, Ohio, by more than three thousand votes over his nearest opponent. As a member of the State Legislature Brown fought against the Black laws, that limited the rights and priviledges of black people. Grand Secretary, and Grand Recorder of the Masonic Grand Lodge. Also a dedicated A.M.E. Church member.

Masonic Documentation: New York City Lodge for Research

◊ ◊ ◊

RICHARD ALGER BROWN
Physician

Graduate: Lincoln University and Howard University Medical College.

Post-Graduate: Tufts University Medical College and Boston University Medical College.

Co-Founder: Vitiligo Clinic.

Charter member: The American Academy of Family Practice.

Honorable member: Frontier International.

Thirty-Second Degree, Ancient and Accepted Scottish Rite of Freemasonry, Prince Hall Affiliation, Northern Jurisdiction, United States of America, and a Shriner.

Documentation: Who's Who Among Black Americans, 1980–81.

◊ ◊ ◊

THOMAS J. BROWN
Most Worshipful Grand Master of Prince Hall Masons of the State of Oregon

Member of The Phylaxis Society.

Thirty-Third Degree, Ancient and Accepted Scottish Rite of Freemasonry, Northern Jurisdiction, Prince Hall Affiliation, United States of America.

Documentation: The Phylaxis Newsletter, Vol. VI, No. 1 (July 1983).

◊ ◊ ◊

WILLIAM WELLS BROWN
Novelist and Playwright

WILLIAM WELLS BROWN, (1816–1884) was a novelist and playwright, born in Lexington, Kentucky. He was the first black in the United States to publish a novel, and also a drama. He was also the first black to publish a travel book.

Brown's father was a plantation owner, and his mother a slave. In his youth he was first hired to a steamboat captain, then later to a printer. The printer was "Elizah P. Lovejoy," an Anti-Slavery Editor. Lovejoy assisted Brown with both his education and his printing.

Books by William Wells Brown:
1. "Clothel" or "The President's Daughter"
2. "The Anti-Slavery Harp" (Collection of Poems.)
3. "An American Slave" (His Autobiography published in London, England.)
4. "The Escape or Leap To Freedom" (Drama.)
5. "The Black Man; His Antecedents; His Genius—His Achievements"
6. "John Brown's Raid on Harpers Ferry—The Proclamation of Freedom"

Documentation: Library of The Masonic Grand Lodge of New York State

◊ ◊ ◊

WILLIARD L. BROWN
Attorney

Past Grand Counselor of The Prince Hall Grand Lodge of West Virginia (1958–66).

Past Potentate of The Shriners, Charleston, West Virginia.

Public Service Commissioner of the State of West Virginia.

State Legal Advisor, N.A.A.C.P., West Virginia.

Councilman, City of Charleston (1947–54).

Recipient: T. G. Nutter Civil Rights Award.

Past Member, Charleston's Human Rights Commission.

◊ ◊ ◊

BLANCHE K. BRUCE
Register of the United States Treasury
and
United States Senator

BLANCHE K. BRUCE, was born March 1, 1841, in dire poverty, in Old Virginia. Nevertheless, from early youth he had a thrist for knowledge, the power of knowledge, and its practical application. He was determined. He believed that determined men can conquer anything. Bruce worked and struggled to attend and graduate from Oberlin College, in Ohio.

In 1870, Blanche K. Bruce, decided to enter politics, and was elected "Sergeant at Arms," of the Mississippi State Senate. Thereafter, he was elected "Commissioner of the Board of Levee," of the Mississippi River. Later, he was elected United States Senator, from the State of Mississippi.

After much distinguished service in the United States Senate, he was offered an appointment as "Assistant Postmaster General," by President Garfield. But Senator Bruce declined. However, he did accept the appointment of "Register of the United States Treasury." Bruce would sometimes comment, "there's money in my name."

Blanche K. Bruce, later recalled that he had taken many giant steps from his birth in slavery, and Freemasonry had contributed beyond a shadow of doubt.

Masonic Documentation: Williamson Prince Hall Collection on Black Masonry

◊ ◊ ◊

BENJAMIN W. BRYANT
Most Worshipful Prince Hall Grand Master
of The State of Colorado and Jurisdiction

Thirty-Third Degree, Ancient and Accepted Scottish Rite of Freemasonry, Northern Jurisdiction, Prince Hall Affiliation, United States of America.

Documentation: The United Supreme Council, Northern Jurisdiction, Prince Hall Affiliation, United States of America.

◇ ◇ ◇

JAMES HARRISON BRYANT
Bishop

Bishop, African Methodist Episcopal Churches, Republic of South Africa.

Bishop, Fifth Episcopal District of The United States of America, (A.M.E. Churches).

Former Pastor of A.M.E. Churches, in Ohio, Kentucky and Maryland.

Past President of The Council of Bishops, A.M.E. Churches.

Vice-President, General Board of A.M.E. Churches.

Thirty-Third Degree, Ancient and Accepted Scottish Rite of Freemasonry, Southern Jurisdiction, Prince Hall Affiliation, United States of America.

Documentation: Who's Who Among Black Americans, 1975–76.

◇ ◇ ◇

IVORY MELVIN BUCK, JR.
Secretary General, The United Supreme Council (Elected 1983) Ancient and Accepted Scottish Rite of Freemasonry, Prince Hall Affiliation, Northern Jurisdiction, United States of America, Inc.

College Administrator: Glassboro State College, Glassboro, New Jersey.

Masonic: Past Master, Oriental Lodge #1, F. & A.M., Prince Hall. Director of Publicity, De Hugo Consistory #2. Potentate, Shrine.

Former: Staff Sgt., Communications, United States Air Force.

Active: Thirty-Third Degree, Scottish Rite of Freemasonry.

◊ ◊ ◊

REV. ISSAC M. BURGAN B.D.
College President

REVEREND ISAAC M. BURGAN, Pioneer, Educator and President of Paul Quinn College. Born October 6, 1848 at Marion, North Carolina.

Self-educated until December 1869, when he entered a select school in Bowling Green, Kentucky. His brilliance attracted the attention of his teachers and the whole school, before he had mastered all the books in the school. After graduation, he united with the church and was licensed to preach. In rapid succession he advanced from class leader, to trustee, and to Pastor.

At commencement "Rev. Isaac M. Burgan," represented The Theological Rhetorical Society, once, The Sodalian Literary Society, twrice. Thereafter he was appointed President of Paul Quinn College, by the Trustees.

Masonic Documentation: New York City Lodge for Research

◊ ◊ ◊

SIMON PETER BURKES
Member: Saint Cyprian Consistory, Number Four
Pittsburgh, Pennsylvania

Thirty-Third Degree, Ancient and Accepted Scottish Rite of Freemasonry, Prince Hall Affiliation, Northern Jurisdiction, United States of America.

Brother Burkes, is the oldest Scottish Rite Mason in the United States, having celebrated his one hundredth and second birthday in 1982.

Masonic Documentation: The Bulletin—Official Organ of The United Supreme Council, Ancient and Accepted Scottich Rite of Freemasonry, Prince Hall Affiliation, Northern Jurisdiction, United States of America.

◊ ◊ ◊

LUTHER C. BURNETT
Urban Planner

Positions
Urban Planner, National Park Service, Washington, D.C.
Urban Planner, Bureau of Outdoor Recreation,
Interior Department

Urban Planner, National Capitol Planning Commission,
Washington, D.C.
Land Surveyor, Detroit Department of Public Works,
Detroit, Michigan
Commissioner of Conservation and Cultural Affairs,
U.S. Virgin Islands

Member: American Institute of Planners and the American Society of Planning Officials.

Award: Governor's Outstanding Award for Service, U.S. Virgin Islands.

Thirty-Second Degree, Ancient and Accepted Scottish Rite of Freemasonry, Prince Hall Affiliation.

Documentation: Who's Who Among Black Americans, 1980-81.

◊ ◊ ◊

LINDEN FORBES SAMPSON BURNHAM
President
The Cooperative Republic of Guyana
Member: English Mechanics Lodge of
Freemasonry of Guyana

LINDEN FORBES SAMPSON BURNHAM was born in Georgetown Guyana. (Formerly British Guiana.) on February 20, 1923.

Education
Queens College
University of London—Honor Student
President, The Bar Association of Guyana
President, The Guyana Labor Union (1964)
Chairman and Founder, People's Progressive Party (P.P.P.)
Honorary Doctorate of Law, Dalhousie University, Canada

Awards
The Jose Marti Award, from the Government of Cuba
The Grand Cordon De L Order, from the Government of Egypt

◊ ◊ ◊

HENRY R. BUTLER
Physician and Surgeon

Worshipful Grand Master of The Most Worshipful Prince Hall Grand Lodge of The State of Georgia.

Thirty-Third Degree, Ancient and Accepted Scottish Rite of Freemasonry, Prince Hall Affiliation, Southern Jurisdiction, United States of America.

Documentation: The Williamson Masonic Collection, The Schomburg Library of Black History and Culture.

◊ ◊ ◊

KENNETH BUTLER
President, Vanguard Oil Company,
Brooklyn, New York

KENNETH BUTLER heads the seventh largest black-owned business in the United States.

Masonic membership: Hiram Lodge #23, Long Island Consistory #61, Abu-Bekr Temple #91.

Philosophy: "I am striving to make the vision of Dr. Martin Luther King, Jr., a reality."

CALVIN OTIS BUTTS, THE THIRD
Minister and Educator

Education
B.A. in Philosophy, Morehouse College, Atlanta, Georgia
Masters in Theology, Union Theological Seminary,
New York City
Doctor of Ministry, Drew University, Madison, New Jersey
Positions
President, Africare, a private organization
dedicated to improving rural African life.
Executive Minister, Abyssinia Baptist Church.
Adjunct Professor, African Studies Department,
City College of New York.
Former Professor of Black Studies at Fordham University.
Former Lecturer, Harvard University, Institute of Politics,
Cambridge, Massachusetts.

Masonic membership: Thirty-Third Degree, Ancient and Accepted Scottish Rite of Freemasonry, Northern Jurisdiction, Prince Hall Affiliation, United States of America. Boyer Lodge, #1. Medina Temple, #19. Past Potentate of the Nobles of the Mystic Shrine of Medina Temple of New York.

Documentation: Antioch Lodge #66 Yearbook, and personal interview and printed resumé.

◊ ◊ ◊

ROBERT H. CAIN
(1825–1887)
(College President)

ROBERT H. CAIN, State Senator, Congressman, Bishop, College President. Born free in Greenbrier County, Virginia.

Cain, moved with his father in 1831, to Gallipolis, Ohio. At the age of thirty-five he entered Wilberforce University and studied for several years, before entering the Ministry of the African Methodist Episcopal Church. He served as Pastor of several Churches in New York.

In 1865, the African Methodist Episcopal Church Council sent Rev. Cain to Charleston, South Carolina to help the emancipated slaves. He traveled throughout the State, organizing Churches, and making converts.

The South Carolina Constitutional Convention met in 1868, and elected Rev. Cain, to the State House of Representatives, and later, the State Senate, where he served for four years. Thereafter, Rev. Cain was elected to the United States House of Representatives, where he served two terms.

And when he finished his service in Congress, his election as the fourteenth Bishop of the African Methodist Episcopal Church was the crowning point in his illustrious career. Bishop Cain, founded, "The Missionary Record," which became an important organ for blacks throughout the State of South Carolina. Thereafter, Bishop Robert H. Cain, was appointed to the Presidency of PAUL QUINN COLLEGE, in Waco, Texas.

Masonic Documentation: The Grand Lodge Library—F. & A.M., State of New York.

◊ ◊ ◊

CHARLES CALDWELL
State Senator

CHARLES CALDWELL, a former slave, who became a Mississippi State Senator, and helped write the Constitution of the State of Mississippi, of 1868.

He was shot at in Jackson, Mississippi, and returned the fire, killing his assailant, the son of a white judge. An all white jury acquited him. Caldwell subsequently served in the "Mississippi State Senate," and Commanded a troop of black militiamen in the City of Clinton.

In 1875, Caldwell tried unsuccessfully to prevent a race riot in Moss Hall. The Riot lasted for four days, with killing widespread, according to the version of the Ku Klux Klan. And Senator Caldwell was among the many killed.

The Senator's wife, Mrs. Margaret Ann Caldwell, told the State Senate Investigating Committee, what she knew about her husband's murder.

Masonic Documentation: New York City Lodge for Research (Prince Hall.)

◊ ◊ ◊

DR. SAMUEL P. CALLAHAN
Dentist and Clergyman

Thirty-second degree Ancient and Accepted Scottish Rite of Freemasonry, for the Southern Jurisdiction of the United States of America, Prince Hall Affiliation and Shriner.

Samuel P. Callahan, was born in Galax, Virginia., on April 15, 1924.

Education
Fisk University—B.A.
Meharry Medical College—Doctor of Dental Surgery.
Wesley Theological Seminary—Bachelor of Divinity.

80

Officer in the United States Navy—1944–1946.
Practicing Dentist—Recipient of the Distinguished Award
for Creative Achievement in Dentistry.
Pastor—Christ is the answer Center
Chairman, N.A.A.C.P., Legal Redress Committee.
Shriner—Prince Hall Affiliation—Alpha Phi Alpha.

◊ ◊ ◊

EUGENE S. CALLENDER
Past Master
**Abercorn Lodge #86, Prince Hall Freemasons
Senior Minister and Chief Executive Officer
Church of the Masters Inc.
City Director—New York, "Cities in Schools."**

REV. EUGENE S. CALLENDER, is the Founder and Chairman of the Board of Directors, of "HARYOU-ACT," the Nation's first Federal Program designed to affect social change among young people in the ghetto. He is the Senior Minister of The Church of the Masters, Inc.

Education
Boston University—B.A.
Westminister Theological Seminary—B.D.
Union Theological Seminary—Graduate Study.
Knoxville College—D.D.
Massachusetts Institute of Technology,
Sloan School of Management,
Certificate in Urban Management.

Positions
President and Chief Executive Officer
New York Urban Coalition.
Deputy Administrator
New York City Housing and Redevelopment Administration.
Executive Director

New York Urban League.
Founder and Pastor,
Mid-Harlem Community Parish.
Chairman: Mayor's Central Harlem Task Force.
Worshipful Master.

Appointed to membership on President Lyndon B. Johnson's Task Force, on "Manpower and Urban Development."

Television Host: "Positively Black."
(N.B.C. T.V.)
Consultant—United States Department of Labor.
Consultant—International Business Machine. (I.B.M.)
Elected—Moderator of the Presbytery of the City of N.Y.
Adjunct Professor, Columbia University,
Corporate Relations and Social Responsibility.

Instructor: New York University—Afro-American Studies.
N.A.A.C.P., Life-member.

Past Master, Abercorn Lodge #68, Prince Hall Masons.

◊ ◊ ◊

JAMES E. J. CAPITEIN
Poet—Writer—Minister—Lecturer

JAMES E. J. CAPITEIN, was born in Africa, kidnapped and taken to Europe, enslaved and sold to a literary man. His owner observed literary ability in young Capitein and decided to educate him. He was sent to Holland to study, and learned to master Latin, Greek, Hebrew, and the Chaldean Tongues.

Besides publishing many volumes of verse and poetry, Capitein wrote and published a quarto volume of his sermons in Dutch. He preached in many Towns, and his collected works was printed in Amsterdam, Holland in 1742.

Capitein was a member of "The Masonic Grand Lodge of Holland."

Masonic Documentation: Mille Volti Di Massoni Di Giordano Gamberini—Roma.

◊ ◊ ◊

FRANCIS L. CARDOZA
Principal of Washington, D.C., High School
Professor of Languages
Secretary of State
State of South Carolina
Treasurer of the State of South Carolina

FRANCIS L. CARDOZA, was born January 1, 1837, in Charleston, South Carolina. He began school at the age of five years, and remained until the age of twelve. Thereafter, he was apprenticed to the carpenter's trade for five years, after which he became a journeyman carpenter. Cardoza worked at the carpentery trade and saved his money, and in the year 1858, went to Glasgow, Scotland to gain an education.

University of Glasgow
University of Edinburgh
University of London

He also won a scholarship in a competitive examination, and moved to London, England. He won fifth prize in Latin Competition among over two hundred competitors, and seventh prize in Greek, before returning to the United States.

Positions
Minister of Temple Street Congregational Church.
New Haven, Conn. August 1, 1864.
Professor of Latin, at Howard University, Washington, D.C.
Principal of the Colored High School of Washington, D.C.

The Constitutional convention of South Carolina, in January 1868, established under the Reconstruction Act, elected, "Francis L. Cardoza, Secretary of State, for the State of South Carolina."

Masonic Documentation: Williamson Masonic Collection— Schomburg Library

◊ ◊ ◊

SIR GERALD CHRISTOPHER CASH
The Governor General of the Bahamas
Knight Grand Cross of the Most Distinguished Order
of Saint Micheal and Saint George
Knight Commander of the Royal Victorian Order
Officer of the Most Excellent Order
of the British Empire
and Justice of the Peace
Thirty-third Degree, Ancient and
Accepted Scottish Rite of Freemasonry,
Prince Hall Affiliation, Northern Jurisdiction,
United States of America
Director, the Central Bank of the Bahamas
Vice-Chancellor of the Anglican Diocese
Vice-President of the Bahamas Olympic Association

GERALD CHRISTOPHER CASH, attended government High School in Nassau. Thereafter, he began teaching at the Eastern Senior High School. After a year of teaching he entered the Law Chamber, as an articuted law student. In October 1940, he was called to The Bahamas Bar, as Counsel and Attorney at Law, of The Supreme Court of the Bahamas.

In 1946, Sir Cash, entered the Honorable Society of The Middle Temp in London, and successfully passed his Bar Examination with Honors.

◊ ◊ ◊

CHARLES FRANKLIN CASTERMAN
Right Worshipful Charles Franklin Casterman
Grand Master of Prince Hall
Masons of the State of Ohio
Grand Secretary and District Organizer
and
Grand Commander of L.D. Easton Consistory #21
Eminent Grand Commander

CHARLES FRANKLIN CASTERMAN, was born in Harrisburg, Louisiana, and he attended the Public Schools, there.

Graduated—Tuskegee Institute—1919.

After graduating from Tuskegee Institute, he entered the United States Postoffice and was gainfully employed until retirement in 1954.

◊ ◊ ◊

OCTAVIUS V. CATTO
Commissioned Major in the United States Army
During the Civil War
Principal of a Philadelphia High School
Equal Rights Advocate
Member of African Lodge #549
of Philadelphia, Pennsylvania

In 1871, Octavius V. Catto, along with several other blacks were killed by a white mob, which sought to prevent them from voting. The right to vote had been recently guaranteed by the passage of the Fifteenth Amendment to the United States Constitution.

This sketch brings to mind the insight of Brother W.E.B. Dubois, when he wrote:
"Throughtout history the powers of single black men flash, here and there, like falling stars, and die, sometime before the world has rightly guaged their brilliance."

Masonic Documentation: The Crisis—Official Organ of N.A.A.C.P. The Harry A. Williamson Collection on Black Masonry.

◊ ◊ ◊

HENRY WILKINS CHANDLER
Lawyer—State Senator—City Clerk Alderman—Delegate

HENRY WILKINS CHANDLER, was born in Bath, Sagadahock County Maine, on September 22, 1852.

Education
Bates College, 1874—B.A. Lewiston, Maine.
Howard University, Law School. LL.B. 1876 Washington D.C.

Pass the Bar Examination, and was admitted to practice law in the State of Florida. Elected Delegate to the Rupublican National Convention in 1884. Thereafter in rapid sucession Henry Wilkins Chandler, was City-clerk, Alderman, then Florida State Senator.

Senator Chandler's speeches were a specimen of eloquence, rhetoric and polish; and the subject was exhausted in every case before he dropped the matter.

Years later, he recalled going to Florida with two dollars and a half, in his pockets, and in less than twenty years amassing more than twenty thousand dollars in Realestate.

Masonic Documentation: The Grand Lodge Library—F. & A.M. State of New York

◊ ◊ ◊

WILLIAM CHAPMAN, JR.

WILLIAM CHAPMAN, JR., Teacher, Scoutmaster, Craftsman in wood. (Makes plaques, gavels, furniture, which adorns many Grand Lodges, Lodge Rooms and Homes of Master Masons throughout the United States.)
Past Master, Wayne Craft Lodge #37.
Past Commander-in-Chief, Wolverine Consistory #6, Ancient Accepted Scottish Rites, Northern Jurisdiction.
Past Illustrious Potentate, Mavracci Temple #13, (A.E.A.O.N.M.S.)
Past President, Masters and Wardens Council.
Past Director, Prince Hall Grand Lodge, Youth Department, Michigan.
Master Mason of the Year. (1968.) Michigan Jurisdiction.

◊ ◊ ◊

WILLIAM CALVIN CHASE
Writer—Editor

WILLIAM CALVIN CHASE, was born February 2, 1854, in Washington, D.C. His father was a blacksmith, and one of Washington's leading citizens. Young Chase worked in a newspaper office as a utility boy, and gained a good general idea of how to operate a newspaper.

Education
Howard University.
Howard University Law School.

After two years in Howard University Law School, Chase began working in the United States Government Printing Office. But when he was not promoted to printer, he filed charges of discrimination based on race and color with the President of the United States.

He became Editor of "The Washington Bee," and the motto of the newspaper was, "Honey for friends, and sting for enemies."

He was considered the "Black Knight," of journalism, from the matchless knight in Walter Scott's "Ivanhoe"

Editor Chase, wrote a criticism on, "Colonel G.W. Williams, History of The Negro Race." In 1885, he was a delegate from the Convention of Black People, to President Grover Cleveland, to request that he review the Emancipation Day parade. And the Honorable Frederick Douglass was elected Emancipation Orator, due largely to the efforts of Editor and Writer William Calvin Chase, who furnished honey for friends, and sting for the enemies of the black people of America.

◊ ◊ ◊

JOHN CHAVIS
(1763–1838)
Minister and Schoolmaster

JOHN CHAVIS, was born free in the West Indies in the year 1763.

He was educated at Princeton University, as well as Washington and Lee University. Chavis was a student of Princeton's President John Witherspoon, who tutored him privately after class. The university at that time permitted a few blacks and Indians to enter its classrooms.

In November 1800, at Timberidge Meeting House, Chavis preached his first sermon, and thereafter was licensed by The Presbytery to preach the Gospel. Thereafter, Chavis opened a school where Greek and Latin could be taught to the sons of the white gentry. Later, he admitted to his school youth of free blacks.

Chavis's Presbyterian Ministry and his role as a Classical Schoolmaster were shortlived. The uprising led by self-taught black preacher Nat Turner, in Southampton County, Virginia, during the summer 1831, prompted the enactment of laws regulating black Ministers and Teachers.

Masonic: African Lodge #459, Philadelphia, Pennsylvania.

Documentation: The Black Presence In The Era Of The American Revolution by Sidney Kaplan. Historical Notes, New York State Grand Lodge (F. & A.M.) Library and Museum.

◊ ◊ ◊

KENNEDY C. CHILDERS, 33°
Waynesboro, Georgia
Educator

K. C. CHILDERS, Educator, masonic leader, agricultural expert, and civic leader was born December 19, 1902 in Bulloch County, Georgia.

Education
Georgia State College, A.B., B.S.
Prairieview A & M College, Texas
Positions
Superintendent & Principal
Masonic Home and School
M. W. Union Grand Lodge of Georgia F&AM
1933–1937
District Deputy Grand Master
Millen Masonic District
M. W. Prince Hall Grand Lodge of Georgia F&AM
1944–Present

In 1968, he organized the Eastern Georgia Farmers Cooperative, Inc., and served as Director for 5 years.

County Agriculture Agent, Burke County, Georgia, 1937–50. State Area Agricultural Supervisor.

Member of Phi Beta Sigma Fraternity

Former Vice President & Chairman, Political Action Committee, Burke County Improvement Association.

He is the chartered Commander-in-Chief of his consistory.

Masonic membership: Past Master, Aurora Lodge No. 54, F. & A.M. Member, New Aurora Chapter No. 60, OES. Past Commander-in-Chief, Lamar Carter Consistory No. 321 AASR. Member, Stoklin Temple No. 22, AEAONMS.

Masonic Documentation: Georgia Masonic Research Center.

◊ ◊ ◊

HENRI CHRISTOPHE
(1767–1820)
King of Haiti
and
Revolutionary Commandering General

KING HENRI CHRISTOPHE'S leadership contributed immensely to the Organic Law of Haiti, Morality, Religion, Education and Industry. It was during his administration that Agriculture and Commerce flourished. He was an extraordinary man during a period of extraordinary men.

Masonic: Member and Officer The Grand Lodge of Haiti.

Biography: *Christophe King of Haiti* by Hubert Cole, New York, 1967.

Masonic Documentation: Bibliotheque Nationale, Paris, France. Museum and Library of The Grand Orient of Haiti (Port au Prince, Haiti).

◊ ◊ ◊

CAESAR A. W. CLARK
Minister & Editor

Pastor, Good Street Baptist Church of Dallas, Texas.

Editor, *National Baptist Voice.*

President, Baptist Missionary and Education Convention of Texas.

Secretary of The Board of Trustees, Bishop College, Dallas, Texas.

Education
B.A., Bishop College, 1946
Doctorate of Religion, Bishop College, 1960

Ebony Poll: One of the fifteen (15) Greatest Black Preachers, *Ebony,* September 1984.

Masonic: Thirty-Third Degree, Ancient and Accepted Scottish Rite of Freemasonry, Prince Hall Affiliation, Southern Jurisdiction, United States of America.

Documentation: The Schomburg Library of Black History and Culture.

◊ ◊ ◊

E. HARRISON CLARK
Tailor—Minister—Teacher and Deputy United States Marshall and Worshipful Grand Master of Prince Hall Grand Lodge of Freemasonry of New York State and Jurisdictions

PAST GRAND MASTER E. HARRISON CLARK, was appointed Deputy United States Marshall by President Franklin Delano Roosevelt, at Hyde Park, New York, after he served as a High School Teacher, in New York City.

His background included being a master tailor, and an able Baptist Minister, and a mason's mason.

Past Grand Master, E. Harrison Clark, was also Grand Inspector General, Thirty-Third degree, Ancient and Accepted Scottish Rite of Freemasonry, Prince Hall Affiliation, Northern Jurisdiction, United States of America.

◊ ◊ ◊

SAMUEL WILCOX CLARK
Twelfth Most Worshipful Samuel Wilcox Clark Grandmaster of the Most Worshipful Grand Lodge of Free and Accepted Masons of the State of Ohio and Jurisdictions

PAST WORSHIPFUL GRANDMASTER SAMUEL WILCOX CLARK, was born on July 25, 1846, in Cincinnati, Ohio. He was initiated and raised in 1870, True American Lodge, Number Two, Cincinnati, Ohio.

Served
Prince Hall Jurisdiction as Worshipful Grandmaster
1879–1888—1898–1902
"Negro Mason In Equity"

This a monumental work on and about Prince Hall Masonry in the context of American Masonry. Past Grandmaster Clark words are as refreshing today as when he first penned them.

"Masons of the world, wheresoever dispersed, the Negro Mason of America stands before you today, as a just and upright Mason, and as such demands that you shall try him by the Square of Virtue, and having tried him, and found him just and true, he further demands that you deny him not, but that you receive him and accept him, accord unto him all the rights that may belong to him. He does not make this demand because he is a Negro, neither does he ask that you do this as a favor, but he demands it because he is a mason, as you are, and because his right to the title of Free and Accepted Mason is equal to yours no more and no less."

The Negro Mason In Equity, is considered one of the most outstanding of any of the numerous treaties from the pen of a black man.

The past Grand Master of the Grand Lodge of Washington (Caucasian) deemed the work of such value that he began quoting therefrom, and in a report which he was chairman, a Special Committee was appointed by the Grand Lodge to investigate that status of Black Freemasonry.

Masonic Documentation and Source of Research: Black Square and Compass. By Joseph A. Walkes. Prince Hall Lodge for Research of New York. Harry A. Williamson's Masonic Library. The Schomburg Center for Research in Black History and Culture.

◊ ◊ ◊

DR. ISODORE HUDDLESTON CLAYBORN, 33°,
Active, FPS
Entrepreneur

Sovereign Grand Commander
Ancient and Accepted Scottish Rite
Southern Jurisdiction
M. W. Grand Master 1965–81
Chairman, Committee on Foreign Correspondence
M. W. Prince Hall Grand Lodge of Texas
Chairman, Fraternal Relations Committee
Ancient Egyptian Arabic Order Nobles Mystic Shrine

DR. ISODORE HUDDLESTON CLAYBORN was born at Waco, Texas, and resides in Duncanville, Texas. The Frater served as Grand Master of Texas for 16 years. During his tenure he caused 10 low-rent housing complexes to be built, 7 in the name of the M. W. Prince Hall Grand Lodge of Texas, and 3 by the United Supreme Council, A.A.S.R., Southern Jurisdiction. The tall handsome Texan is by profession, a real estate entrepreneur. He serves as a member of the Board of Directors of Guaranty Bank of Dallas, and the Legal Defense Fund.

Honors
Grand Commander of Liberia,
by President William V. S. Tubman.
Honorary Doctorate of Humane Letters, Bishop College,
April, 1973.
One of the 100 Most Influential Black Americans, *Ebony* Magazine.
Grand Band of Liberia, by William R. Tolbert.
Past Imperial Potentate, Zakat Temple No. 164.
The Gold Medal Award, United Supreme Council,
A.A.S.R., S.J.
Honorary Citizen Award, Fredicksburg, Virginia.
John G. Lewis, Jr. Award for 1982. The Phylaxis Society.
Silver Nail Recipient, Maria Morgan Branch, YWCA.

Masonic membership: Past Master, Paul Drayton Lodge #9, F. & A.M. Member, Red Rose Chapter #405, OES. Member, Circle of Unity Court #48, H of J. Member, Trinity Chapter #1, RAM. Member, Mystic Tie Commandery #3, KT. P C-in-C, Dale Consistory #31, AASR, SJ. Noble Advisor, Zarat Temple #164, AEAONMS. Fellow, The Phylaxis Society.

Documentation: Georgia Masonic Research Center.

◊ ◊ ◊

ETHELL COBBS, JR.
Most Worshipful Grand Master of the State of Michigan
Most Worshipful Prince Hall Grand Lodge of Free and Accepted Masons

Executive Editor, "The Michigan Voice of Prince Hall."

Thirty-Third Degree, Ancient and Accepted Scottish Rite of Freemasonry, Prince Hall Affiliation, Northern Jurisdiction, United States of America.

Masonic Documentation: The Michigan Voice of Prince Hall.

◊ ◊ ◊

HON. MR. JUSTICE C.O.E. COLE
Judge

Retired Chief Justice of The Supreme Court of The Republic of Sierra Leone.

District Grand Master of Freemasonry of The Republic of Sierra Leone and The Gambia. Jurisdictions of The United Grand Lodge of England.

Awards: Order of The British Empire and Order of The Royal Society of Lawyers.

◊ ◊ ◊

NATHANIEL COLE
(NAT KING COLE)
Singer—Pianist
Prince Hall Mason, Los Angeles, California

NATHANIEL COLE, was born in Montgomery, Alabama, on March 17, 1917. He started his career at an early age as pianist and church organist, in Chicago, Illinois, where his father was the Minister, and his mother, the Church's Choir Director.

While attending Phillips High School, Nat King Cole, as he was commonly called, formed his own band, and also played in his brother's sextet. In 1936, he joined the touring revue of *Shuffle Along*, and when the show closed in Hollywood, he became a pianist in a night club. The King Cole Trio was formed in the late 1930's with Oscar Brown on the guitar, and Wesley Prince on the bass.

Cole's deep voice and smooth renditions of, *Nature Boy, Mona Lisa, Too Young, Answer Me, My Love, Rambling Rose*, and many others made Nat King Cole a household word.

Nathaniel Nat King Cole's last motion picture was, *Cat Ballou*, starring Jane Fonda, before he died from lung cancer in 1965.

Brother Nathaniel Cole was a member of Thomas Waller Lodge #49, of Los Angeles, California.

◇ ◇ ◇

RAYMOND T. COLEMAN
Grand Historian of Prince Hall Grand Lodge of Massachusetts and Jurisdiction

Secretary of William G. Butler Masonic Lodge.

Editor: The Craftsman, The Official Publication of The Prince Hall Grand Lodge of Massachussetts and Jurisdiction.
President, The Fraternal Publishing and Printing Company of Boston, Massachusetts.
Editor, The Phylaxis, The Official Magazine of The Phylaxis Society.
A Society for Prince Hall Freemasons Who Seek More Light And Have Light To Impart.
Commissioner of Zoning for The City of Boston, Massachusetts.
Former President of The Roxbury Chamber of Commerce.

Member of The Board of Directors:
Roxbury Community College
Small Business Development Corporation
Area Planning Action Council.

Consultant: Graphics, Media and Advertising.

Former Managing Editor of The Tri-City-Star, of Boston and The Boston Sun.

Masonic Documentation: Statement furnished by Grand Historian Raymond T. Colman.

WILLIAM DAVID COLEMAN
President
President of The Republic of Liberia, 1896–1900

Grand Master of The Masonic Grand Lodge of The Republic of Liberia.

Member: Saint Paul's Lodge #2 Clay-Ashland, Monserrado County.

Documentation: Proceedings from The Grand Lodge of Liberia.

◊ ◊ ◊

CECIL WAYNE CONE
Educator

CECIL WAYNE CONE, was born in Bearden, Arkansas, on May 21, 1937.

Education
Shorter College, B.A.
Smith College, B.D.
Garrett Theological Seminary. D.D.
Emory University, Ph.D. 1974.

Positions
Minister, Mount Zion A.M.E. Church.
Minister, Allen Temple A.M.E. Church
Minister, Saunders Memorial A.M.E. Church.
Professor of Theology, Jackson Theological Seminary
Dean, Jackson Theological Seminary

Member
National Council of Black Churchmen
Society for the Study of Black Religion
Congress of the African People
American Academy of Religion

Fellow
Rockefellor Doctoral Fellowship—1970–1972.

Member
Binford Lodge #26, F. & A.M. Prince Hall Affiliations.

◊ ◊ ◊

JAMES E. COOK
Clergyman and Dean

Dean of Religion at Lomax-Hannon Junior College, 1961–67.

Pastor, Warner Temple, A.M.E. Zion Church, Lancaster, South Carolina.

Trustee of Lomax-Hannon Junior College.

Member of the Board of Christian Education of A.M.E. Zion Churches.

Masonic: Wingfiled Lodge #23-A, Consistory #19. Thirty-Third Degree, Ancient and Accepted Scottish Rite of Freemasonry, Southern Jurisdiction, Prince Hall Affiliation, United States of America, Class 1972. United Supreme Council.

Certificate for Distinguished Work in Religion, Lomax-Hannon Junior College.

◊ ◊ ◊

ALDRAGE BENJAMIN COOPER
Research Chemist
Member—Prince Hall Progressive Lodge #17, New Brunswick, New Jersey

Aldrage Benjamin Cooper, was born on January 27, 1906, in Wilkes Barre, Pennsylvania. He is a Research Chemist.

The Author: Chronology of Prince Hall Masonry in New Jersey, 1953.

◊ ◊ ◊

SAMUEL CORNISH
1796–1859

SAMUEL E. CORNISH, minister and journalist. Born in Delaware.

Education
The Free African School.
Princeton University.

SAMUEL CORNISH shared with John B. Russwurm, the founding of "FREEDOM'S JOURNAL" in New York in 1827. This newspaper was considered by many as the "People's Voice, reporting news, and fighting back against lies, misrepresentations, and slander. He was founder of the "African Presbyterian Church," in New York City, and served as its Paster.

Cornish was considered one of the outstanding writers among pioneers of black journalism in the United States.

Publisher and Editor: "The Weekly Advocate," renamed "The Colored American."

The later years of Cornish was occupied with his work for abolition of slavery, and the support of the idea of a College for

Black youth. He was also a Trustee for the Free Black Schools, in New York City.

Masonic Documentation: Williamson Prince Hall Collection.

◊ ◊ ◊

JOSEPH MASON ANDREW COX
Poet—Writer—Playwright—Lecturer
College Professor—Television Producer

Grand Historian of the state of New York and jurisdiction. Member and Historian of Antioch Lodge, #66, Prince Hall Freemasonry.

Member: King David Consistory, Number Three, Ancient and Accepted Scottish Rite of Freemasonry, Prince Hall Affiliation, Northern Jurisdiction, (Thirty-Second Degree.) United States of America.

Member: The Grand Lodge Historical Committee of the Prince Hall Grand Lodge, State of New York.
Life Member of the Phylaxis Society, A Society of Prince Hall Freemasons who seek more light and have light to impart.

Producer and Moderator, "Focus On Thought Profound" popular television show. (From 1980-1982.) Talk show of Distinguished people.

Books published:
Bouquet of Poems.
Land Dimly Seen.
The Collected Poetry of Joseph Mason Andrew Cox.
Ode to Dr. Martin Luther King, Jr. (Drama in Three Acts)
Profound Fantasy And Reality Remembered.
New And Selected Poems, 1966-1978.
Great Black Men Of Masonry, Qualitative Black Achievers Who Were Freemasons.

United States Representative, World Poetry Conference. Expo #67, Montreal, Quebec., Canada.

First Prize, Daniel S. Mead International Writer's Contest.
Fourth Prize, World Poetry Contest, Cambridge, England.
Awarded the Statue of Victory, World Culture Prize 1985.

Doctorate of Art Psychologhy, China Art College, World University. Ph.D., Art Psychology 1972, Hong Kong, Crown Colony.

Member
The Poetry Society of America.
(Formerly the Executive Board.)
The Authors League of America.
The American Academy of Poets.
The International Academy of Poets. (London, England.)
The International Academy of Arts, Letters And Science.
(Rome, Italy.)
The United Poet Laureate International. (Philippines.)

Biography Appears:
Notable Americans of the Bicentenial Era.
International Biographical Dictionary.
International Book of Honor.
Encyclopedia of Contemporary Personalities.
Four Languages, Rome, Italy.
International Who's Who of Poets and Writers.
Four Thousand Notable Americans.
5,000 Personalities of the World.

The poetry and writing of "Joseph Mason Andrew Cox," has been translated into ten languages and is house in major libraries and collections throughout the world.

◊ ◊ ◊

GEORGE W. CRAWFORD
Lieutenant Grand Commander, The United Supreme Council,
Northern Jurisdiction
and
Past Grand Master of Prince Hall Masons
of The State of Connecticut

Thirty-Third Degree, Ancient and Accepted Scottish Rite of Freemasonry, Northern Jurisdiction, Prince Hall Affiliation, United States of America.

Documentation: New York Prince Hall Lodge for Research.

◊ ◊ ◊

WILLIAM R. CROSS
Business Executive

Contractor, Remodeling and building homes and buildings.

Former General Manager, J. T. S. Brown & Sons Distillery, in Kentucky.

Chairman, The Board of Education, Bardstown, Kentucky.

Past Master, Euclid Lodge #13, Prince Hall, F. & A.M.

Member of The Mayor's Advisory Board.

◊ ◊ ◊

JAMES D. CROSSON
Judge

Judge of The Circuit Court of Cook County, Chicago, Illinois.

Former Administrative Assistant to the Chief Judge of the Municipal Courts of Chicago.

Law Partner: Gassaway, Crosson, Turner & Parsons.

Former Referee: Municipal Court of Chicago, Illinois.

Trustee: John Marshall Law School, and the Chicago Y.M.C.A.

Masonic: Freemasonry, Prince Hall Affiliated, F. & A.M.

◊ ◊ ◊

ALEXANDER CRUMMELL

ALEXANDER CRUMMELL, Rector of Saint Luke Church, Washington, District of Columbia. Author. Professor of Mental and Moral Science In The College of Liberia.

Bishop Hood said, "Crummell was among the most scholarly black men of his age." He was the son of royal paternity on one side, and free born maternity on the other side. He was therefore born free in the City of New York.

In 1862, Crummell published a volume of speeches and addresses, most which were delivered in Africa. His writing was chaste, scholarly, instructive and entertaining. They seemingly flowed from a heart full of tenderness and love toward mankind, and also showed a simple faith in Christ, that is both touching and tender.

Masonic Documentation: Williamson Masonic Library—Schomburg Library.

PAUL CUFFEE
(1759-1817)

Freemason, Captain, Shipbuilder and Shipowner, also Philanthropist, who made a patentable improvement on the modern ship compass. He was born on the Island of Cullyhunk, nine miles off New Bedford, the son of a slave. He was among the first to support African Colonization of Freedmen as a solution to problems arising from settling Americans of African Ancestory.

Cuffee a free black man who in 1797, bought a farm, and on the land built a school for free black children, and was one of the seven black freeman signing the petition to the Massachusetts legislature.

"By reason of long bondage and hard slavery, we have been deprived of enjoying the profits of our labors or the advantages of Inheriting Estates from our parents, as our neighbors, the white people do, and yet, we have been and are now taxed both in our polls, and the small pittance of estate which through much hard labor and industry, we have got together to sustain ourselves."

Later, Paul Cuffee, and his brother John filed a taxpayers suit against the State of Massachusetts, for the right of Free blackmen to vote. They lost the case. But several years, thereafter, the legislature adopted a bill granting the right to free black men to vote.

Paul was a boy of thirteen years, at the time of his father's death. He scarcely knew the letters of the alphabet, but with the aid of a tutor, he learned to read and write. But from an early age, the salt of the sea was in his blood. He studied navigation and mastered the rudiments of latitude, lead, and lookout. And shipped out aboard the whaler bound for Mexico, or the Gulf of Mexico, as he was lead to believe. (And in the Century to follow, black men and men of color, including a few members of his own family played an important part in the American fishery—as seamen, mates, harpooners, and occasionally captains.) Let the record show, that one, Lewis Temple, a black ironworker of New Bedford, Massachusetts, revolutionized the technique of the whale hunt, with his invention of the Toggle Harpoon.

Paul Cuffee's second voyage was to the West Indies. And on his third voyage his ship was captured by the British, and he spent three months in a New York prison. He fought for the rights of his people, after his release and continued planning his career as a merchant mariner. First he built a deckless ship from keel to gun-wale.

1810, Captain Paul Cuffee, sailed his ship "The Traveller," out of Massachusetts, bound for Sierra Leone, in West Africa, with a crew of thirty-eight American blacks, and after fifty five days, landed safely on African soil. Thereafter, consulted by President Andrew Jackson and Henry Clay. His place is assured both in Masonic history, and in the history of human accomplishments.

Masonic Documentation: Williamson Collection on Black Masonry. (Prince Hall.)

◊ ◊ ◊

NORRIS WRIGHT CUNEY
The First Grandmaster of the Most Worshipful Grand Lodge of Free and Accepted Masons of Texas and Jurisdictions.

Former School Director for Galveston County, Texas.

Alderman: Board of Alderman
City of Galveston, Texas.
Inspector of Customs—Port of Galveston, Texas.
Collector of Customs for the Port of Galveston, Texas.

First Grandmaster Norris Wright Cunney, was born in Galveston, Texas, on May 12, 1846, and died on May 3, 1898, in Galveston, Texas.

Editorial note: The Grand Lodge of Texas was organized by and under the authority and jurisdiction of the Prince Hall Charter, which was granted by the United Grand Lodge of England.

Masonic Documentation: Texas Masonic Quarterly—Prince Hall Journal.

◊ ◊ ◊

MALCOLM G. DADE
Clergyman

Rector Emeritus, The Episcopal Church of Saint Cyprian, Detroit, Michigan.

Thirty-Third Degree, Ancient and Accepted Scottish Rite of Freemasonry, Northern Jurisdiction, Prince Hall Affiliation, United States of America.

Administrator: Board of the House of Correction, Detroit, Michigan.

Honorary Canon of The Cathedral of Saint Paul.

Certificate of Tribute, Michigan State Legislature, 1967.

Documentation: Who's Who Among Black Americans, 1980–81.

◊ ◊ ◊

CHARLES F. DAILY
Merchant, Importer and Exporter

Grand Master of Free and Accepted Masons of The State of Florida and Jurisdictions. Past Master of Saint John Lodge #51.

GRAND MASTER DAILY was born in Saint Thomas, West Indies, in 1820.

He was a merchant of produce who imported and exported between the United States and Europe.

Grand Master received his first three masonic degrees in a Lodge in Liverpool, England, and his Scottish Rite degrees including his thirty-third in Glasgow, Scotland. He was Knighted at Greenock, Scotland. His final membership was under The Grand Orient of France.

Documentation: The Williamson Collection (Masonic Prince Hall) of The Schomburg Library of Black History and Culture.

◊ ◊ ◊

ULYSSES GRANT DAILY, M.D.

ULYSSES GRANT DAILY, (1885–1961.) Medical Doctor and Surgeon, born in Donaldsonville, Louisiana. And graduated from Northwestern University Medical School, in 1906, and upon graduation was appointed "Demonstrator in Anatomy" at Northwestern University Medical School.

Thereafter, he served as surgical assistant to the famous Doctor Daniel Hale Williams, first man to perform open heart surgery and the Founder of Provident Hospital, in Chicago, Illinois. But Daily didn't stop there. He continued advanced studies in

Surgery in London, Paris and Vienna. In 1926, he set up his own hospital. His surgical skill and brilliant mind brought him recognition as one of the most distinguished surgeons in the United States.

In 1954, Dr. Daily was named honorary "Consul to Haiti." Later, "Health Advisor" to Pakistan, India, Ceylon and Africa. He also wrote numerous technical articles in Medical publications throughout the world.

Masonic Documentation: Williamson Masonic Collection— Schomburg Library.

◊ ◊ ◊

SAMUEL T. DANIELS
Labor Leader
and
The Most Worshipful Grand Master
of The State of Maryland and Jurisdiction.

Business Representative of Baltimore Municipal Employees Local #144, American Federation of Labor and Congress of Industrial Organization.

Executive Secretary, Maryland State Commission on Interracial Problems and Relations.

Board Member, National Council of Christians and Jews.

Commissioned First Lieutenant and served in the Korean War.

Educational Research Assistant, Baltimore Equal Employment Opportunity Commission.

Thirty-Third Degree Ancient and Accepted Rite of Freemasonry, Prince Hall Affiliation, Northern Jurisdiction, United States of America.

Documentation: The Phylaxis, Vol. XI, No. 2, Second Quarter 1985.

◊ ◊ ◊

ROBERT LENZY DARBY
Editor, Masonic Scholar, Researcher, Writer
Editor, The Phylaxis Newsletter

ROBERT L. DARBY hails from Augusta, Georgia. He received his degrees in the Rising Star Lodge #18 at Lawton, Oklahoma, in 1961.

Fellow, The Phylaxis Society.

Founder and Director, The Georgia Masonic Research Center.

Quality Control Inspector of the Georgia Power Company.

Masonic membership: Past Master, Bannaker Lodge #3, F. & A.M. Past Commander-in-Chief, Lebanon Consistory #28, Ancient and Accepted Scottish Rite of Freemasonry. Past Potentate, Stolkin Temple #22, AEAONMS. The Augusta District Past Master's Council. Commander-in-Chief of the year (1980), Georgia Council of Deliberation.

◊ ◊ ◊

CHARLES ALFONZO DARGAN, 33°
New York City
19th Imperial Potentate
Ancient Egyptian Arabic Order Nobles Mystic Shrine
1969–1971

CHARLES A. DARGAN was born December 2, 1902, in the area now known as Daytona Beach, Florida. He was educated at Edward Waters College, Jacksonville, Florida. He has worked as assistant public relations director of Opportunities Industrialization Center in Washington, D.C., and is a retired railroad worker. He initiated the current Legal Defense Fund program of the shrine.

Masonic membership: Past Master, Boyer Lodge #1, F. & A.M. Member, Eureka Chapter #17, RAM. Past Commander, Ivanhoe Commandery #5, KT. Past Potentate, Medina Temple #19, AEAONMS

Masonic Documentation: Georgia Masonic Research Center.

◊ ◊ ◊

EDWARD B. DARNELL
Recording Secretary of the United Supreme Council
of
The Ancient and Accepted Scottish Rite
of Freemasonry, (Prince Hall Affilation)
Northern Jurisdiction,
United States of America.

Deputy Director—The City Airport of Detroit, Michigan.

Sovereign Grand Inspector General, Thirty-Third Degree, Ancient And Accepted Scottish Rite of Freemasonry, Prince Hall Affiliation, Northern Jurisdiction of the United States of America.

Editor: The Phylaxis Newsletter.
Fellow: The Phylaxis Society.
Past Master: Unity Lodge #28.
Past Commander-in-Chief, of the Wolverine Consistory.
Number Six, Valley of Detroit, Orient of Michigan.

Elected: To The United Supreme Council for the Northern Jurisdiction.
Honorary Member of The United Supreme Council, Southern Jurisdiction.

Brother Darnell, a former United States Marine who earned his Master's Degree, and a Specialist Degree from three different Institutions of Higher Learning.

Past Potentate of Marracci Temple #13, Oasis of Detroit, Desert of Michigan, and is the General Chairman of the Standing Committee on Temples for the Imperial Council; and Imperial Director of Voter Registration. Recipient of the Imperial Council's Legion of Honor Award in 1973. Cited—Who's Who Among Black Americans in 1974.

◊ ◊ ◊

HORACE ALEXANDER DAVENPORT
Judge

Judge of the Thirty-eighth Judicial District of the Commonwealth of Pennsylvania.

Former Law Partner, Gerber, Davenport & Wilenzik.

Member: Pennsylvania Bar Association, and the Civil Rights Commission of Pennsylvania Bar Association.

Former Director: Montgomery County T.B. & Health Association.

Former Director: Montgomery Hospital.

Area Captain: The Salvation Army.

Masonic membership: Mount Pisgal Lodge #32, F. & A.M., Prince Hall Affiliation.

◊ ◊ ◊

HARRY E. DAVIS
Attorney
Member
Excelsior Lodge #11, Prince Hall Freemasonry

Thirty-second degree, Ancient, Accepted Scottish Rite of Freemasonry, Prince Hall Affiliation, United States of America.

Member: Excelsior Lodge #11, Prince Hall Masonry, of Cleveland, Ohio.

Author: "Freemasonry Among Negroes In The United States."

Masonic Documentation: "Masonic Biographical Sketches." Alphonse Cerza, P.M.

◊ ◊ ◊

JOHN WARREN DAVIS
(1888–1980)
Educator

DR. JOHN WARREN DAVIS, President of West Virginia State College, Board Member of the National Science Foundation. Appointed by President Harry S. Truman, to the National Advisory Board on Education. Director of Technical Assistance to the Republic of Liberia.

Born: February 11, 1888, in Milledgeville, Georgia. Died July 12, 1980.

Education
Milledgeville High School.
Morehouse College, Atlanta, Georgia.
University of Chicago, Chicago, Illinois.
Member of "Phi-Beta-Kappa."
Prince Hall Mason (33 degree.)
Professor at Morehouse College, in Atlanta, Georgia.

When Dr. John Warren Davis, was appointed President of West Virginia State College, the enrollment was twenty-one students, and during his thirty-four year tenure, he guided and directed its development, and expanded the student enrollment to nineteen thousand students, and built its academic accreditation to the recognition as one of America's outstanding land grant colleges, with an enviable cultural center.

Director of Education, for the N.A.A.C.P., Legal and Educational Fund. Recipient of Fourteen Honorary Doctorates. National Board Member of The National Urban League, and N.A.A.C.P. Dr. Davis accompanied Dr. Mary McLeod Bethune on her initial visit to the "White House," to present the status of Black people to the President of the United States, The Honorable Franklin Delano Roosevelt. Distingushed member of—The Phylaxis Society—Thirty-Third Degree, Ancient and Accepted Scottish Rite of Freemasonry, Prince Hall Affiliation, Northern Jurisdiction, United States of America.

Masonic Documentation: Schomburg Library of Black History and Culture.

◊ ◊ ◊

JONATHAN DAVIS, M.D.
(1820-1874)
Worshipful Grand Master,
Prince Hall Grand Lodge of Pennsylvania

JONATHAN DAVIS, was an outstanding free black American in the nineteenth century who was a prominent physician and pharmacist, who practiced medicine in Philadelphia, Pennsylvania. He was a Prince Hall organizer, and Worshipful Grand Master of the Prince Hall Grand Lodge of Pennsylvania.

In 1860-1861, Boyd's Medical Directory listed Jonathan Davis, Medical Doctor, and he was also listed in several other medical directories. These listings were made before Davis was awarded an "Honorary Degree of Medical Doctor" by Eclectic College of Medicine, of Philadelphia, in 1869. However, an "Honorary Degree" in Medicine was unusual then, as now. We must not forget that black slaves brought from Africa knowledge of herbs, bark, and plants which could and were used as remedies for sickness, and treatment for disease.

While active in the medical profession, Davis was dedicated to Prince Hall Freemasonry, and he became an organizer in and for the fraternity, as it was becoming permanent in the middle of the nineteenth century. These were the years of slavery, and the emergance of the anti-slavery movement.

Davis and six other Masonic brothers formed the Supreme Prince Hall Masonic Council, in the District of Columbia. This is documented in "The History of Freemasonry Among Colored People in America." By William H. Grumshaw. And The Jonathan Davis Consistory—Number One, District of Columbia, in more than forty Consistories in the United States, Liberia and Germany.

In addition to participating in organizational endeavors in the District of Columbia, while living and practicing medicine in Philadelphia, Dr. Davis was among the first of the pioneers in the expansion of Prince Hall Masonry, Southward and Westward. It was at Charlestown, South Carolina, that he assisted in the establishment of its Grand Lodge, in June 1867, but it wasn't legally approved until the legislature of the State of South Carolina approved it by The Act of 1872, dealing with organizations. This firmly and legally established the Prince Hall Grand Lodge in the State of South Carolina.

Jonathan Davis, a great man left his footprint in the sands of Time, and as we see them while his name and fame marches on and on to successors, today and tomorrow.

◊ ◊ ◊

OSSIE DAVIS
Author—Actor—Director—Playwright

OSSIE DAVIS, Born in Cogdell, Georgia—December 18,1917.

Actor
Rose McClendon Players.
The Defenders.
Night Gallery.
The Sheriff.

Director
Cotton Comes to Harlem.
Black Girl.
Countdown at Kusini.

Author
Purlie Victorious. (Broadway Comedy.)

Co-Writer and Director
Today is Ours.

Co-Host
Ossie Davis & Ruby Dee Story Hour.

Membership
N.A.A.C.P., and Prince Hall Freemasons.

◊ ◊ ◊

OSSIE B. DAVIS
(Clergyman)

OSSIE B. DAVIS, Born in Starkville, Illinois, on May 14, 1922.

Education
Rust College—A.B.—1948
University of Indiana—M.A.—1955
Gammon Theological Seminary—B.D.—1964
Emory University—D.D—1968
Various Church Pastorates since—1950

Positions
Principal—Perkins Elementary School—1951–55
Principal—Goodman Jr. High School—1955–59
Principal—Montgomery High School—1959–62

Co-Chairman
National Freedom Riders—Southern Christian Leadership Conference.

Probation Counsellor—Fulton County Delinquency Treatment Center.
Delegate—Democratic National Convention
Thirty-second degree—Prince Hall Freemason Affiliation
Scottish Rite—Southern Jurisdiction

◊ ◊ ◊

ROSCOW A. L. DAVIS
Most Worshipful Prince Hall Grand Master of The Grand Bahamas and Jurisdiction

Thirty-Third Degree, Ancient And Accepted Scottish Rite of Freemasonry, Northern Jurisdiction, Prince Hall Affiliation, United States of America.

Documentation: The United Supreme Council, Northern Jurisdiction, Prince Hall Affiliation, United States of America.

◊ ◊ ◊

WILLIAM L. DAWSON
Congressman and Democratic Official

WILLIAM L. DAWSON, United States Congressman and Vice-Chairman of the Democratic National Committee.

Born: April 26, 1886, Albany, Georgia.

Education
Fisk University.
Kent Law School.
Northwestern University.

Dawson entered the United States Army as a Lieutenant with the American Expeditionary Forces in 1917. He also served with the 369th Infantry in the famous Argonne offensive and the Vosges Mountains, was wounded and gassed.

Elected Alderman—Chicago City Council. 1944 Congressman Dawson was appointed Vice-Chairman of the Democratic National Committee.

Doctor of Law degrees from numerous Universities, and many organizations besides the Prince Hall Freemasons.

Masonic Documentation: New York State Grand Lodge Library— F. & A.M.

◊ ◊ ◊

C. F. DAY
Author and Writer
Thirty-Third Degree Ancient and Accepted Freemason—Member of the Grand Masonic Lodge of France.

C.F. DAY, was a thirty-third degree Freemason, member of the Grand Masonic Lodge of France. He was both writer and author.

His published works:
"The Rights and Wrongs of Freemasonry and the Regular Formation of Scottish Rite Masonry."

Masonic Documentation: Prince Hall Lodge for Research of New York.

◊ ◊ ◊

MARTIN ROBINSON DELANY
(1812–1885)
Medical Doctor—Author—Editor—Major Literary Man, Lieutenant Governor of South Carolina

Major in the United States Army—the One Four Regiment of South Carolina, Commissioned by President Abraham Lincoln and Major Delany continued in Military Service on the staff of General Daniel E. Shickle Lieutenant Colonel on the staff of Governor Scott of South Carolina. Inspector of Customs.

Author: The Orgin and Object of Ancient Freemasonry, its introduction into the United States and legitmacy among colored people.

Martin Robinson Delany, was born May 6, 1812, in Charleston, Virginia. He boasted having descended partially from African Kings and Chieftains. His maternal ancestry being Mandingo, his paternal, Golah.

He attained independence of thought at an early age. Later, he graduated from Harvard University Medical College, and was the first black medical student to matriculate from the renown college of medicine.

Member of Saint Cyprian Masonic Lodge #13, of Pittsburgh, where he earned his first Thirty Masonic Degrees. Thereafter he earned his two additional degrees and received his Thirty-Third Masonic Degree.

While in England he was elected to membership in the following: Fellow, The Royal Society.

Delany was the publisher of two weekly newspapers His philosophy was vividly set forth in this poem he wrote to Frederick Douglass, editor of "The North Star."

> Be Thou Like The First Apostle
> Be Thou Like The Heroic Paul
> If Free Thought Seeks Expression
> Speak Boldly—Speak It All!
> Face Thine Enemies And Accusers
> Scorn The Prison Rack Or Rod
> And If Thou Hast Truth To Utter
> Speak And Leave The Rest To God.

Founder: Pittsburgh, Pennsylvania African Educational Society, Primarily because black people were barred from schools in the city of Pittsburgh.

Edited and wrote numerous articles to news-media and the government, and to the Governors of all Southern States on the Conditions and Deprivation imposed on the Black Minority by the White Majority.

Charter Member—Mount Nebo Royal Arch Masonic Chapter #12, F. & A.M.

◊ ◊ ◊

OSCAR DE PRIEST
(1871–1951)
United States Congressman

OSCAR DE PRIEST, was born in Florence, Alabama in 1871. He served as Alderman in Chicago, Illinois, before being elected to Congress, in 1929. He served with distinction until his defeat in 1934.

Education
Public Schools of Alabama.
Business Course in Kansas.

When Oscar De Priest, was elected to Congress, he was considered the spokesman for eleven million black people. During the Administration of President Hover, Congressman De Priest and his wife were invited to join other Congressmen and their wives at a White House Tea. This incident immediately, received a nationwide reaction of sharp disapproval.

Congressman was a Thirty-Third Degree, Ancient and Accepted Degree of Scottish Rite Freemasonry, Nothern Jurisdiction, Prince Hall Affiliation, United States of America.

After De Priest's defeat for re-election to Congress, he served, again as Alderman in the City Council of Chicago, from the Third Ward. Thereafter, he withdrew from politics and returned to his realestate business.

Masonic Documentation: Williamson Collection on Freemasonry—Schomburg Library.

◊ ◊ ◊

OSCAR STANTON DEPRIEST
Thirty-Third Degree, Ancient and Accepted Scottish Rite, Freemasonry, Prince Hall Affiliation, Western Consistory, U.S.A. and Commander-in-Chief of Chicago's Western Consistory Number Twenty-Eight.

OSCAR STATON DePRIEST, Thirty-Third degree, Ancient and Accepted Scottish Rite of Freemasonry, and the son of the late Congressman Oscar DePriest, is Commander-in-Chief, of Chicago's one thousand member Western Consistory, which is considered the world's largest.

Masonic Documentation: Masonic News Quarterly.

◊ ◊ ◊

W. B. DERICK
Minister and Scholar

REVEREND W.B. DERICK, Minister of The African Methodist Episcopal Church, Scholar and Orator, was born on the Island of Antigua, in the British West Indies, on July 27, 1843. This was approximately, nineteen years after the Emancipation was conferred on the Islands by the British Parliament in 1834.

Derick's father, Thomas J. Derick, Sr., belonged to a highly respectable family of large planters and land owners. Young Derick attended a very select private school, and thereafter went to sea with a Captain who was a friend of the family. After several voyages he returned and studied with a fine classical scholar. Years later, he became the Minister of The African Methodist Episcopal Church. His Sermons, Addresses and his Speeches were scholarly and profound and excerpts were carried in:

The New York Times.
The New York Sun.
The New York Herald.
The New York Evening Telegraph.
The Christian Recorder.
The Boston Advocate.
The New York Freeman.

Masonic Documentation: Williamson Collection on Freemasonry.

◊ ◊ ◊

McKINLEY A. DE SHIELD, SR.
**Postmaster General of The Republic of Liberia (1951-1975)
Worshipful Grand Master of
The Grand Lodge of Masonry
of the Republic of Liberia**

Awarded "The Order of Liberian Pioneers" by President Tolbert.

◊ ◊ ◊

SAINT JULIAN F. DEVINE
Charleston, South Carolina City Alderman
Prince Hall Mason—Thirty-Third Degree Shriner

SAINT JULIAN F. DEVINE, was born in Bonneau, South Carolina, on July 5, 1916.

Education
Public Schools of Bonneau, S.C.
Washington School of Arts.
United States Armed Forces.

Membership
Charleston, South Carolina, City of Charleston. Serving on The Committee on Transportation, and The Committee on Education and Housing.

Position
Alderman, South Carolina, city of Charleston.
Serving on The Committee on Transportation
and
The Committee on Education and Housing.

◊ ◊ ◊

EUGENE DICKERSON, JR., 33°
Washington, D.C.
**24th Imperial Potentate
Ancient Egyptian Arabic Order Nobles Mystic Shrine
1978–1980
Grand Eminent Commander
John W. Freeman Grand Commandery, K. C. (D.C.)
1954–1956
M. E. Grand High Priest
King Cyrus Grand Royal Arch Chapter of Virginia
1953–1955
Worthy Grand Joshua
Heroines of Jericho
1955–1957**

EUGENE DICKERSON, JR., masonic scholar, lecturer, and teacher was born in Gloucester, and reared in Harrisburg, Virginia.

Education
Public schools of Harrisonburg, Va.
Dunbar High School, Washington, D.C.
Howard University

Masonic membership: Omar Lodge #226, Harrisonburg, VA. Past High Priest, St. Joseph Chapter #45, RAM (Va). Past E. Commander-Sinion Commandery #1, KT (D.C.) Member, Jonathan Davis Consistory #1, AASR (D.C.) Past Potentate, Mecca Temple #10, AEANOMS.

Masonic Documentation: Georgia Masonic Research Center.

◊ ◊ ◊

JAMES A. DICKERSON, SR.
Grand Inspectors General,
Ancient Accepted Scottish Rite, of Freemasonry, Prince Hall Affiliation, Northern Jurisdiction.
Licensed Real estate Broker
Mortgages—Sales—Management

Achievements: Past Master, Boyer Lodge.#1—1963. Past High Priest, Eureka Chapter #17—1963. President, First Masonic District Association of New York. Past Grand High Priest of the Most Excellent Prince Hall Grand Chapter, Holy Royal Arch Mason.

Member, King David Consistory, Number three, Ancient Accepted Scottish Rite, of Freemasonry, Prince Hall Affiliation, Northern Jurisdictions, of the United States of America.

Member of Alpha Council, Number One, Royal and Select Masons, of New York City, New York.

Honorary Member, Progressive Lodge #64, Mount Vernon, N.Y. Thirty-Third Degree, Ancient Accepted Scottish Rite, Prince Hall Affiliate, Northern Jurisdiction, United States of America.

◊ ◊ ◊

CHARLES C. DIGGS, JR.
Congressman

Hon. CHARLES C. DIGGS, JR., Member of Congress from Detroit, Michigan. Born: Detroit, Michigan—December 2, 1922. Graduated from Wayne State University, and Detroit College of Law.

Licensed Mortician. Member of the Michigan Bar. Former Michigan State Senator. Former Chairman of the Congressional Black Caucus. Prince Hall Freemason. Grand Lodge of Michigan. Listed: "Who's Who Among Black Americans."

Documentation Masonic: "The Crisis." The Schomburg Collection on Black History and Culture

◊ ◊ ◊

JOHN WESLEY DOBBS
**Grand Master of Prince Hall Masons of Georgia
(1932)
(Unanimously re-elected annually.)
(Active Thirty-third degree Mason.)
Grand Minister of State—United Supreme Council
Scottish Rite Free Masonry—Southern Jurisdiction
and
Past Imperial Potentate
Ancient Egyptian Arabic Order,
Nobles of the Mystic Shrine, North and South America.**

JOHN WESLEY DOBBS, was born near Marietta, Cobbs County, Georgia. He was educated in the Public Schools of Savannah, Georgia, and at Morehouse College, in Atlanta, Georgia. He was employed in the Railway (United States) Mail Service for thirty-two years, and was Honorably retired with Pension.

Achievements
Life-member and National Vice-President, N.A.A.C.P.
Director, Citizens Trust Bank of Atlanta, Georgia.
Past Vice-President of the State Central Committee of the Republican Party in Georgia.
Member of "Omega Psi Phi, Greek Letter Fraternity.

Grand Master John Wesley Dobbs, worked untiringly to educate the black people of Georgia, on the power of the ballot. Reminding them, "That a Voteless People—Is a Helpless People." Today there are more than two hundred thousand black voters in the State of Georgia.

Masonic Documentation: Most Worshipful Grandmaster, X.L. Neal, of the Prince Hall Grand Lodge of Georgia. (The State of Georgia.)

◊ ◊ ◊

JAMES C. DODD
Architect

Owner: Dodd & Associates, Architects and Planners.

Owner: Urban Construction Company, Sacramento, California.

Past President, Central Valley Chapter, American Institute of Architects.

Vice-President, National Organization of Minority Architects.

Chairman of The Board of Governors, California State Community Colleges.

Thirty-Second Degree Prince Hall Mason and recipient of The Prince Hall Masonry Award for Architectural Design (1971).

Architectural Achievement Award, N.A.A.C.P. (1972).

Vice-President of The Sacramento Branch, N.A.A.C.P.

Member of the California Coordinating Council for Higher Education.

HERBERT M. DOUGLASS
Most Worshipful Grand Master of Prince Hall Masons of The State of New Jersey and Jurisdictions

Thirty-Third Degree, Ancient and Accepted Scottish Rite of Freemasonry, Northern Jurisdiction, Prince Hall Affiliation, United States of America.

Documentation: United Supreme Council, N.J., Prince Hall Affiliation, United States of America.

◊ ◊ ◊

PAUL DRAYTON
First: Grand Master of the Grand Lodge of New York State.

PAUL DRAYTON, was also a member of Boyer Grand Lodge, and when The National Grand Lodge of America was erected in 1845, he became an active member.

Worshipful Grand Master, Paul Drayton, of the Grand Lodge of New York State, was fair in complexion, and could have passed for white. However, he never did. Nevertheless, during his period as Grand Master, he visited North Carolina, and erected a number of Lodges in the State for Blacks. This caused quite a controversy, in both North Carolina, and New York State. The State of North Carolina accused the Grand Master of making Masons of Black men.

Masonic Documentation: Prince Hall Lodge for Research of New York.

◊ ◊ ◊

WILLIAM EDWARD BURGHARDT DUBOIS
(W.E.B. Dubois—1868-1963.)
(Made a Freemason on sight by the Worshipful Grandmaster.)
(Prince Hall Grand Lodge.)

W.E.B.DUBOIS, Educator, Author, Historian, Social Scientist and Leader and Organizer.
Born: February 28, 1868—Great Barrington, Massachusetts.
1890—B.A. Harvard University. (cum laude) He was one of the six elected commencement speakers. his thesis: Jefferson Davis: Representative of Civilization.

1892-94 Graduate Study—University of Berlin. (Germany) History and Economics.
1894-96 Professor of Greek and Latin—Wilberforce University.
1896—Doctorate of Philosophy (PH.D.) degree at Harvard University. Dissertation: Suppression of African Slave Trade. (1638-1870)
1896-97 Assistant Professor, Sociology—University of Pennsylvania.
1897-1910 Professor of Economics and History at Atlanta University.
1900—Secretary—First Pan African Conference in England.
1905-09 Founder and General Secretary of "The Niagara Movement."
1909—Among the Original Founders and Incorporators of the N.A.A.C.P. National Association for the Advancement of Colored People.
1910—Founder and Editor of "The Crisis" magazine, until 1934.
1921—Secretary—Pan African Congress—London, Brussels and Paris.
1923—Spingarn Medalist; Special Minister Plenipotentiary and Envoy Extraordinary Representing the United States at the Inauguration of the President of Liberia. Third Pan African Congress in London, Paris and Lisbon.
1934-44 Chairman, Department of Sociology—Atlanta University.

1940—Founder and Editor: Phylon Magazine (Altanta.) Accredited from N.A.A.C.P., as Consultant to the Founding United Nations; seeks firm Anti-Colonial commitment on the part of the United States. Presides at the Fifth Pan African Congress in Manchester, England.
1947—Edits on behalf on the N.A.A.C.P., and presents to the United Nations "An Appeal To The World" protesting segregation and Racial Discrimination in the United States.

Dr. W.E.B. DuBois died on August 27, 1963 in Accra, Ghana, and was given a State Funeral, the day a quarter million people marched on Washington, demanding an end to segregation and discrimination. Finally, what is it in the life of William Edward Burhardt DuBois, that emerges as his most outstanding achievement?

The answer is, he stood fast by his principles and ideals to the end, that his convictions about them grew stronger, that his defense of them grew more and more vigorous with the passing years. In conclusion, Dr. DuBois's greatest virtue was his committed empathy with all of the oppressed, and his Divine dissatisfaction with all forms of injustice. In essence, the spirit that perseveres to the end is sustained by a threefold force of feeling, of will, and of mind.

Masonic Documentation: W.E.B. DuBois Papers. The University of Massachusetts, and The Williamson Prince Hall Masonic Collection.

◊ ◊ ◊

EDWARD D. DUGGER, JR., 33°
Dayton, Ohio
1919–1975
36th M. W. Grand Master
M. W. Prince Hall Grand Lodge of Ohio
1965–1967
Past M. E. Grand High Priest
Grand Holy Royal Arch of Ohio

EDWARD D. DUGGER, JR., masonic leader, athlete, engineer, and humanitarian, was born in Medford, Massachusetts in 1919. He retired as Chief of Scientific and Information Office at Wright Patterson Air Base, Ohio.

Education
Tufts University

Member of Omega Psi Phi Fraternity.

National Collegiate record holder, ICAAAA champion, New England champion and National AAU champion in low and high hurdles.

Board member of Dayton Athletic Club, United Fund, Selective Service Board, NAACP, and Kidney Foundation.

Masonic membership: Past Master, Ancient Square Lodge #40, F. & A.M. Member, Unity Chapter #95, OES. Past Commander-in-Chief, Miami Consistory #26, AASR. Past Grand Thrice Ill. Master-Royal & Select Masons. Past Potentate, Amer Temple #107, AEANOMS.

Masonic Documentation: Georgia Masonic Research Center.

◊ ◊ ◊

ALEXANDER DUMAS
Writer — Dramatist — Novelist
Masonic Grand Lodge of France

ALEXANDER DUMAS, born in Paris, France, in 1802. At the age of fifteen he began working as a clerk, and at the age of eighteen he began his writing career. He wrote much, but received no praise, nor compensation for his work. But in 1826, at the age of twenty-four years, his fame as an author began with, "The Novelles." In 1829, Dumas, wrote and produced the historical play, *"Henry, the Third."*

The absence of colorphobia in France, during the Life and Times of Writer and Dramatist Alexander Dumas, his illustrious name entered the ranks of world literature without any question as to skin-color, the French people just referred to his works.
The Three Musketeers. Published in Eight volumes.
The Count of Monte Cristo. Published in Twelve volumes.
Le Reine Margot. Published in six volumes.

Sketches of all three Dumas's can be found in various places, including, but not limited to:
"Americana Encyclopedia."
"Encyclopedia Britannica."
"Chamber's Encyclopedia."
"Afro-American Encyclopedia."

The Life and Adventures of Alexander Dumas, by Perry Fritzgerald (1873.) Alexander Dumas Attributed his greatness to the role that his mother played in his life. However on second thought, how can we objectively evaluate the truly remarkable role mother's play in the history of their son's loves?

It is written:
Demosthenes — father was a blacksmith.
Euripides — father was a vegetable merchant.
Socrates — father was a mediocre sculptor.
Columbus — father was a woodcarver.
Carver's — father was a black slave.

Shakespeare's—father was a butcher.
Cromwell's—father was a brewer.
Douglass's—father was a black slave.
Pushkin's—father was a black General.

Greatness of all these men have been accorded by those who speak of them, and for them, as attributing their remarkable achievements, and extraordinary talents to the gentility of their mothers.

Masonic Documentation: Mille Volti Di Massoni Di Giordano Gamberini—Roma—1975

◇ ◇ ◇

OSCAR J. DUNN
Lieutenant Governor of the State of Louisiana
1868–1871
Worshipful Grand Master of Masons in the State of Louisiana and Jurisdiction
1864–1867
Past District Deputy Grand Master of Masons in the State of Ohio.

OSCAR J. DUNN, was conceded to be one of the most brilliant men of his time. He was known throughout Louisiana for his political statue. And he was near being Governor of the State of Louisiana, when he died suddenly. It was alleged that Grandmaster Dunn was poisoned by his political enemies.

Lieutenant Governor Dunn, a member of Eureka Lodge, and in 1869, he succeeded in having Eureka Grand Lodge, incorporated by an Act of the Legislature as the sole source of Ancient Free and Accepted York Masonry in the State of Louisiana.

Masonic Documentation: Worshipful Grand Master, Earle L. Bradford, Grand Master of Prince Hall Masons of the State of Louisiana and its Jurisdictions.

J.J. DURHAM
Blacksmith—Minister—Medical Doctor

J.J. DURHAM, born April 13, 1849, near Woodruffs, Spartanburg County, South Carolina.

Apprenticed at an early age to learn the Blacksmith's trade. He worked by day, and studied at night until he learned to read and write.

1867, Durham was converted and joined Pilgrim Baptist Church, in Greenville County. The same year he was licensed to preach, and entered the ministry, as an assistant minister. In 1868, Minister Durham was called to preach at Foster's Chapel, in the City of Spartanburg, South Carolina. A few years later he paid an instructor to teach him Latin and Algebra. And when South Carolina College, opened to black students, Reverend Durham enrolled. Thereafter the degrees were after his name.

Atlanta University, A.B.
Fisk University, A.M.

Thereafter, Minister J.J. Durham enrolled in, "Meharry Medical College," in Nashville Tennessee, and completed all his medical courses in two years, graduating in March 1862, Valedictorian of his class, and with the degree, "Medical Doctor." He was also a member of the debating team, and later a National Debater.

◊ ◊ ◊

FRANCOIS "Papa Doc" DUVALIER
Physician and Surgeon
(Ph.D. & M.D.)
President of the Republic of Haiti.
Minister of Public Health of Haiti
Masonic Membership—Grand Lodge of France.

FRANCOIS DUVALIER, was born in Port-au-Prince. Haiti, on April 14, 1907. He was the son of a teacher, and the grandson of a tailor.

Education
Lycee Alexander Petion, Port-au-Prince.
University of Haiti Medical School.
University of Michigan, United States of America.

Internship: Hospital, Saint Francois de-sales.

He wrote for the newspaper, "Action Nationale." The articles were considered brilliant, witty and thought-provoking. Thereafter he specialized in tropical diseases.

1946—Director of Public Health—Republic of Haiti.
1948—Minister of Public Health—Republic of Haiti.
1957—Elected President of the Republic of Haiti.

During the Administration of President Duvalier, the bond and the ties with Africa were strengthened. He envisioned Africa in the vanguard of the Colonial and neo-colonial liberation movement.

Masonic Documentation: Mille Volti Di Massoni Di Giordano Gamberini, Roma, 1975

◊ ◊ ◊

JOHN W. EDGHILL
21st Imperial Potentate
Ancient Egyptian Arabic Order Nobles Mystic Shrine
1972-1974

"CHAMP" EDGHILL was born in New York City in 1921 and reared in Atlantic City, New Jersey. He was a professional boxer for a number of years with a record of 75 wins, 1 loss, and 12 draws. At one time, he was ranked the number 7th world welter weight contender by *Ring Magazine.*

Education
Public schools of New Jersey and New York
B.S., West Coast University-Los Angeles

Joined the American Tobacco Company in 1951.

Past Exalted Ruler, I.B.P.O.E. (Elks) of New York.

Member, Kiwanis Club.

Past Commander, Kenneth Hawkes Post #61, American Legion of Atlantic City, New Jersey.

Masonic membership: Mount Pisgal Lodge #83-Brooklyn, New York. Long Island Consistory #61, AASR. Abu-Bekr Temple #71, AEAONMS, Brooklyn, New York.

At age 51, he was the youngest noble ever elected Imperial Potentate.

Masonic Documentation: Georgia Masonic Research Center.

◊ ◊ ◊

RAYMOND P. ELIE
Grand Master, Banker, Executive

Grand Master, The Grand Orient of the Republic of Haiti.

Director, The National Bank of the Republic of Haiti.

Director, The Central Bank of the Republic of Haiti.

Director, General Purchase for the Republic of Haiti.

Vice-President, Board of Directors of The Flour Mill of Haiti.

Masonic Documentation: Personal interview and Archives of the Grand Orient of the Republic of Haiti.

◊ ◊ ◊

EDWARD KENNEDY ELLINGTON
(Duke)
(1899–1974)
Composer—Musician—Orchestra Leader

EDWARD KENNEDY ELLINGTON, was born on April 29, 1899, in Washington, D.C. He wrote his first musical composition at the age of fifteen. The title was "Soda Fountain Rag." He later organized his orchestra, and kept it together for almost fifty years, in a fashion unparalleled by any other artist in the history of music. He acquired the nickname "Duke," because of his regal bearing and his immense dignity. His artistic talent was recognized early, and he was offered a scholarship at The Pratt Institute of Fine Arts.

Thirty-Second Degree, Ancient and Accepted Scottish Rite of Freemasonry, Prince Hall Affiliation, Southern Jurisdiction, United States of America.

Active in: The Acatia Grand Lodge, District of Columbia.

Listed are a few of Duke's popular compositions:
   Mood Indigo   Solitude   Daybreak Express
   Liberian Suite   Blue Bells of Harlem   Deep South
                       Suite
              Sophisticated Lady

Concert at The Cathedral of San Francisco and in Synagogues with Duke Ellington's Music sung in Hebrew.

                Conducted
          The London Philharmonic
              Paris Opera
             LaScala Opera

Duke fused jazz with formal concert idiom.

Duke was born into a deeply religious family, and he began piano lessons when he was seven years old.

Gold Medal Humanitarian Award from President Lyndon Baines Johnson, at the White House. Doctor of Music Degrees from both Columbia and Yale Universities. Conducted a Sacred Concert at Westminster Abbey.

Duke Ellington was honored at the White House on his seventieth birthday as guest of President Richard Nixon. He was presented with a medal and citation.

Derek Jewell, biographer of Duke Ellington:
"There will never be a definitive biography of Duke Ellington, who was the least definitive of geniuses."

◊ ◊ ◊

ROBERT BROWN ELLIOT
The Second—Grand Master of the Prince Hall Grand Lodge of the State of South Carolina

Member of the South Carolina State Constitutional Convention of 1868, which operated under Federal Constitutional guidelines.

Member of the State of South Carolina House of Representatives (1868–1870).

Congressman from the State of South Carolina to the United States House of Representatives, Washington, D.C.

Speaker of the United States House of Representatives (1875–1876).

Grand Master, Robert Brown Elliott, was the second Worshipful Prince Hall Grand Master in the State of South Carolina.

◊ ◊ ◊

EDGAR E. EVANS
Educator

Professor, Alabama State University, 1949–1972.

Fellow, Royal Society of Health, 1965.

Member: American Academy of Political Science, and American Society for the Study of Education.

Life member, N.A.A.C.P.

Thirty-Third Degree, Ancient and Accepted Scottish Rite of Freemasonry, Southern Jurisdiction, Prince Hall Affiliation, United States of America.

Documentation: Who's Who Among Black Americans, 1975–76.

MELVIN H. EVANS
Physician
Commissioner of Health of the U.S. Virgin Islands
Senior Assistant Surgeon, U.S. Public Health Service
Governor of the U.S. Virgin Islands

MELVIN H. EVANS, born Christiansted, Virgin Islands, August 7, 1917.

Education
Howard University, B.A., 1940, Magna Cum Laude
Howard University, College of Medicine, M.D., 1944, Honor Student
University of California, M.P.H., 1967

Positions
Chief Municipal Hospital Physician, 1948–1951
Senior Assistant Surgeon, U.S. Public Health Service
Commissioner of Health, 1959–1967
Appointed governor of the U.S. Virgin Islands

The first elected governor of the United States Virgin Islands.

Masonic Documentation: Freemason

◊ ◊ ◊

MEDGAR WILEY EVERS
(1925–1963)
N.A.A.C.P. Field Director
Thirty-Second Degree Ancient and Accepted Scottish Rite of Freemasonry, Prince Hall, Affiliation Southern Jurisdiction

MEDGAR WILEY EVERS, was born July 2, 1925, in Decatur, Mississippi.

Education
Alcorn Agricultural and Mechanical College in Southwest, Mississippi. He was editor of the Alcorn College Herald, President of the Junior Class and Vice-President of the Student Forum.

Medgar Evers was the first black applicant for the University of Mississippi Law School since the Reconstruction years when the State was represented on all governmental levels by black men.

He let the sit-in at Woolworth's lunch counter in Jackson, Mississippi. Organized over two thousand angry blacks to a church meeting where he was the key speaker. Later, he gave the Southern Civil Rights struggle new vigor and leadership.

Medgar Evers College, of the City University of New York, is named and stands as a monument and memorial to his courage, honor and determination.

After his death from a sniper's bullet, his body was viewed from the Mississippi State Prince Hall Masonic Grand Lodge.

◊ ◊ ◊

LOUIS FAIR, JR.
(1895–1978)
Past Most Worshipful Grand Master
State of New York

LOUIS FAIR, JR., Past Most Worshipful Grand Master, State of New York. Born: New York, N.Y., May 5, 1895.

Past Grand Master Louis Fair, Jr., was termed a dreamer who put foundations under his dreams. He combined vision with reality. It was through his vision that the Most Worshipful Prince Hall Grand Lodge of the State of New York grew and prospered. Here examples were set, precedents established and knowledge defined for other Grand Lodges to follow. This was done in other jurisdictions. The concrete accomplishments, lofty projects and enriching endeavors became akin to a powerful lighthouse for all to see on America's turbulent sea during the transfigured night.

The Masonic Climb of Louis Fair, Jr.:
    Entered Apprentice, 9/22/1922
    Fellowcraft, 10/22/1922
    Master Mason, 11/28/1922
    Past Master, Adelphia Union Lodge #14
    District Deputy Grand Master, 1934–1936
    Junior Grand Warden, 1936–1937
    Senior Grand Warden, 1938
    Deputy Grand Master, 1940–1942
    Grand Master, 1942–1952

Past Grand Master Louis Fair, Jr's. illustrious name is imprinted in the annals of Prince Hall Masonry because of his untiring efforts and sharp and penetrating insight that made his dreams living realities. Prince Hall Grand Lodge now owns, free and clear, the magnificent Temple at 454 West 155th Street, New York City. The money was raised within one year. He also purchased six valuable lots adjacent to the Temple for promotional purpose, foreseeing and hoping that key positions would be available for the brethren of the craft upon their development. The nine hundred and sixty-four acres at Roscoe, New York, was another of the Past Grand Master Fair's acquisitions.

This property, valued at more than a half-million dollars, will serve as a haven for the aged and indigent Prince Hall Masons, their widows and orphans. He also organized the Voluntary Immediate Relief which has paid more than one hundred thousand dollars in the First Masonic District.

When Louis Fair, Jr., became Grand Master of the Most Worshipful Prince Hall Grand Lodge of the State of New York and its jurisdictions in June 1942, there were approximately two thousand members on the roster, and the balance in the treasury was less than three thousand dollars. In ten years of Grand Master Fair's administration, the membership swelled to over six thousand members and the staggering sum of two hundred thirty-three thousand, nine hundred sixty-eight dollars and three cents. These are a few of the many accomplishments of Past Most Worshipful Grand Master of the State of New York, Louis Fair, Jr.

Masonic Documentation: The Harry A. Williamson Collection of Black Masonry. Prince Hall Grand Lodge of the State of New York.

◇ ◇ ◇

W. CHARLES FENNICKS
Assistant Managing Editor, Voice of Prince Hall.
Former Assistant Principal of Lee County High School, State of Alabama.
Quality Control Inspector, Ford Motor Company.

Past Master, Corinthian Lodge #38, Detroit, Michigan. Member—The Wolverine Consistory, Number six. Member—Marracci Temple, Thirteen.

Masonic Documentation: The Michigan Voice of Prince Hall.

◇ ◇ ◇

EUGENE ALPHONSO FFOLKES
Past District Grand Warden (Masonic) of Jamaica.
Past Master of Jamaica Lodge #7254 E.C.
Consulting Engineer.
Partner, Folkes & Harrison Engineering Associates.

Education
Jamaica College
McGill University
Durham University. (Masters of Science degree.)

Watchword
"A smooth sea never makes a successful mariner, nor is a man perfected without adversity."

Masonic Documentation: International Guide To Who's Who In The Caribbean. (West Indies.) Personalities In The Caribbean.

◊ ◊ ◊

JOSEPH SIMEON FLIPPER
College President, Lawyer, Bishop, Masonic Leader, Dean

Deputy Grand Master, Most Worshipful Union Grand Lodge of The State of Georgia, F. & A.M. 1887–1888.

Bishop of The African Methodist Church and Dean at Turner Theological Seminary.

President, Morris Brown College, Atlanta, Georgia.

Attorney at Law.

Masonic Documentation: Georgia Masonic Research Center.

◊ ◊ ◊

ALONZO D. FOOTE, SR.
Lieutenant Colonel, United States Army (Ret.)
Treasurer of The Phylaxis Society

Fellow of The Phylaxis Society.

Thirty-Third Degree, Ancient and Accepted Scottish Rite of Freemasonry, Prince Hall Affiliation, Northern Jurisdiction, United States of America.

Imperial Potentate, The Shrine, Desert of Seattle.

Documentation: Tenth Anniversary Journal, The Phylaxis Society.

◊ ◊ ◊

B. ALBERT FORD
Grand Minister of State
United Supreme Council

Ancient and Accepted Scottish Rite of Freemasonry (Prince Hall Affiliations) Northern Jurisdiction, United States of America, Inc. and Thirty Third Degree, Ancient and Accepted Scottish Rite of Freemasonry (Prince Hall Affiliation) Northern Jurisdiction, United States of America.

◊ ◊ ◊

JOHNNY L. FORD
Mayor
Mayor of Tuskegee, Alabama

Former Executive Director and Coordinator of Tuskegee Model Cities Program.

Chairman of Alabama's Black Mayor's Committee.

Masonic membership: Silver Trowell Lodge #10, F. & A.M.

Member, Governor of Alabama's Manpower Committee.

Member; Tuskegee Airmen's International.

Documentation: Who's Who Among Black Americans, 1975–76.

EDWARD FORSTER
1902–1982
Grand Master and Certified Public Accountant

Past Grand Master of the Republic of Guinea, West Africa.

Past Certified Public Accountant (C.P.A.) of the Republic of Guinea, West Africa.

Past Treasurer and Warden of All Saints Church of the Republic of Guinea, West Africa.

Past Certified Public Accountant (C.P.A.) of Founis Corporation of the Republic of Guinea, West Africa.

Masonic Documentation: Masonic Archives of the Republic of Guinea, West Africa, and Daughter Millicent During.

◊ ◊ ◊

JAMES FORTEN
(1766–1848)
Inventor—Manufacturer—Philanthropist
Masonic Organizer
Member and Office of the African Lodge #459, Philadelphia, Pa.

JAMES FORTEN, was born free in 1866, at Philadelphia, Pennsylvania. His friends included, but were not limited to Richard Allen, Absalom Jones, Paul Cuffee, and William Lloyd Garrison.

Forten briefly attended the school of the anti-slavery Quaker, Anthony Benezet. At the age of fifteen he enlisted as a powder boy on the Royal Louis, a privateer, commanded by Captain Stephen Decatur, and sailing the high seas. During an engagement at sea, the ship was captured, and Forten taken prisoner with other officers and crew members. After seven months on a floating hell prison ship, he was exchanged, which was rare in the case of a black, as they were generally sold as slaves in the West Indies. But he walked home from the Port of Philadelphia, after being freed.

After a long and distinguished career as inventor, manufacturer, philanthropist and masonic organizer, Forten recalled as he neared age sixty, that his great-grandfather was brought from Africa and enslaved, but his grandfather obtained his freedom. And he was born free, and was a great man, enchanced by Prince Hall Freemasonry.

Masonic Documentation: Historical Society of Pennsylvania. The Harry A. Williamson Collection of Black Masonry.

◊ ◊ ◊

AMOS FORTUNE
(1706-1801)

AMOS FORTUNE, Tanner and Bookbinder, born in Woburn, Massachusetts, a slave. He became a master tanner, and purchased his freedom when he was sixty years old.

Ams Fortune was a master tanner, and business was good. He paid his Church and Town taxes regularly and in 1744, purchased a half-acre of land near the Wilmington road.

In 1781, Fortune moved to Jaffery, New Hampshire. There he set-up his tannery and prospered. As his business progressed, he took in apprentices, black and white. After joining the Church, he became one of the first citizens of Jaffery. There were other free blacks in the Town, but none had done as well as Amos Fortune, and he reached out for them. He had read and knew enough law to act as an attorney and counsellor for brothers in distress.

Thereafter, Fortune became a Founder of the Town's Social Library, and began his free service of rebinding the books in the collection. His tombstone read: "Amos Fortune born free in Africa, enslaved in America, he purchased his freedom, professed Christianity, lived reputably and died hopefully at the age of ninety-one, on November 17, 1801.

Masonic Documentation: New Hampshire Historical Society. Massachusett's Historical Society.

◊ ◊ ◊

TIMOTHY THOMAS FORTUNE
(1856–1928)

TIMOTHY THOMAS FORTNE, Mail-clerk, Printer, Journalist, Editor. Born in Marianna, Florida in 1856. Considered by many as the Dean of Black American Journalist.

Education: Attended the first black school opened in Marianna, Florida. Howard University, Washington, Dictrict of Columbia.

Newspaper apprenticeship with, "The Courier," in Marianna, Florida, and journalism became an integrated part of Timothy T. Fortune. He immediately absorbed the information he was assembling in type. After becoming a master printer, he left the trade to become a mail-clerk, and saved enough money to enter Howard University. While in Washington, D.C., he met Frederick Douglass, and Booker T. Washington, and other famous black American Leaders.

Fortune later edited a book on "The Speeches of Booker T. Washington." He also edited the paper issued by "Marcus Garvey," the Jamacian who strongly influenced black people with his, "back-to-Africa-Movement."

The day came when, President Theodore Roosevelt, would say, "Tom Fortune, keep that pen of yours off me."

Masonic Documentation: Williamson Masonic Collection, Schomburg Library.

◊ ◊ ◊

SAMUEL FRAUNCES
(1722–1795)
Chief Steward for President George Washington at the White House.
Tavern-owner and Revolutionary Patriot.
Member of Holland Lodge, Number eight, of New York City, New York.

SAMUEL FRAUNCES, a West Indian black man who was owner and keeper of "Fraunces Tavern," in the Wall Street area, of New York City, between 1762 to 1765 and from 1789 to 1794. He also served as Household Steward to President and General George Washington.

Fraunces was a Freemason and a member of Holland Lodge, number #8, of New York City, New York.

Masonic Documentation: "Ten Thousand Famous Masons."

◊ ◊ ◊

BENJAMIN THOMAS FREDERICK
Worshipful Master, Antioch Lodge #66, 1981
Superintendent in the New York Post Office

BENJAMIN THOMAS FREDERICK, was born in Brooklyn, New York on May 26, 1931, and was formally educated in the New York City School System. He servered in the United States Army during the Korean Conflict.

Masonic record: Member of Anticoh Lodge, since 1972. Member of Widow's Son Chapter, Number One, Royal Arch Masons. Antioch Study Club, one of his many sources of Masonic light, and Master Frederick urges all members of the craft to avail themselves to the teaching and instructions the Study Club affords.

Master Benjamin Thomas Frederick, advanced from the beginner's status in the United States Post Office in 1957, through dedicated service, love for learning and untiring effort to Superintendent in the New York Postal Service.

He possesses an unshakable faith in mankind's destiny, and refuses to believe that we are so tragically bound to the starless midnight of racism, exploitation and war, that we cannot see the bright daylight of Brotherhood, Peace and Equality, here and now!

◊ ◊ ◊

THEODORE FREEMAN
Past Master of Carthaginian Lodge #47, Prince Hall Affiliation

Founder and Organizer of Abu Bekr Temple #91, A.E.O.N.M.S., and First Illustrious Potentate.

Member of Medina Temple #19.

Thirty-Third Degree, Ancient and Accepted Scottish Rite of Freemasonry, Prince Hall Affiliation, Northern Jurisdiction, United States of America.

Documentation: New York State Grand Lodge Library and Museum (F. & A.M.)

◊ ◊ ◊

HERBERT H. FRITGERALD
Detective

President, Brother Officer Law Enforcement Society.

Member, New Jersey Narcotic Enforcement Officers Association.

Member, Trenton Housing Authority Commission.

Board of Director, Model City Policy Commission.

Advisory Board Member, Industrial Home for Boys.

Master Mason, King David Lodge #15, F. & A.M. (Prince Hall).

Thirty-Second Degree Freemason, Ophir Consistory #48, Trenton, N.J.

Documentation: Who's Who Among Black Americans, 1980–81.

◊ ◊ ◊

JAMES E. FULLER
(1846–1909)
Most Worshipful Prince Hall Grandmaster of the State of Virginia
City Councilman of Norfork, VA.

JAMES E. FULLER, was the first black City Councilman of Norfork, Virginia during the Reconstruction period. He started the first colored school, or school for blacks in the City of Norfork, and area.

Councilman James E. Fuller, played a major role in the erection of a monument in old West Point Cemetery in honor of black Union Soldiers who gave their lives during the Civil War. There is a movement led by Prince Hall Masons to establish, "The James E. Fuller Memorial Day," in the City of Norfork, Virginia.

Masonic Documentation: Southern Masonic Review.

◊ ◊ ◊

SUMNER A. FURNISS
Past Sovereign Grand Commander
United Supreme Council Ancient and Accepted of Scottish Rite of Freemasonry,
Northern Jurisdiction.
Thirty-third Degree, Ancient and Accepted of Scottish Rite of Freemasonry,
Prince Hall Affiliation, United States of America, Northern Jurisdiction.

Past Worshipful Grandmaster, of Prince Hall Masons of Indiana and Jurisdictions.

◊ ◊ ◊

HOMER E. GAINES
Businessman

Self-employed owner of two Gasoline and Service Repair Stations.

Most Worshipful Grand Master of The State of Michigan and Jurisdiction (1957–1958).

Chairman of The Cathedral Maintenance Committee.

Mason Gaines is Past Master, Past Commander-in-Chief, Past Potentate, and a member of Detroit Chapter, Number One, Holy Royal Arch Masons.

Grand Lecturer for six years in the Grand Lodge of the State of Michigan.

Thirty-Third Degree, Ancient and Accepted Scottish Rite of Freemasonry, Northern Jurisdiction, Prince Hall Affiliation, United States of America.

◊ ◊ ◊

HENRY HIGHLAND GARNET

HENRY HIGHLAND GARNET, President of Avery College and United States Minister and Consul-General to Liberia, was born in 1815 to slave parents. His grandfather was a Mandingo Chief, kidnapped from Africa's West Coast by slave-traders. When he was nine years of age, his family and seven other slaves excaped to the North by Wagon and on foot.

The family first settled in New Hope Pennsylvania, but within a few years moved to New York City. And at the age of eleven, Garnet was enrolled in the African Free School. After years as a student he took a job as a cook and steward on a schooner. Returning he studied "Greek and Latin" in the High School. Garnet completed his studies at Oneida Institute and graduated with honors. Thereafter he settled in Troy, New York, where he taught school and edited a weekly newspaper.

Garnet spoke before "The United States Congress," and also served as the "President of Avery College." He was appointed by President James A. Garfield, as United States Minister and Consul-General to Liberia. He died and was buried in Africa. In America, HENRY HIGHLAND GARNET, was eulogized by Alexander Crummel and others.

KENNETH ALLEN GIBSON
Mayor of the City of Newark, New Jersey.
Former Chief Engineer of the City of
Newark Housing Authority.

Grand Inspector General, Thirty Third Degree, Ancient and Accepted Scottish Rite of Freemasonry. Prince Hall Affiliation, Northern Jurisdiction, United States of America.

Former Chief Structural Engineer of the City of Newark, New Jersey.

Mayor Gibson was born in Enterprise, Alabama on May 15, 1932.

Education
B.S. in Engineering, Newark College of Engineering

Board of Directors
Newark Y.M.C.A. and Y.W.C.A.
Newark Urban Coalition.
Frontiers International.

Masonic Documentation: The Phylaxis Society. New York State Masonic Library and Museum.

◊ ◊ ◊

RUSSELL SIDNEY GIDEON
Sovereign Grand Commander, United
Supreme Council, Ancient and
Accepted Scottish Rite of
Freemasonry, Prince Hall Affiliation,
Northern Jurisdiction.

Thirty-Third Degree, Ancient and Accepted Scottish Rite of Freemasonry. Prince Hall Affiliation, Northern Jurisdiction, United States of America.

Registered Pharmacist
President of Gideon's Madison Drug Company.
Past Imperial Potentate, A.E.A.O.N.
Lieutenant Grand Commander A.A.S.R.

Life Member, of the National Association for the Advancement of Colored People.

Member of the Board of Directors:
Seattle Urban League.
East Madison, Y.M.C.A.

Masonic Documentation: Ebony and The Schomburg Library.

◇ ◇ ◇

RICHARD D. GIDRON
President and Chief Executive Officer
Dick Gidron Cadillac, Incorporated
and
Member of Boyer Lodge, Number One
First Masonic District
Prince Hall Freemasonry.

RICHARD D. GIDRON, was born in Chicago, Illinois, on October 10, 1938. He graduated from Saint Paul Elementary School, and Booker T. Washington High School.

Higher education
Stratton College.
General Motors Institute of Technology.

Majoring in Business Management and Dealership Management.
Assistant Treasurer and Director of Consumer Affairs, State of New York.

Community activity
Board of Directors—Police Athletic League.
Board of Directors—Young Men's Christian Ass'n.
Board of Directors—Bronx Boys Club of America.
Board of Regents—Saint Peter's College.

Life member of the National Association for the Advancement of Colored People.

Masonic Documentation: Prince Hall Sentinel.

◊ ◊ ◊

T.G. GIVENS
Masonic Leader of Texas

Right Worshipful "T.G. Givens," Past Worshipful Grandmaster of the Prince Hall Grand Lodge of Texas and Jurisdictions.
and
Commander-in-Chief—North Star Consistory—Number #245 Paris, Texas.

Past Grand Lodge Communications Officer.
Past Chairman of the Grand Lodge Finance Committee.
Past Chairman of the Grand Lodge Scholarship Committee.

Member, Senior Warden and Worshipful Master . . . Olive Branch Lodge Number #19—Paris, Texas.

Education
Degrees from Prairie View College, in Texas.

Principal: Gibbons High School, Paris, Texas.

◊ ◊ ◊

CARLTON B. GOODLETT, 33°
San Francisco, California
Medical Doctor
Publisher
California Voice
San Francisco Sun Reporter
President
National Newspaper Publishers Association
1973-1978
Chairman of the Board
New Journal & Guide Newspaper
Norfolk, Virginia

CARLTON B. GOODLETT, newspaper editor, civil rights activist, advisor to 6 presidents, and advocate of world peace, was born July 23, 1914, in Chipley, Florida, and reared in Omaha, Nebraska.

Education
Central High School, Omaha
Howard University, B.S.
University of California, Ph.D.
Meharry Medical College, M.D.

In 1966 Dr. Goodlett ran in the gubernational primary elections of California and came in third in a field of six Democrats.

President, National Black United Fund.

Past President, San Francisco NAACP.

Assistant Publisher, The Big Red Newspaper, New York City.

Former Director, San Francisco Council of Boy Scouts.

Chairman, California Black Leadership Conference.

Member, Board of Trustees, Talladega College.

Member, Board of Overseers, Medical School of Morehouse College.

Masonic membership: Hannibal Lodge #1, F. & A.M. Golden Gate Consistory #295, AASR. Thutmore Temple #74, AEAONMS.

Masonic Documentation: Georgia Masonic Research Center.

◊ ◊ ◊

LESTER R. GRANGER
Executive Secretary, National Urban League

MASON GRANGER built the National Urban League into a Leading Minority Social Service Organization.

Thirty-Third Degree, Ancient and Accepted Scottish Rite of Freemasonry, Northern Jurisdiction, Prince Hall Affiliation, United States of America.

◊ ◊ ◊

RAYMOND L. GRAY, SR.
Executive

President, Local Union #2049, A.F.G.E., A.F.L.-C.I.O., Naval Ordnance Lab.

Executive Committee Member, American Federation of Government Employees (Fourteenth District).

Assistant Educational Director, Department of National Office (A.F.G.E.).

Member of The Board of Directors, A. Philip Randolph Institute.

Worshipful Master, Warren Lodge #8, F. & A.M. Prince Hall.

Right Worshipful Grand Trustee, Prince Hall Grand Lodge.

Member of The Board of Directors of Stoddard Baptist Home.

Documentation: Who's Who Among Black Americans, 1975-76.

◊ ◊ ◊

WILLIAM GRAY
Congressman

Chairman, Finance Committee—United States House of Representatives

Thirty-Third Degree, Ancient and Accepted Scottish Rite of Freemasonry, Prince Hall affiliated, Northern Jurisdiction, United States of America.

Documentation: The Bulletin, Official Organ United Supreme Council, Ancient and Accepted Scottish Rite of Freemasonry (Prince Hall Affilitation) Northern Jurisdiction, United States of America., Inc.

◊ ◊ ◊

FLAVE K. GREEN 33°
District Deputy Grand Master
of The First Masonic District
of New York State

Subway Motorman with New York City Transit Authority (Ret.).

Worshipful Master of Antioch Lodge #66, in 1971.

Master of The Year Award from The Most Worshipful Prince Hall Grand Lodge.

Thirty-Third Degree, King David Consistory #3, A.A.S.R.

Past District Deputy Grand Lecturer.

Member of The Phylaxis Society.

Sergeant (Ret.) #332 Fighter Group, Stationed in Italy.

Documentation: Yearbook 1982, Antioch Lodge #66, F. & A.M., Prince Hall.

◊ ◊ ◊

J. EDWARD GREEN
Masonic Leader

Past Master and Treasurer, Boaz Lodge #65, F. & A.M.

Life Member, The Phylaxis Society.

Past Potentate, Sahara Temple #2, Pittsburgh, Pa.

Treasurer, Menlick Chapter #29, H.R.A.M.

Captain General, Cyrene Commandery #9 K.T.

Thirty-Third Degree, Ancient and Accepted Scottish Rite of Freemasonry, Northern Jurisdiction, Prince Hall Affiliation, United States of America.

◊ ◊ ◊

WILLIAM OLIVER GREEN
1906–1982
Most Worshipful Grand Master of the Prince Hall Grand Lodge of the State of Michigan

Thirty-Third Degree, Ancient and Accepted Scottish Rite of Freemasonry, Prince Hall Affiliation, Northern Jurisdiction, United States of America.

Member, The Phylaxis Society.

Illustrious Potentate, Marracci Temple #13.

Worshipful Master, Doric Lodge #22.

Documentation: The Phylaxis Newsletter, Vol. 5, December 1982.

◊ ◊ ◊

CLIFTON S. GREENE
Business Executive

Owner, Cliff Greene's Wine and Liquors Corporation.

Chief Executive Officer, Greene and Harris Enterprises, Inc.

Built a multi-million dollar Housing Development for the elderly in Brooklyn's Bedford Stuyvesant Section.

First black man in the United States to file with the Federal Communications Commission for an Ultra High Frequency T.V. Station.

Masonic membership: Widow's Son Lodge #11, Long Island Consistory #61.

Thirty-Second Degree, Prince Hall Freemason.

Documentation: Who's Who Among Black Americans, 1980–81.

◊ ◊ ◊

JAMES E. GREENE
Senator
Vice-President of the Republic of Liberia

Former Superintendent of Education, Sinoe County.

Chairman of The True Whig Party of the Republic of Liberia.

Commander-in-Chief, Valley of Mesurado Consistory #237, Prince Hall Freemasonry of Liberia.

◊ ◊ ◊

NELSON E. GREENE
Funeral Director and Businessman

Commissioner of Alexandria Redevelopment and Housing Authority (1966–69).

Director and Owner, Greene Funeral Home.

Director of the City of Alexandria Board of Trade.

Member of The National Funeral Director's Association.

Member of Virginia Morticians Association.

Thirty-Second Degree, Prince Hall Freemason and a Shriner.

◊ ◊ ◊

WILLIAM ALBERT GREENE
Masonic Leader

Commander-in-Chief, Sardonias Consistory #41.

Most Excellent Grand High Priest, State of New Jersey.

Past Master, Integrity Lodge #51, Patterson, New Jersey.

William Greene Order of Pythorgans, Newark, New Jersey.

Thrice Illustrious Master, Haggai Council, Patterson, New Jersey.

Sir Knight Palestine Commandery #13, Jersey City, New Jersey.

Thirty-Third Degree, Ancient and Accepted Scottish Rite of Freemasonry, Northern Jurisdiction, Prince Hall Affiliation, United States of America.

Documentation: One Hundredth Anniversary Journal, United Supreme Council, Prince Hall Affiliation, Northern Jurisdiction.

◊ ◊ ◊

RICHARD THEODORE GREENER
(A.A.—LL.B.—LL.D.)

RICHARD THEODORE GREENER, Lawyer, Chief Civil Service Examiner, Dean of the Law School, at Howard University. Prized Essayist. Born in Philadelphia, Pennsylvannia. Lived in Boston, Mass.

Education
Grammer School of Cambridge, Massachusetts.
Phillips Academy, Andover, Massachusetts.
Howard University, B.A. Cambridge, Mass. 1870
at the age of twenty-six.

Achievements
Principal, Institute for Colored Youth, Philadelphia, Penn.
Principal, Summer High School, Washington, D.C.
Associate Editor, "New National Era." Newspaper.
Instructor, Law Department, Howard University.
Professor, Metaphysics and Logic,
University of South Carolina.
Professor, Department of Greek and Latin,
South Carolina University.

Attorney Greener, was considered a great orator. He was a popular spokesman for the Republican party.

Masonic Documentation: Williamson Collection, Schomburg Library.

RICHARD T. GREENER
United States Counsel General to Moscow, Russia.
Officer, Shekinah Lodge #5,
Charleston, South Carolina.
District Deputy Grand Master of Colored Masons of Georgia.

RICHARD GREENER, was one of the great black men of Masonry. Yet, the present generation is without knowledge of this distinguished black man.

He delivered the principal address before the Masonic Craft in Savannah, Georgia. The occasion was the celebration of the Feast of St John's Day, in June 1876, at the invitation of Eureka Lodge, number #1. An overflow crowd packed the Savannah Theatre; the other bodies participating were:

>Mount Moriah #16.
>Pythagoras #14.
>Hilton #2.

Along with The Grand Lodge of Georgia. Richard Greener, the District Deputy Grand Master was well received.

Masonic Documentation: Prince Hall Lodge for Research of New York. Williamson Masonic Collection on Black Masonry.

◊ ◊ ◊

WILLIAM R. GREENWOOD
Thirty-Third Degree, Ancient and Accepted
Scottish Rite of Freemasonry,
Prince Hall Affiliation, Western Jurisdiction of
the United States of America.
Vice-President and Manager of
Lowry Air Force Facility
of Colorado National Bank.
Assets $450,000,000.

WILLIAM R. GREENWOOD, is President of his own financial management firm in Denver, Colorado, and he is also the General Chairman of the Citizen's Budgetary Committee and Board Member of Dynamic Growth, Inc. He has developed a six million dollar luxury one story condominium building.

As Budget Director, William R. Greenwood, developed the budget and the financial plan for Titan 1, Missile Site, of the United States Air-force Academy.

Masonic Documentation: Official Bulletin of The United Supreme Council of Ancient and Accepted Scottish Rite of Freemasonry. (Prince Hall Affiliation.)

◊ ◊ ◊

WILLIAM H. GRIMSHAW
**Grandmaster of Black Masons in Washington, District of Columbia.
Commander of a Lodge of the Grand Army of the Republic.
Doorkeeper at the Entrance of the Reading Room of the Library of Congress**

Grimshaw's first book titled, "The Official History of Freemasonry Among The Colored People of North America," was considered a monumental work. He became a writer who was recognized as a Historian of Masonry among Black Americans, and one who was believed and accepted for his authorship and regarded as an authority. When his book was published in 1903, and thereafter his status soared.

Masonic Documentation: Williamson Prince Hall Masonic Collection.

◊ ◊ ◊

HERBERT M. GROCE, JR.
Rector and Grand Chaplain

Rector: Saint Andrew's Episcopal Church of New York.

Grand Chaplain of the Grand Lodge of Free and Accepted Masons of The State of New York.

Member: Allied Lodge #1170, F. & A.M. Thirty-Second Degree, Ancient Scottish Rite. Shriner in Mecca Temple #1. Knight of Malta.

Education
LaSalle College, Philadelphia, Penn.
Thomas A. Edison College, New Jersey.
Seton Hall University, New Jersey.
General Theological Seminary, New York.
Institute of Theology,
Cathedral Church of Saint John The Divine,
New York, New York.

Director: The Lincoln Center for the Performing Arts, The University of Medicine and Dentistry of New Jersey, The Radio Corporation of America, and The Singer Company of New York.

Masonic Documentation: Allied Lodge #1170, F. & A.M., The Grand Lodge Library and Museum of New York State.

◊ ◊ ◊

NEVILLE SHERLOCK GROSVENOR
Master-Mason, Prince Hall Memorial Lodge #100 of Barbados.

Managing Director, Advocate News of Barbados.
General Manager.
Voice Publishing Company, Limited.
Motto: "Every opportunity is a challenge."

Masonic Documentation: The International Guide to Who's Who in the West Indies. "Personalities in the Caribbean."

◊ ◊ ◊

EDWARD A. HAILES, SR.

EDWARD A. HAILES, SR., Minister and Sovereign Grand Keeper of the Archives, United Supreme Council, Ancient and Accepted Scottish Rite of Freemasonry, Prince Hall Affiliations for the Southern Jurisdiction. An ordained Baptist Minister in 1951, and Pastor of Union Baptist Church of New Bedford, Massachusetts until 1963.

Education
Virginia State College and Virginia Union University
Boston University and Harvard University.

Positions
Executive Director, Washington branch, N.A.A.C.P.
Executive Director, Washington, D.C. Center, Opportunities Industrial Center, a non-profit, self-help, independent organization for the unemployed and the underemployed.

Served on the Commission on Criminal Justice, Standard and Goals in the area of Civil Disorders.

Member: National Housing Corporation, N.A.A.C.P.
President, Washington, D.C., Branch N.A.A.C.P.

Biography
Who's Who Among Black Americans.
Who's Who In America.
International Who's Who Among Intellectuals.
Who's Who In Religion.

Candidate for the National Board of Directors of the National Association for the Advancement of Colored People.

◊ ◊ ◊

ALEX HALEY
(Writer and Author)

ALEX HALEY, taught himself to write during a twenty year career in the United States Coast Guard. After retiring with an Honorable Discharge, and the rating of "Chief Journalist," which was created for him. He then began as a Magazine Writer and Interviewer, before undertaking his first book, "The Autobiography of Malcolm X," which sold more than two million copies.

Alex Haley, spent twelve years researching and writing, "ROOTS," which had been hailed even before publication as, an epic work destined to become a classic of American Literature.

Earlier, Haley had interviewed and written sketches on the Life of Miles Davis, and other Superstars. He was born in Henning, Tennessee, in 1921.

Thirty-Third Degree, Ancient and Accepted Scottish Rite of Freemasonry, Prince Hall Affiliation, Southern Jurisdiction, United States of America.

Haley's—Roots—The Saga of an American Family.

Masonic Documentation: The Schomburg Collection of Black History and Culture.

AMOS T. HALL
Worshipful Grand Master, Amos T. Hall
Prince Hall Grand Lodge
of the State of Oklahoma
and
Associate District Judge in Oklahoma

AMOS T. HALL, distinguished civil rights lawyer, in the Southwest. Represented the National Association for the Advancement of Colored People, in numerous cases involving civil and constitutional law.

Past Master, and Past Worshipful Grand Master of Prince Hall Grand Lodge of the State of Oklahoma, and thirty-third degree Mason.

In 1971, Attorney and Grand Master, Amos T. Hall, was appointed Associate District Judge in Tulsa, Oklahoma.

AMOS T. HALL, PRESIDENT

Speaking as President of the Conference of Grand Masters, said: "Bogus Masonry is the most disturbing problem facing Masons today. It preys on the weak and uninformed. It offers empty honor and inducements to those with mercenary minds. It can and must be fought with:

              Legislation—Litigation—Education

Today finds Prince Hall Masonry occupying a place of leadership and influence unequaled by any other organization." (Los Angeles, California, 1954.)

◊ ◊ ◊

PRINCE HALL
(1735–1807)
Patroit—Organizer—Abolitionist
Founder of the African Masonic Lodge in the United States of America.
First Worshipful Master of the African Masonic Lodge in the U.S.A.

PRINCE HALL is thought to have been born in Barbados, although no documentation to that effect has been found. However, it is known that he worked as a laborer and a leather dresser, and studied at night. Hall educated himself to become a leader in the movement which led to the erosion of slavery in the North. Prince Hall, remained a champion of the cause of liberty and brotherhood until his death at age seventy-two, in 1807.

Great black men come in schools. And they are the answer to some great felt need. Man has been called, the creature of circumstances. But what do you think of a man who can make the circumstances of life, the willing servant of his lofty purpose? Prince Hall was such a man. He made his circumstances. Yes, he was a man of genius, but also much more.

During Prince Hall's lifetime, his contribution toward the creation of a black consciousness and black pride were monumental. But his most important was the organization of the first black Masonic order, or Lodge, one year before the Declaration of Independence, which now bears his name.

Prince Hall and thirteen other blacks were initiated as Masons in the year of 1775, by John Hatt, of the Irish Lodge, number 441, which was attached to the British regiment stationed near Boston, and had authorization by Batt, and John Rowe, Provisional Grand Master of North America to form the African Lodge number one. In 1784, after the war they were granted a charter from the Grand Lodge of England, as African Lodge number 459, with Prince Hall as Master.

Subsequently, Hall helped to form other African Lodges, in Philadelphia and Providence, and was instrumental in creating the first interstate organization of black people in America. This was a milestone in the development of a collective identity in the continuing struggle for recognition of the rights of blackmen, and the full realization of freedom for all Americans.

Freemasons of color, therefore, trace their heritage through Prince Hall, and have erected an imposing monument to the Masonry of this great black American Patriot. This is a fitting and proper dedication to continue his work, on the part of more than a half million members, of more than forty Grand Lodges of Prince Hall Freemasons across America. Although, a monument of granite has been erected in memory of Prince Hall, in Copp's Hill burying ground, in Boston, Mssachusetts, the bright light of peace, brotherhood and freedom must become a reality to fulfill the legacy of Prince Hall.

◊ ◊ ◊

TITUS C. HALL
Major General United States Air Force

Commander for Reconnaissance and Electronic Warfare Systems, Headquarters Aeronautical System Division, Air Force System Command at Wright-Patterson Air Force Base, Ohio.

Thirty-Third Degree, Ancient and Accepted Scottish Rite of Freemasonry, Northern Jurisdiction, Prince Hall Affiliation, United States of America.

Education
B.A., Engineering at Tuskegee Institute, Alabama.
M.S., Systems Engineering Management,
University of Southern California.

Former Commander, of #2700, Air BaseWing, Wright-Patterson Air Force Base in January 1976.

Former Director of Material Management, San Antonio Air Logistics Center, Kelly Air Force Base, Texas.

Documentation: The Lowry Airman, April 17, 1981, Denver, Colorado. The Winter Bulletin, Official Organ, United Supreme Council, Ancient and Accepted Scottish Rite of Freemasonry, Prince Hall Affiliation.

◊ ◊ ◊

WEST ALEXANDER HAMILTON
Thirty-Third Degree, Ancient and Accepted of Scottish Rite of Freemasonry, Southern Jurisdiction, Prince Hall Affiliation, United States of America.

Colonel, United States Army, U.S.A.
Co-Owner, Hamilton Printing Company.

Former Member, District of Columbia Board of Education.
Former Professor of Military Science and Tactics, Morgan State College.
Former Professor of Military Science and Tactics, Prairie View College.
(Advanced in the United States Army from Private to Colonel.)
Earned his Master's Degree at the American University.

Masonic Documentation: Masonic News Quarterly, Southern Jurisdiction.

◊ ◊ ◊

FRANK HAMPTON, SR.
Business Executive—City Councilman
Masonic Officer.

FRANK, HAMPTON, SR., was born in Houston, Texas., on January 2, 1923.

Education
Edward Waters College, in Florida.

Achievements
Owner: Hampton Gulf Service Station.
Owner: Hampton Fuel Oil Corporation.
Owner: Hampton Villa Apartments.
Owner: H & L. Advertising & Public Relations Firm.
City Councilman from the eighth district
of Jacksonville, Florida.

Led the fight for black police officers in Jacksonville in 1953. Filed legal action to place blacks in City and State government executive postitions. Led the fight to desegregate Florida golf courses. Filed court suit to open Florida golf tournaments to black golfers.

Appointed Chairman of the Committee to investigate racial discrimination, in hiring, wages, job classifications, and working conditions, by Gulf Oil, for Angola and other parts of Africa, long before the freedom movement began, and before independence came.

Thirty-third degree, Ancient and Accepted Scottish Rite of Freemasonry, Prince Hall Affiliation, of the Southern Jurisdiction.

◊ ◊ ◊

LIONEL HAMPTON
Grand Inspector General of the Thirty-third Degree of the Ancient and Accepted Scottish Rite of Freemasonry Prince Hall Affiliation Northern Jurisdiction of the United States.

LIONEL HAMPTON, Orchestra leader, Composer, Businessman and Thirty-three degree Prince Hall Mason, born 20 April 1908. America's Goodwill Ambassador to Europe and the Far East is also President of "The Lionel Hampton Enterprises, Inc."

Lionel Hampton was awarded the Doctor of Music degree at Howard University, in Washington, D.C. Besides being a great solo performer, he is constantly looking to develop new artist. Lionel is inspired and inspiring, both as a musician and as a man.

The Lionel Hampton Community Development corporation which includes, but is not limited to Hampton Houses which consist of a thirty-nine story building and two eight story buildings, that accomodates three hundred and fifty families. This nineteen million dollar project was needed and welcomed to New York's Harlem. In 1980, The Gladys Hampton Houses with living accommodating two hundred and ten families. This project lends a face lifting to Harlem.

Masonic Documentation: King David Consistory number three, Valley of New York. Prince Hall Lodge for Research of New York.

◊ ◊ ◊

WILLIAM H. HANCOCK
Wealthy Building Contractor

WILLIAM H. HANCOCK, was the first black man initiated into a Masonic Lodge in the State of North Carolina. He received his degrees in Saint John Lodge #3 (White Lodge) Newborne, North Carolina, in the year 1867.

Documentation: Lodge Minutes of Saint John Lodge #3, Newborne, North Carolina. Harry E. Davis, "A History of Freemasonry Among Negroes In America."

◊ ◊ ◊

WILLIAM C. HANDY
(1873–1958)
Lifetime Member of Hiram Lodge, Number Four, Under the Jurisdiction of The Prince Hall Grand Lodge of New York. Thirty-Third Degree, Ancient and Accepted Scottish Rite of Freemasonry, Prince Hall Affiliation, Norther Jurisdiction, United States of America. President of Handy Brothers Music Company, Inc. New York, N.Y.

WILLIAM C. HANDY, was born in Florence, Alabama, in 1873, the son of a Baptist Minister. He composed the "Memphis Blues, Saint Louis Blues, and The Beale Street Blues."

Author
Negro Authors and Composers of the United States.
W.C. Handy Collection of Negro Spirituals.

The United States Government honored W.C. Handy, with a six cent U.S. Postage Stamp.

Nathaniel King Cole, a charter member of Thomas Waller Lodge, number Forty-Nine of Los Angeles, California, played the role of W.C. Handy, in the film, "St Louis Blues."

One hundred and fifty thousand people watched the funeral procession, and the thirty piece Prince Hall Masonic Bass Band, which led the cortege up Lenox Avenue, where more than two thousand and five hundred mourners attended the church for his service, which included notables from all walks of life. The Mayor, Congressmen and high ranking Masons, both Black and White. W.C. Handy was buried with Masonic Rites.

Masonic Documentation: The Williamson Masonic Collection.

◊ ◊ ◊

RICHARD A. HARDY
Thirty-Second Degree, of Scottish Rite Freemasonry, Prince Hall Affiliation, Northern Jurisdiction, Unites States of America.
Past Worshipful Master, Antioch Lodge #66, F. & A.M.
District Deputy Grand Lecturer.
Editor: Antioch Newsletter.
Director of Masonic Information—Antioch Lodge.

RICHARD A. HARDY, was born on April 4, 1909, at Raleigh, North Carolina, and is a Certified Aide to Handicapped Persons. He is currently on the Staff of the Westside Ecumenical Ministry to the Elderly, (W.E.M.E.) an Interdominational non-profit Corporation.

Past Master Hardy, as an avid reader, forceful speaker, and a scholarly writer, whose talents are constantly demanded.

Masonic Documentation: Interview with Past Master Hardy.

◊ ◊ ◊

HARRISON L. HARRIS
Past Grand Secretary of Prince Hall
Grand Lodge of Virginia and Jurisdictions

Past Grand Secretary Harrison L. Harris, authored a "Masonic Textbook" published at Petersburg, Virgini in 1902. It comprised a historical sketch of Masonry and the Organization of Masonic Grand bodies, particularly by black people.

Masonic Documentation: The Phylaxis Society.

◊ ◊ ◊

RICHARD GORDON HATCHER
Mayor
Mayor of the City of Gary, Indiana

Former Deputy Prosecuting Attorney of Lake County, Indiana.

Former City Councilman of Gary, Indiana.

Founder, National Black Caucus of Locally Elected Officers.

Thirty-Third Degree, Ancient and Accepted Scottish Rite of Freemasonry, Southern Jurisdiction, Prince Hall Affiliation, United States of America.

Life Member and Leadership Award, N.A.A.C.P.

Biography in *Who's Who Among Black Americans*.

Documentation: Georgia State Masonic Research Center.

◊ ◊ ◊

AUGUSTUS F. HAWKINS, 33°
Congressman
Thirty-third degree Ancient and Accepted Scottish Rite of Freemasonry. Prince Hall Affiliation.

AUGUSTUS F. HAWKINS, was born in Shreveport, Louisiana, on August 31, 1907.

Education
University of California—A.B.—Economics.
University of Southern California, Graduate Study the Institute of Government.

Former member of California State Assembly, from Los Angeles.

Presently, United States Congressman, from 21st Congressional District.

Congressman Hawkins has authored and co-authored more than three hundred laws, while in the California State Assembly and the U.S. Congress. California Low Cost Housing Programs, Removal of Racial Designations from all State Documents, and the State's anti-discrimination laws.

In Congress, he serves on the Education and Labor Committee.

◊ ◊ ◊

LEWIS HAYDEN
Grand Master of Prince Hall Grand Lodge of Massachusetts.
Grand Secretary of Prince Hall Grand Lodge of New York.

LEWIS HAYDEN, was born a slave, he married in slave status. But he and his wife escaped. Thereafter, he began a career with and in the "Underground Railroad," an escape route for slaves seeking freedom. He devoted considerable time to the anti-slavery movement. He was determined that other black men find freedom.

Lewis Hayden became the author of several very rare brochures. He thereafter began correspondence with the German Grand Lodge, and convinced Brother Joseph G. Findel, the great German Historian, that the claim of black brethren was indesputable, and as a result, Brother Findal, became a champion of the Black Masonic cause in Germany, and his writings and speeches ably sustain his unshakable determination to sustain his convictions.

Masonic Documentation: Williamson Collection on Black Masonry. The Schomburg Library of Black History and Culture.

◊ ◊ ◊

LEMUEL HAYNES

REV. LEMUEL HAYNES, the first black Minister of a Congregational church in the United States of America. Theology early fascinated this Bible struck youth, yet in 1774, at the age of twenty-one, when his period of service to the Deaconship was completed, he enlisted as a minuteman, and spent one day, a week training on the village green. Soon after the skirmish at Lexington, with Captain Ball's Militia Company, he joined the army at the seige of Boston, and learned both Latin and Greek.

When Reverend Haynes received his call from a Church in the West Parish of Rutland, Vermont, he encountered the popular free-thinkers of the day, which included but wasn't limited to Thomas Paine, author of The Rights of Man, and Age of Reason, fame, and he achieved a transatlantic reputation as a skillful and ruthless polemicist in theological disputes. Thereafter, Middlebury College, bestowed the Honorary Master of Arts degree, upon him, the first ever granted to a black in America.

Timothy Mather Cooley, Doctor of Divinity, began his eulogy of The Reverend Lemuel Hayes with these words:

"In various periods of time, there have been Africans whose intellectual powers, and extraordinary attainments would be an ornament to any age, and to any country. Among warriers few have held higher rank than Hanno and Hannibal. The poetic works of Terence, were admired in the Augustan Age, and have survived the devastation of two hundred years. Cyprian, Bishop of Carthage, whose memory is dear to all Christendom and Augustine, Bishop of Hippo, the successful defender of the church from Pelagius, and his heresies, were Sons of Africa. This tribute to a Great Black Man of Masonry, transcends race, color and time. Dead, yet alive, Lemuel Haynes.

Masonic Documentation: Black Presence In The American Revolution 1770–1800 Sidney Kaplan. Black Spuare and Compass, Joseph A. Walkes.

◊ ◊ ◊

ALTON LEE HAYWOOD, SR.
Grand Secretary of The Most Worshipful Prince Hall Grand Lodge of New York and Jurisdiction. (1951) Past Master of Joppa Lodge #55.

Staff Member of the City of New York Water Resource Department.

Education
Johnson C. Smith University
Charlotte, North Carolina.
City College of the City University of New York.
New York, N.Y.

Member
King David Consistory, Number #3.
Medina Temple, Number #19.
(A.E.A.O.N.M.S.)

Masonic Documentation: Information supplied by The Dinner Committee Honoring Past Master Henry G. Walton of Hiram Lodge, #4, and Past Master Alton Lee Haywok, Sr., of Joppa Lodge, Number #55.

◊ ◊ ◊

WILLIAM A. HEATHMAN
Treasurer General, United Supreme Council, Northern Jurisdiction, Prince Hall Affiliation, United States of America

Past Grand Master of The State of Rhode Island and Jurisdiction.

Thirty-Third Degree, Ancient and Accepted Scottish Rite of Freemasonry, Northern Jurisdiction, Prince Hall Affiliation, United States of America.

Documentation: New York Prince Hall Lodge for Research.

◊ ◊ ◊

BUTLER THOMAS HENDERSON
Executive Director
The Earl Warren Legal Training Program
New York, New York.
Thirty-third Degree, Ancient and
Accepted Scottish Rite of Freemasonry
Prince Hall Affiliation, Northern Jurisdiction,
United States of America.

BUTLER THOMAS HENDERSON, was born in Knoxville, Tennessee, on June 20, 1919. He was educated at Morehouse College, the University of Arkansas, and New York University. He was awarded the degree, Doctor of Law, in 1973, at the University of Arkansas, in Pine Bluff, Arkansas.

Positions held
Assistant director, United Negro College Fund
New York, N.Y.
Director, United Board for College Development
Atlanta, Georgia.
Associate Professor, Economics, Morehouse College
Atlanta, Georgia.
Assistant to the President, Morehouse College
Atlanta, Georgia.
Chairman, Department of Economics and Business
University of Arkansas, at Pine Bluff, Arkansas.

Membership
Shriner, Prince Hall Affiliation.
Life-member, N.A.A.C.P.
Trustee—Morristown College, Morristown, Tennesee.

Masonic Documentation: Personal resume and resume.

◊ ◊ ◊

JACOB R. HENDERSON
Business Executive

United States Housing Manager, United States Housing Authority.

President, Henderson Travel Service, Inc.

Former Fiscal Accounting Clerk, United States Housing Authority.

Board Member, Butler Street Y.M.C.A., and Radio Moderator.

Member of The City of Atlanta Charter Commission.

Shriner and Thirty-Third Degree, Ancient and Accepted Scottish Rite of Freemasonry, Southern Jurisdiction, Prince Hall Affiliation, United States of America.

Documentation: Georgia State Masonic Research Center.

◊ ◊ ◊

MORRIS HENDERSON
Health Executive

Project Director, St. Louis Comprehensive Neighborhood Health Center.

Executive, National Association of Neighborhood Health Centers.

Member, Greater St. Louis Crime Commission.

President of Missouri State Conference of N.A.A.C.P. Branches.

Thirty-Second Degree, Ancient and Accepted Scottish Rite of Freemasonry, Prince Hall Affiliation.

Certificate of Appreciation, Missouri Governor's Advisory Committee.

Certificate of Appreciation, St. Louis Police Department.

Biography in *Dictionary of International Biography, Two Thousand Men of Achievement,* and *Who's Who In Health Care.*

Documentation: Who's Who Among Black Americans, 1980-81.

◊ ◊ ◊

CHARLES V. HENDLEY
Lawyer and Most Worshipful Grand Master of Alabama, and Jurisdictions Prince Hall Masonry and Sovereign Grand Inspector General Thirty-Third and Last Degree Scottish Rite of Freemasonry United States of America.

WORSHIPFUL GRAND MASTER CHARLES V. HENDLEY, increased the membership to more than forty thousand Prince Hall Masons, and put the Alabama Grand Lodge on a sound and constructive financial program. He was born in Huntsville Alabama.

Education
Howard University, Washington, D.C.
Howard University Law School, Washington, D.C.

Attorney Hendley became a Prince Hall Mason by joining Eureka Lodge, number five (5) in Washington, D.C. He later was elected Worshipful Master, and Grand Trustee. His distinguished record before the Courts of Alabama, and the United States Supreme Court is a monument to his brilliancy of mind, and extraordinary ability.

Masonic Documentation: Prince Hall Sentnel.

◊ ◊ ◊

MILTON HENRY, 33°
St. Paul, Minnesota
M. W. Grand Master
M. W. Prince Hall Grand Lodge of Minnesota
1975–76
Historian
Thomas H. Lyle Chapter, The Phylaxis Society
Chairman, Committee on Foreign Correspondence
M. W. Prince Hall Grand Lodge of Minnesota

MILTON HENRY was born November 19, 1919, at Pine Bluff, Arkansas, and raised at Carbondale, Illinois.

Education
Public schools of Carbondale
B.S., Southern Illinois University
M.S.W., St. Louis University

The Frater works as supervisor of Child Protective Services, Hennepin County, Minneapolis.

Noble Henry was a member of the United States Army with the 96th Infantry Division during World War II, and saw action in the South Pacific.

He was the first Prince Hall Grand Master of Minnesota to meet with a committee of caucasian grand lodge officers to discuss the matter of fraternal recognition.

During his tenure as Grand Master, a headstone was placed at the grave of Thomas H. Lyle, first Grand Master of Minnesota.

He was made a mason in Tuscan Lodge No. 44 of Carbondale, and is an Honorary Past Grand Master of Illinois.

Masonic membership: Past Master, Pioneer Lodge #1. P C-in-C, North Star Consistory, #14, AASR. Past Potentate, Fezzan Temple #26, AEAONMS.

Documentation: Georgia Masonic Research Center.

◊ ◊ ◊

JOSIAH HENSON
Key Character—Stowe's Uncle Tom's Cabin
and
Secretary in a Canadian Prince Hall Masonic Lodge.

JOSIAH HENSON, was the remarkable hero, of Harriet Beecher Stowe's "Uncle Tom's Cabin," the celebrated novel, that President Abraham Lincoln, said caused the Civil War.

Henson labored in anti-slavery causes. Henson traveled throughout Canada and England. And at his death, he was an active member of Mount Moriah Lodge, number four, Dresden, Ontario., Canada, which is under the jurisdictions of the Prince Hall Craft, in the Province of Ontario.

The record shows that Josiah Henson, was secretary of his Canadian Lodge in 1866, and the Prince Hall Day, souvenir Book, concludes that his degrees were received in Boston, Massachusetts.

Harriet Beecher Stowe's character, "Topsy", was a black girl named Dinal, from the same plantation where, Henson had lived. And Simon Legree, was Bruce Litton, who broke Henson's arm and so maimed him for life, that he could thereafter never touch the top of his head.

In 1960, The Grand Lodge of the Provience of Ontario, Prince Hall affiliation noted the passing of the historical figure, Josiah Henson:

"The history of we of Color, while inextricably interwoven with the history of both the United States, and Canada, has received for too little mention in the records of the past; as a result this omission has not only been detrimental to our race, but has denied educational values to our people, of facts pertaining to we of color.

◊ ◊ ◊

MATTHEW HENSON
Explorer
Member: Celestial Lodge #3, Prince Hall Masonry
New York, New York.

MATTHEW HENSON, was born in Charles County, Maryland, on August 8, 1866.

Henson accompanied Admiral Robert E. Perry, to the North Pole, and was one of the most valuable aids in the expedition that discovered our northmost point.

Author: A Negro Explorer to the North Pole.

Masonic Documentation: Prince Hall Lodge of Research of New York.

◊ ◊ ◊

JEROME LEWIS HERBERT
Past Master
Chairman: Research and General Information
Grand Lodge
Prince Hall Masons, State of California,
Chief Potentate of Egyptian Temple, #5.
A. E. A. O. N. M. S.

JEROME LEWIS HERBERT, graduated from Prairie View State College, in 1915, enlisted in the United States Army and advanced to First Lieutenant in the U.S. Infantry. He is the past master of Garrison Lodge #45.

Masonic Documentation: Prince Hall Masonic Digest.

◊ ◊ ◊

DAVID JAMES HICKMAN

Thirty-third degree Ancient and Accepted Scottish Rite of Freemasonry, Prince Hall Affiliation. Southern Jurisdiction, and Deputy Grand Master of Prince Hall Masons, of the State of Mississippi, and Chairman of the Department of Mathematics, at Jackson State College, in Jackson, Mississippi.

Deputy Grand Master, David James Hickman, of the Grand Lodge of Mississippi, earned his Doctorate of Philosophy, in Mathematics, at the University of Notre Dame.

Masonic Documentation: Grand Lodge Library, F.A.M. State of New York. Brother Allan Boudreau, Librarian and Curator.

◊ ◊ ◊

GRADY B. HINKLE
Real Estate Broker and Housing Official

Member of Greater Indianapolis Housing Development Corporation.

Former President of The Brokers Association of Indiana.

Education: Lain's Institute of Technology, Indiana.

Masonic membership: Past Master of Meridian Lodge #33. Secretary of Constantine Consistory #25.

District Deputy Grand Master of the State of Indiana.

Grand Minister of State of The United Supreme Council.

Thirty-Third Degree, Ancient and Accepted Scottish Rite of Freemasonry, Prince Hall Affiliation, Northern Jurisdiction, United States of America.

Documentation: The Summer Bulletin (1975), United Supreme Council.

◊ ◊ ◊

IRA S. HOLDER, JR.

President of the John F. Kennedy Democratic Club, Uniondale, New York.

Past Master of Widow Sons Lodge #11.

Past District Deputy Grand Master of the Second Masonic District (1977–1980).

Documentation: The Prince Hall Sentinel, Summer 1986, Vol. 36, No. 2.

IRA S. HOLDER, SR.
Grand Historian New York State
Prince Hall Grand Lodge.
(1969-1973)
Member of the Bicentenial Commission
Commemorating the Memory and Anniversary
of Patron Saint Prince Hall's
Entry into the Masonic Fraternity
Along with Fourteen Other Black Men
Grand Lodge Appointment Member
Secretary of the Barbados
Committee for the Formation of
Prince Hall Memorial Lodge U.D. in 1963
Fellow of the Phylaxis Society.

IRA S. HOLDER, SR., was born in Barbados, West Indies, on September 27, 1900. He received his formal training and education in both, Barbados and Guyana, as an apprenticeship in Printing and Bookbinding. Later he studied to become a tailor.

He is a member of the Widow Sons Lodge, number #11, F.A.M., and also a member and fellow of The Phylaxis Society, and Chairman of the membership committee.

1975—Certificate of Literature, The Phylaxis Society.

1975—Elected a Fellow, of the Phylaxis Society for his service to the Society, Humanity, and Prince Hall Masonry.

1978—Awarded a Certificate of Appreciation for Outstanding and dedicated Service to the Society for 1978.

Ira S. Holder, Sr., is a lecturer, and many of his lectures have been published in The Phylaxis Society Magazine.

◊ ◊ ◊

JUSTIN HOLLAND
Deputy Grand Master of the Most Worshipful Prince Hall Grand Lodge of Ohio
Chief of Foreign Affairs of the Grand Lodge of Ohio.

JUSTIN HOLLAND, was born in Norfold County, Virginia, in 1819.

Education
Oberlin College, Oberlin Ohio.
Master Mason—Eureka Lodge #14, Cleveland, Ohio.

Brother Holland, assisted with the organization of Excelsior Lodge number eleven, and he was the first secretary of the lodge. In 1870, he was elected Worshipful Master, and served for three years. 1875–1881, Brother Holland was elected Deputy Grand Master, and was accredited and recognized Chief of the Foreign Affairs of the Grand Lodge, 1881 to 1883.

Justin Holland was a fine writer, logical and forceful reasoner, an accomplished linguist, a most untiring worker, and a finished master in the art of diplomacy. The work of securing recognition of the Grand Orients, and Grand Lodges of Europe and South America, are due more to Brother Holland's scholarly and tactful labors, than all other efforts and influences combined.

◊ ◊ ◊

BERNUS EUGENE HOLMES, 33°
Savannah, Georgia
Georgia Youth Director
Ancient Egyptian Arabic Order Nobles Mystic Shrine

BERNUS EUGENE HOLMES was born at Savannah, September 25, 1950.

Education
Tompkins High School, 1968
B.S., Savannah State College, 1972
M.A., Central Michigan University, 1980

The Frater works as a United States Probation Officer. He is the first Black appointed to that position in the Southern District of Georgia, which comprises 43 counties.

He is a member of the N.A.A.C.P. and the Frank Callen Boys Club.

Membership in professional organizations include, Coastal Law Enforcement Association, American Probation and Parole Association, and the Federal Probation Association.

Masonic membership: Pythagoras Lodge #11. Georgia Chapter #1, RAM. St. Philip Commandery #9, KT. Ezra Consistory #27, AASR. Omar Temple #21, AEAONMS.

Masonic Documentation: Georgia Masonic Research Center.

◊ ◊ ◊

BENJAMIN LAWSON HOOKS
Executive Director, National Association for the Advancement of Colored People. (N.A.A.C.P.) Former, Federal Communication's Commissioner. Lawyer and Former Judge.

Brother Hooks was born in Memphis, Tennessee, on January 31, 1925.

Education
Lemoyne College, B.A., Memphis, Tennessee.
DePaul University. J.D. Chicago, Illinois.

Attorney Hooks was the first black Judge of Shelby County Criminal Court, in the State of Tennessee.

The Right Worshipful Grand Secretary of the Most Worshipful Prince Hall Grand Lodge of Tennessee and Jurisdiction. (State of Tennessee.)

Minister on Leave
Middle Baptist Church, Memphis, Tennessee.
Greater New Moriah Baptist Church, Detroit, Michigan.

Brother Hooks resigned his Federal Communication Commissionership to accept the Directorship of the National Association for the Advancement of Colored People.

◊ ◊ ◊

JOHN HOPE
(1868–1936)
**Grand Inspector General, Thirty-third Degree
Ancient and Accepted Scottish Rite of Freemasonry
Prince Hall Affiliation, Southern Jurisdiction
United States of America.
Founder and President of Atlanta University
and the Atlanta University System
President of Morehouse College. (1907)**

JOHN HOPE, was born in Atlanta, Georgia in 1868.

Education
Worcester Academy, Worcester, Massachusetts.
Brown University, Providence, Rhode Island. (BA.MA.)
(Scholarship Student)
Elected to Phi-Beta-Kappa.

President Hope's dream came true in 1929, when Morehouse College and Spelman College, and Atlanta University agreed to affiliate and function as members of the Atlanta University System.

Masonic Documentation: Williamson Masonic Collection of Schomburg Collection.

195

STERLING JAMES HOPKINS
(1895–1955)
Grandmaster of the Prince Hall Grand Masonic Lodge of the State of California.
(From 1949 until 1955)

STERLING JAMES HOPKINS, was born in the State of Georgia, on July 4, 1895.

Past Master of the Orange Valley Lodge, number #13. Profound Thinker, Eminent Jurist, Skilled Craftman.

Worshipful Grandmaster of Prince Hall Masons of the State of California, from 1949 until his death in 1955.

Masonic Documentation: Prince Hall Masonic Digest.

◊ ◊ ◊

WALTER SPURGEON HORNSBY III
President
Pilgrim Health & Life Insurance Company
Augusta, Georgia

WALTER SPURGEON HORNSBY III was born September 6, 1941, in Augusta, Georgia. He was the first Black to enter college at age 15 under the Ford Foundation Early Admissions Program.

Education
A.B., Morehouse College, Atlanta, 1961
Further study at University of Michigan in Actuarial Science

Member, Omega Psi Phi Fraternity

Listed in *Who's Who in Life Insurance,* 1972 to present.

Vice-President, Program, Georgia-Carolina Boy Scouts.

Masonic membership: Bannaker Lodge #3, F. & A.M. Lebanon Consistory #28 AASR. Stolkin Temple # 22 AEONMS.

Masonic Documentation: Georgia Masonic Research Center.

◊ ◊ ◊

CHARLES HAMILTON HOUSTON
1895–1950
Attorney at Law

General Counsel, National Association for the Advancement of Colored People. Attorney Houston as Chief of the Legal Department directed the effort which built the foundation for the case of Brown *vs.* The Board of Education, in 1954.

Dean at Howard University Law School, in Washington, D.C.

Education: Amherst College, Phi Beta Kappa, and Class Valedictorian. Harvard Law School, The First Black on the Law Review Editorial Board. Harvard Law School, earned Doctorate in Jurisprudence. Thereafter awarded a traveling Fellowship to Europe and another Degree. When he returned to America he joined his father's law firm in Washington, D.C.

Thirty-Third Degree, Ancient and Accepted Scottish Rite of Freemasonry, Prince Hall Affiliation, Southern Jurisdiction, United States of America.

Judge, Governor and Brother William Hastie, summarized his influence this way: "Attorney Houston guided us through the legal wilderness of second glass citizenship. He was our Moses of the journey. He also lived to see us close to the Promised Land of full equality under law, closer than even he dared hope, when he set his course, and so much closer than would have been possible without his genius, and his leadership."

Documentation: "Simple Justice," by Richard Kluger. The Schomburg Library of Black History and Culture.

◊ ◊ ◊

COURTNEY PARRIS HOUSTON, JR.
Treasurer General
The United Supreme Council
and
Teacher

Ancient and Accepted Scottish Rite of Freemasonry, Prince Hall Affiliation, Northern Jurisdiction, United States of America, Inc.

Former Administrative Supervisor, United States Army Air Force.

Education: Hampton Institute, Virginia. Central State college, Ohio. Temple University, Penn. University of Delaware, Delaware.

Past Master and Treasurer, Prudence Lodge #6, Dover, Delaware.

Deputy Grand Master of the State of Delaware.

Member of Corinthian Consistory #5, Wilmington, Delaware.

Active, Thirty-Third Degree, Ancient and Accepted Scottish Rite of Freemasonry, Northern Jurisdiction, Prince Hall Affiliation.

Documentation: The United Supreme Court, N.J., United States of America.

WILLIAM HENRY HOWE, 33°
Philadelphia, Pennsylvania
1890–1981
20th Imperial Potentate
Ancient Egyptian Arabic Order Nobles Mystic Shrine
1971–1972

WILLIAM HENRY HOWE was born in Columbus, Georgia, on January 24, 1890. He was reared in Apalachicola, Florida and moved to Pennsylvania in 1916. He died June 2, 1981.

Education
Public schools of Apalachicola, Florida
Cheyney State Training School

He was a member of the United States Army during World War I and received an Honorable Discharge.

Masonic membership: Past Master, King David Lodge #52, F. & A.M. Member, King Solomon Chapter #1, RAM. Member, De Molay Consistory #1, AASR. Past Potentate, Pyramid Temple #1, AEAONMS.

Masonic Documentation: Georgia Masonic Research Center.

◊ ◊ ◊

CLAUDE HUDSON
Dentist and Civic Leader

National Life Membership, National Association for the Advancement of Colored People.
National Board of Directors, National Association for The Advancement of Colored People.

Thirty-third Degree, Ancient and Accepted of Scottish Rite of Freemasonry, Southern Jurisdiction, Prince Hall Affiliation. United States of America.

Past President, Los Angeles Branch, N.A.A.C.P.

Masonic Documentation: Masonic News Quarterly, Southern Jurisdiction. Prince Hall Affiliation.

◊ ◊ ◊

CHARLES DUNCAN HUGHES
Chartered Life Underwriter

Branch Manager: Maritime Life Assurance Company.

Master Mason: Hope Masonic Lodge Sar-la-Mar, Sussex Lodge Kingston, Jamaica.

Member
Life Underwriters Association of Jamaica.
Life Underwriters Association of Canada.
National Association of Life Underwriters of the United States of America.

Masonic Documentation: International Guide to Who's Who in the West Indies.

◊ ◊ ◊

ROBERT J. HUNTER
State Employee

Administrative Assistant to the State Senate of Pennsylvania.

Lawyer, Member of the Pennsylvania Bar.

Owner and Manager of Hunter's Employment Agency.

Pennsylvania Grand Lodge Mason of The Year Award.

1972 Masonic Public Relations Award, State of Pennsylvania Grand Lodge.

Thirty-Third Degree, Ancient and Accepted Scottish Rite of Freemasonry, Northern Jurisdiction, Prince Hall Affiliation, United States of America.

Received Keys to The Cities: Houston, Texas, 1971. Detroit, Michigan, 1974. Newport News, Virginia, 1974.

◊ ◊ ◊

CARTER LASEY JACKSON
Grand Treasurer, Most Worshipful Prince Hall Grand Lodge State of New York and Jurisdictions Deputy Commissioner Security Health and Hospital Corporation.

Positions in Freemasonry: Past Master, Hiram Lodge, Number #4. King David Consistory, Number #3, of the Ancient and Accepted Scottish Rite, Afiliated with Prince Hall Freemasonry, Northern Jurisdiction. Grand Inspector General, Thirty-third degree.

◊ ◊ ◊

MAYNARD HOLBROOK JACKSON
Attorney at Law
Mayor of Atlanta, Georgia
Thirty-third Degree, Ancient and Accepted Scottish Rite, of Freemasonry, Prince Hall Afiliation, Southern Jurisdiction.

The education of Mayor Maynard Holbrook Jackson, of Atlanta, Georgia: Morehouse College, Deleware State College and Howard University Law School.

He was admitted to practice law in the State of Georgia in 1965. Thereafter he became a partner in the law firm of: "Emory, Jackson, Patterson, Parks and Franklin."

1970-74—Vice-Mayor of Atlanta, Georgia. 1974-Present—Mayor of Atlanta, Georgia. President, of the National Conference of Democratic Mayors. Chairman, National Gun Control Center. Member of the American Bar Association. Atlanta Urban League—N.A.A.C.P. N.O.W.—National Welfare Rights Organization. Trustee—Morehouse College. Member—Alpha-Phi-Alpha.

Masonic Documentation: Masonic News Quarterly, Prince Hall. Southern Jurisdiction.

◊ ◊ ◊

DR. RAYMOND E. JACKSON, 33°
M. W. Grand Master
M. W. Prince Hall Grand Lodge of New York
1934-1936
13th Imperial Potentate—AEANONMS
1939-1955

RAYMOND E. JACKSON, masonic leader, musician, and union official, was born August 3, 1900 in Buffalo, New York.

He received the honorary doctorate of humanities degree from Wilburforce University in 1949, and he was youngest Past Master to be elected Grand Master of New York.

He was the first Black in the United States to represent Black musicians in the American Federation of Labor.

Masonic membership: St. John's Lodge #16-Buffalo. Bison Consistory #29 AASR. Hadji Temple #61 AEANOMS.

Masonic Documentation: Georgia Masonic Research Center.

◇ ◇ ◇

DANIEL CHAPPIE JAMES
General, United States Army Airforce
Commander, of the United States Army Air force
Deputy Chief of Staff, Air Defense Command Division.

DANIEL CHAPPIE JAMES, was born February 11, 1920, at Pensacola, Florida.

Education
Tuskegee Institute, Air Command Staff College, 1942 B.S.

Positions
Commander, Sixtieth Flight Interceptor Squard.
Assistant Director of Operations, 81st Flight Wings.
Royal Airforce, Bentwater, England.
Deputy Chief of Staff, Air Defense Command Division.
Commander of Operations, Davis Monthan Airforce Base.
Commander, Thirty-third Tactical Flight Wing,
Elgin, Army Airforce Base.

Honors and Awards
United Negro College Fund
Distinguished Service Award.
American Academy of Achievement Award.

Bishop Wright Air Industry Award.
Distinguished Flying Cross Award,
Two Oak leaf clusters.

General Daniel Chappie James was made a, "Mason on Sight," by Worshipful, James Black, the Grand Master of the Most Worshipful Prince Hall Grand Lodge of Illinois, Public School, #183, in Brooklyn, New York, has been named, General Daniel Chappie James Public School.

◊ ◊ ◊

WILLIAM DE COURCEY JEFFERS
(Agriculturist.)
Master Mason, Member of
Saint Anthony Freemason Lodge
Officer-in-Charge, of the
Camden Park Experimental Station,
Department of Agriculture, Kingstown, Saint Vincent.

Education
Montserrat Secondary School.
Ohio State University,
Master of Science degree in Horticulture
(vegetable crops)
Agricultural Research.

Served as Acting Director of Agriculture for Saint Vincent.

Masonic Documentation: International Guide To Who's Who In The West Indies.

◊ ◊ ◊

AUGUSTUS G. JENKINS, JR.
President—Jenkins Funeral Home, Incorporated
Founding Member—The Black Tennis Foundation
Member, Antioch Lodge #66, Prince Hall Masonry

BROTHER JENKINS is a former High School and Collegiate Tennis player with Tennis roots deep in the Public Parks of New York City. He was a Physics Major, before graduating from Central State University, in Ohio.

Work experience
Design Specialist, for The National Cash Register Company. (Computer Division). System Engineer, International Business Machine.

Brother Jenkins, sits in an advisory capacity on several civic and community organizations.

Masonic Documentation: The Black Tennis Foundation.

◊ ◊ ◊

ARTHUR D. JEWELL
Educator

Professor of Electrical Engineering, Howard University, Washington, D.C.

Principal of Carver Vocational High School, Wilmington, Delaware.

Vice-Principal, Philadelpia's McKinley High School, Philadelphia, Penn.

Systems Analyst Project Leader for Ordnance for The United States Marine Corp's Supply Activity, in Philadelphia, Penn.

Thirty-Third Degree, Ancient and Accepted Scottish Rite of Freemasonry, Northern Jurisdiction, Prince Hall Affiliated, United States of America.

Documentation: The United Supreme Council, August 1975. Northern Jurisdiction, Prince Hall Affiliation, United States of America.

◊ ◊ ◊

CHARLES C. JOHNSON, 33°
1863–1928
Medical Doctor and Registered Pharmacist
M. W. Grand Master
M. W. Prince Hall Grand Lodge of South Carolina
F. & A.M., 1893–1928

CHARLES C. JOHNSON was born in Orange County, Virginia in 1863. Grand Master Johnson authored a book entitled "A Warning," concerning the existence of a body of men within his jurisdiction who claimed descent from the "Old National Compact" or National Grand Lodge, movement.

Education
Howard University, Pr Cer 1881, A.B. 1885, M.D. 1888.

Masonic membership: Lebanon Lodge #6 F. & A.M., Columbia, SC. C. C. Johnson Consistory #136 AASR, Columbia, SC.

Masonic Documentation: Georgia Masonic Research Center.

◊ ◊ ◊

CLEVELAND JOHNSON, JR.
Grand Inspector General of the Thirty-Third Degree, Ancient and Accepted Scottish Rite of Freemasonry, Northern Jurisdiction, Prince Hall Afiliation, United States of America
Commander-In-Chief
of
King David Consistory, Number Three (3) Ancient and Accepted Scottish Rite of Freemasonry Prince Hall Afiliation, United States of America

CLEVELAND JOHNSON, JR., has joined New York State University Agricultural and Technical College, at Farmingdale, New York, as the Executive Assistant to the President of the University.

The Bulletin, United Supreme Council, AASR. Prince Hall Afiliation.

◊ ◊ ◊

HILERY RICHARD WRIGHT JOHNSON
**Worshipful Grandmaster of the Republic of Liberia
President of the Republic of Liberia
President of Liberia College
Classical Scholar and Professor of French, German and Mathematics**

Worshipful Grandmaster Johnson was a Professor at Liberia College at the same time Professors Blyden, Crumwell and Freeman were on the faculty and Honorable Joseph Jenkins Roberts, who was later to become President of the Republic, was President of Liberia College.

In the canvass of 1884, Hilery Richard Wright Johnson, secured the majority of votes and was elected President of the Government of Liberia.

Masonic Documentation: The Private Papers of President William Tolbert of Liberia. The Schomburg Library of Black History and Culture.

◊ ◊ ◊

J. ROSAMOND JOHNSON
(1873–1954)
**Internationally Acclaimed Composer
Member of Hiram Lodge, #4 of New York City
Grand Inspector General, Thirty-Third Degree
Ancient and Accepted Scottish Rite of Freemasonry
Prince Hall Affiliation.
Northern Jurisdiction, United States of America**

J. ROSAMOND JOHNSON, studied music at the New England Conservatory of Music, in Boston, Massachusetts. Thereafter, he became Director of Music for The Music School Settlement of New York.

He collaborated with his brother James Weldon Johnson, by setting his poetry to James's music to make what is now considered the Black National Hymn, "Lift Every Voice and Sing."

Johnson also wrote: "Under the Bamboo Tree", "Nobody's Looking but the Owl and the Moon", and "Congo Love Song."

In 1913, J. Rosamond Johnson, directed a musical comedy in London, at the Hammerstein Opera House. This was an overwhelming success. He arranged the music for his brother's collection: "The Book of American Negro Spirituals in 1925."

Masonic Documentation: The New York City Masonic Lodge for Research. The Williamson Collection, Schomburg Collection.

◊ ◊ ◊

JACK ARTHUR JOHNSON
(1878–1946)
World Heavyweight Champion
Master Mason Grand Lodge, Glasgow Scotland

JACK ARTHUR JOHNSON, born 1878, Galveston, Texas. His birth date was one year after the Official ending of the Reconstruction, and fifteen years after the Emancipation Proclamation. He was the first black man to win the World Heavyweight Championship. When Johnson defeated World Champion Tommy Burns in Australia, in 1908, for the Championship, the world was alarmed.

Jack Arthur Johnson, had broken the color-line. However, the color-bar had received legal approval by the United States Supreme Court decision in the case of "Plessy vs. Ferguson." It was in this case that the Court upheld segregation in public transportation. In the years to follow, the Court's principals were applied to every facet of American life.

Jack Arthur Johnson was a barrier breaker. When he was initiated into Freemasonry in Glasgow, Scotland, it created controversy, widespread controversy in white America's Freemasonry, and the minutes of the Grand-Lodges, and Lodges, in numerous jurisdictions have so recorded.

But "Johnson", was a people's champion, who stayed warm in the hearts of countless millions, long after he had retired. And for that he deserves a monument. One who acts and speaks for a cause deserves a monument. In the landscaped cemetery a towering oak casts ample shadow over Jack Arthur Johnson's monument, which is picturesque massive granite, a huge block, and carries but one word "Johnson".

◊ ◊ ◊

JAMES J. JOHNSON
Public Relations Officer

Public Relations Officer of The Port Authority of New York and New Jersey.

Worshipful Master of Hiram Lodge #4. Thirty-Second Degree, King David Consistory, #3. Shriner, Medina Temple #19, Noble of the Mystic Shrine.

Born and educated in Joplin, Missouri.

Documentation: Prince Hall Lodge for Research and a personal interview.

◇ ◇ ◇

JOHN H. JOHNSON
(Publisher)
Quality Trade Books
and
Ebony—Jet—Ebony, Jr.
Associate Editor
The Bulletin, Official Organ,
The United Supreme Council,
Ancient and Accepted Scottish Rite of Freemasonry,
Prince Hall Affiliation,
Northern Jurisdiction, United States of America
Chairman and Chief Executive Officer,
Supreme Life Insurance Company of America
Chairman, Radio Station, "W.J.P.C.",
Chicago's First and only black owned radio station

Education
University of Chicago. Northwestern University.

Member of the Board of Directors: Greyhound Corporation, Bell and Howell Company, Zenith Radio and Television Corporation, Marina City Bank and Twentieth Century Fox Films Corporation.

Thirty-Third Degree, Ancient and Accepted Scottish Rite of Freemasonry, Prince Hall Affiliation, Northern Jurisdiction, United States of America.

Awards

Spingarn Medal, National Association for the Advancement of Colored People. Russwurm Award, National Newspaper Publishers Association. Horatio Alger Award, American Schools and Colleges.

◊ ◊ ◊

MARSHALL SULLIVAN JOHNSON, MPS, 33°,
Active
Pittsburgh, Pennsylvania
22nd Imperial Potentate
Ancient Egyptian Arabic Order Nobles Mystic Shrine
1974–1976

MARSHALL S. JOHNSON was born in Connellsville, Pennsylvania.

Education
Public schools of Connellsville, PA.
B.A., Lincoln University

Member, Kappa Alpha Psi Fraternity.

The Hall of Fame, United Golfers Association.

Member of Big Brothers of Allegheny County, and served on the board of directors, Square and Compass Federal Credit Union.

Organized the Imperial Council's Department of Recreation in 1955, and served as the director for 13 years.

Retired in 1971 as a Postal Service Superintendent.

Noble Johnson died November 9, 1982.

Masonic membership: Past Master, St. Cyprian Alpha Lodge #13, F. & A.M. Past President, 7th Masonic District, MWPHGLPA. Past Commander-in-Chief, St. Cyprian Consistory #4, AASR. Past Potentate, Sahara Temple #2, AEANOMS.

Masonic Documentation: Georgia Masonic Research Center.

◊ ◊ ◊

MELVIN M. JOHNSON
Sovereign Grand Commander
United Supreme Council, Northern Jurisdiction, Prince Hall Affiliation, United States of America

Past Worshipful Grand Master of Prince Hall Masons of Massachusetts.

Thirty-Third Degree, Ancient and Accepted Scottish Rite of Freemasonry, Prince Hall Affiliation, Northern Jurisdiction, United States of America.

Documentation: New York Prince Hall Lodge for Research.

◊ ◊ ◊

ROBERT H. JOHNSON
Administrative Assistant

Past Grand Master of Prince Hall Free and Accepted Masons in the State of Minnesota and Jurisdictions.

First member of The Phylaxis Society in the State of Minnesota and Jurisdictions.

Administrative Assistant to The Thomas H. Lyles Chapter of The Phylaxis Society.

Documentation: Tenth Anniversary Journal, The Phylaxis Society.

◊ ◊ ◊

ABSALOM JONES
The First Worshipful Grandmaster of The Prince Hall Grand Lodge of Pennsylvania.
The First Worshipful Master of the Second African Masonic Lodge, 459, of Philadelphia, Pennsylvania.
Founder of The First Episcopal Church for Blacks in the United States of America

ABSALOM JONES was born a slave in Sussex, Delaware, on 6 November 1746. And as a child he learned to read and write. Thereafter he bought a Speller and a Testament. After going to Philadelphia, Pennsylvania with his Master, and working as an apprentice, he saved money and bought is freedom, married another slave and bought her freedom. They worked together for the same former master, saved money and bought several houses, and had rented them by the time "Richard Allen", rode into Philadelphia to begin his historical work. Jones was by then prominent among blacks, as well as the black members of Saint George's Methodist Church.

Absalom Jones and Richard Allen became co-workers and co-leaders, in the striving for a black or African church. They also united to achieve justice, equality and education for blacks. Jones later assisted Allen in the organization of the "Free African Society."

Absalom Jones and Richard Allen jointly authored a classic titled, "A Narrative of the Proceedings of Black People during the calamity in Philadelphia in 1794" a memorable and magnificent rebuttal of scanderous misrepresentation of the role of black people during the Crisis.

Masonic Documentation: "The Black Presence During The American Revolution, 1770–1800." By Kaplan. "Prince Hall Lodge of Research of New York."

Editorial note: Absalom Jones and Richard Allen were pulled from their knees while at worship and prayer at the caucasian Saint George's Methodist Episcopal Church, in Philadelphia, Penna., in November 1787. And because of bigotry and racism they withdrew from the caucasian church and began a black solidarity movement.

◊ ◊ ◊

DANIEL W. JONES
Certified Public Accountant

Trustee of Prince Hall Grand Lodge of New York State (1966–1969).

Past Master, Prince Hall Lodge #38.

Chairman of the Committee on Budget of the Prince Hall Grand Lodge of New York.

Secretary of the Prince Hall Temple Association.

Former, Certified Public Accountant, employed by the City of New York.

Thirty-Third Degree of Ancient Accepted Scottish Rite of Freemasonry, Northern Jurisdiction, United States of America.

Documentation: Prince Hall Sentinel, Vol. 36, No. 3, Fall 1986.

◊ ◊ ◊

JOHN JONES
The Eighth: Worshipful Grand Master of the Grand Lodge of the State of Ohio.

JOHN JONES LODGE, number seven, at Chicago, Illionis was named in both his memory and his honor.

In 1866, Grand Master John Jones, published a sixteen page pamphlet under the title of, "An Argument in Relations to Freemasonry Among Colored Men in the Country, Showing Its Regularity, Legitimacy and Legality."

Masonic Documentation: "Prince Hall Lodge for Research of New York."

◊ ◊ ◊

LAWRENCE A. JONES, SR., MPS, 33°
Kansas City, Missouri
M. W. Grand Master
M. W. Prince Hall Grand Lodge of Missouri, F. & A.M.

LAWRENCE A. JONES, SR., was born in Kansas City, Missouri on September 22, 1924. He was a licensed embalmer and funeral director for the states of Kansas and Missouri.

Education
Public schools of Kansas City, Missouri
Worsham College of Mortuary Science, Chicago, 1945

Past president and member of the Missouri and Kansas Funeral Directors Assn.

Masonic membership: Past Master, Blue Valley Lodge #64, F. & A.M. Member, Mount Oread Chapter #6, RAM. Member Queen of Sheba Chapter #19, OES. Past Commander-in-Chief, Kansas City Consistory #7, AASR. Past Potentate, Allah Temple #6, AEAONMS

Masonic Documentation: Georgia Masonic Research Center.

◊ ◊ ◊

LEONARD T. JONES
Teacher, Masonic Officer, Police Officer

Adjunct Professor, Criminal Justice, Community College of Philadelphia.

Author: *The Handbook For Non-Teaching Assistants* and *The Handbook For Internal Security Officers.*

Grand Historian and Keeper of The Archives of The Most Worshipful Grand Lodge of The State of Pennsylvania.

First Worshipful Master and Life Member of Herbert E. Millen Lodge #151 (Free and Accepted Masons).

Past Commander-in-Chief, De Molay Consistory #1.

Thirty-Third Degree, Ancient and Accepted Scottish Rite of Freemasonry, Northern Jurisdiction, Prince Hall Affiliation, United States of America.

Lieutenant, The Philadelphia Police Department. (Homicide Division.)

Police Liaison Officer, assigned to The Narcotics Bureau, United States Treasury Department, 1950–1952.

Documentation: The Winter Bulletin, Official Organ of The Supreme Council, Scottish Rite of Freemasonry, Northern Jurisdiction, Prince Hall Affiliation, United States of America.

◊ ◊ ◊

RALPH H. JONES
Historian

Member of The World Methodist Historical Society.

Author: *Rev. Charles A. Tindly's Biography*. Mason Tindley's biography treats the life and work of black America's most important sacred music composers.

Exhibitor: The Pepperpot Man. The Afro-American Historical and Cultural Museum which relates to the black experience in Pennsylvania for over three centuries (1681–1981).

Thirty-Third Degree, Ancient and Accepted Scottish Rite of Freemasonry, Northern Jurisdiction, Prince Hall Affiliation, United States of America.

Documentation: The Winter Bulletin, Scottish Rite of Freemasonry.

RALPH WALDO EMERSON JONES
President
Gambling College
Thirty-Third Degree, Ancient and Accepted Scottish Rite of Freemasonry
Prince Hall Affiliations, Southern Jurisdiction
United States of America

DR. JONES was born on August 6, 1905, in Lake Charles, Louisiana. Education: Southern University, B.S., 1924. Columbia University, M.A., 1935. Louisiana Technical University, Ph.D., 1969.

Dr. Jones has served Grambling College for more than fifty years, during which time he was Band Director, Coach, Instructor, Dean of Men, and Academic Dean.

Masonic Documentation: Ebony Success Library, One Thousand Successful Blacks.

◊ ◊ ◊

RENRIC H. JORDAN, JR.
United States Postal Service (Ret.)
Worshipful Master of Antioch Lodge #66, in 1961

Secretary of Antioch Lodge #66, from 1972 to 1983.

Thirty-Second Degree, King David Consistory #3, A.A.S.R., Prince Hall. Shriner, Medina Temple #19, A.E.A.O.N.M.S.

Awarded a plaque in recognition of dedicated service to Antioch Lodge #66.

Documentation: Yearbook, 1982, Antioch Lodge #66, F. & A.M. and Who's Who Among Black Americans, 1975–1976.

◊ ◊ ◊

SIDNEY A. JONES, JR.
Judge
**Associate Judge of the Circuit Court of Cook County
Thirty-Third Degree, Ancient and Accepted Scottish Rite of Freemasonry,
Prince Hall Affiliations, Northern Jurisdiction, United States of America**

Past President of Cook County Bar Association. Life-Member of The National Association for the Advancement of Colored People. Trustee, Atlanta University, Atlanta, Georgia.

Masonic Documentation: Ebony Success Library, One Thousand Successful Blacks.

◊ ◊ ◊

JACK A. KELLEY
Law Enforcement Officer

Coordinator of Law Enforcement Training at California State University.

Vice-Chairman, Board of Directors of Model City.

Past Potentate, Saphar Temple #117, Prince Hall Affiliation (Shriner).

Officer, Association of Black Educators of Fresno, California.

1942, All Western Basketball Star

1942, Honorable Mention Little American Football League.

◊ ◊ ◊

ROBERT KENDALL, Ph.D.
Thirty-Third Degree, Ancient and Accepted Scottish Rite of Freemasonry, Southern Jurisdiction, Prince Hall Affiliation, The United States of America

Past Master, Thomas A. Simms, Jr. Lodge #170, of Kentucky. Past Commander-in-Chief, of Phoenix Consistory # 92, Hopkinsville, Kentucky.

Most Worshipful Junior Grand Warden of The Most Worshipful Grand Lodge of Kentucky.

Retired from the United States Army, with the Rank of Master Sergeant. Earned his Doctorate of Philosophy (Ph.D.) at the George Peabody College for Teachers, Vanderbilt University, Nashville, Tennesee.

Masonic Documentation: Masonic News Quarterly, Southern Jurisdiction.

◊ ◊ ◊

WILLIAM OSCAR KENDALL
(Legislator)
Member of the House of Assembly
Master Mason, Free and Accepted Masonry of Guyana

Director: Guyana and Trinidad Life and Fire Insurance Company. Director: Banks and Breweries Limited. Director: Industrial Development Corporation.

Minister of Communications and Public Works, (1954–1957.) Legislative Member of Trade and Industry Commission.

Member of the "New Amsterdam Town Council."

Masonic Documentation: "International Guide To Who's Who In The West Indies."

◊ ◊ ◊

WORSHIPFUL BROTHER ABDULLA M. KHIMYI, WORSHIPFUL MASTER
Past District Grandmaster of East Africa.
Lodge Zanzibar, Number 3897.E.C.
of
United Grand Lodge of England
District of East Africa

Lodge Philosophy: "May every brother who has merit find encouragement." "May every mason attain the summit of Masonry."

Masonic Documentation: Masonic Review of East Africa.

◊ ◊ ◊

THOMAS KILGORE, JR.
Minister and Educator

Pastor, The Second Baptist Church of Los Angeles, California.

Professor, University of Southern California School of Religion.

Chairman of The Board of Trustees, Morehouse College, Atlanta, Georgia.

Past President, Progressive National Baptist Convention.

Board Member, Golden State Mutual Life Insurance Company.

Director of The Office of Special Community Affairs of the University of Southern California.

Education
B.A., Morehouse College, 1935
M.A., Howard University, 1944
Doctorate, Union Theological Seminary, 1957

Member: Phi Beta Kappa.

Masonic: Thirty-Third Degree, Ancient and Accepted Scottish Rule of Freemasonry, Prince Hall Affiliation, Southern Jurisdiction, United States of America.

Ebony Poll: One of the fifteen (15) Greatest Black Preachers, *Ebony,* September 1984.

Documentation: The Schomburg Library of Black History and Culture.

◊ ◊ ◊

LLOYD H. KIMBROUGH
Masonic Leader

Most Worshipful Grand Master of Prince Hall Freemasons of The State of Ohio (1948) and Thirty-Third Degree, Ancient and Accepted Scottish Rite of Freemasonry, Prince Hall Affiliation, Northern Jurisdiction, United States of America.

Contributing Editor
*The Prince Hall Masonic Informer,
Journal of Freemasonry,* Official Organ of The Most Worshipful Grand Lodge of The State of Ohio (1948)

Documentation: The Williamson Masonic Collection (Prince Hall), The Schomburg Library of Black Culture and History.

C.D.B. KING
Secretary of State of The Republic of Liberia, and Delegate to the Peace Conference and the Representative of Liberia at The League of Nations. President-Elect, of The Republic of Liberia. Deputy Grand Master of the Grand Lodge, Ancient, Free and Accepted Masons of Liberia.

Right Worshipful Arthur A. Schomburg, was Chairman of the Committee that arranged the Reception and Banquet tended by The Grand Lodge of Prince Hall Masons to Honor, Deputy Grand Master King, and Mrs. King, who was the Grand Worthy Matron of the General Grand Chapter, of the Eastern Star.

Masonic Documentation: The Phylaxis, Volume Seven, Number Four., Fourth Quarter 1981.

◊ ◊ ◊

MARTIN LUTHER KING, SR.
(1900–1984)
Minister

Minister of The Ebeneezer Baptist Church of Atlanta, Georgia.

Masonic Membership: H. B. Butler Lodge #23, Atlanta, Ga.

Father of Dr. Martin Luther King, Jr., Nobel Peace Prize Winner, who led and inspired a movement for social, economic and political change, and who America honors with a National Holiday on 15 January each year.

Rev. King, Sr. (Daddy King, as he is affectionatly called) is the American success story of a man who rose from the poverty of black rural life at the turn of the century in Georgia to become a successful Minister and an effective Civil Rights Leader in the Movement for social, economic and political change.

He was a personal friend and avid supporter of President Carter, and also delivered the eulogy at the funeral of New York's former Governor and United States Vice President Nelson Rockefeller at The Riverside Church in 1979.

Dr. King, imbued within his son Martin the idea and knowledge that mankind isn't doomed in the starless night of racism, poverty and ignorance, but can unite and work for the bright day of freedom, equality and brotherhood, here and now, on this good earth.

Masonic Documentation: Georgia State Masonic Research Center.

◊ ◊ ◊

HARRY KNIGHT
Masonic Leader
Worship Master, Euclid Lodge #70, F. & A.M. Prince Hall.
Member of King David Consistory #3, A.A.S.R.M.

Thirty-Third Degree, Ancient and Accepted Scottish Rite of Freemasonry, Prince Hall Affiliation, Northern Jurisdiction, United States of America.

Brother Knight, created a Sir Knight in Ivanhoe Commandery, in 1901, and was the first Secretary of Consolidation of Excelsior and Widow's Son Chapter, Royal Arch Masons.

Documentation: Heritage Antioch Lodge #66, F. & A.M., Prince Hall Affiliation.

JOHN LANGSTON

JOHN LANGSTON, was the illustrious son of John Mercer Langston. Brother Langston was Inspector General of the Freedman's Bureau. Congressman elected to the House of Representatives from the State of Mississippi.

Author
Freedom and Citizenship 1893, Collected Speeches and From Virginia Plantation to National Capitol. 1894.

Prince Hall Mason, member of Saint Marks Lodge #7.

His father John Mercer Langston, was one of the Organizers and the First Worshipful Master of Saint Marks Lodge #7.

◊ ◊ ◊

JOHN MERCER LANGSTON
Organizer and First Worshipful Master of Saint Marks Lodge #7.
Lawyer—College Professor—Dean—Consul General College President

JOHN MERCER LANGSTON, born in slavery, on December 14, 1829, Louisa County, Virginia.

Education
Oberlin College, Oberlin, Ohio, B.A. 1884.

Langston sought admission to the law schools of New York State, but was denied because of skin color. Law Schools in New York State at that time only admitted white law students. He was also denied admission to the law schools of the State of Ohio.

Nevertheless, Langston read law nights, and after a number of years of dedicated study, offered himself to the Law Examiners, which was novel for a black person, at that time, in America's history. After considerable deliberation, he was admitted to the practice of law.

Positions
Dean and Professor of Law, at Howard University.
Consul General to the Republic of Haiti.
President, Virginia Normal Institute.

Admitted to practice law before the United States Supreme Court. John Mercer Langston, spoke and wrote fluently in French, Spanish, Greek, Latin and Hebrew, and possessed a great library. Besides, he was a member and fellow, of England's Philosophical Association Victorian Institute, which was the mark of a distinguished and remarkable man.

◊ ◊ ◊

LEWIS HOWARD LATIMER
**Inventor — Draftsman — Poet — Freedom Fighter
Freemason, Member of the Grand Lodge of England**

LEWIS HOWARD LATIMER, was born in Flushing, New York in 1848. A towering giant whose work we have yet to measure. But where would the world be without Latimer's priceless treasure?

An associate of Thomas Edison, and the inventor of the carbon filament for light. Latimer drafted the original drawings for Alexander Graham Bell, and countless other scientist and inventors. A pioneer in the electrical industry. He supervised installations in Montreal, London and New York.

Lewis Howard Latimer, whose father was an escaped slave, and also a Freemason, later, a member of the Grand Lodge of England. His name was, "George W. Latimer", a courageous and honorable man.

Monuments to Lewis Howard Latimer: 1. Latimer Federal Housing Development, in Flushing, New York. 2. Latimer Public School, #56, Brooklyn, New York. New York City Board of Education. 3. The Latimer Electrical Society, in the Electrical worker's Union, District six. New York, N.Y.

The illustrious name of Lewis Howard Latimer, is now before the United States Postal Advisory Committee, submitted by Senator Robert Kennedy, later resubmitted by Senator Edward Kennedy, of Massachusetts for designation in Latimer's memory and honor.

Masonic Documentation: Mille Volti Di Massoni di Giordano Gamberini. Concise Dictionary of American Biography.

◊ ◊ ◊

DAVID LEARY
Sovereign Grand Commander

DAVID LEARY, of Philadelphia, Pennsylvania, was the first black man to receive the thirty-third degree, and that was in the year 1850. It was conferred by Count De Saint Laurent, who himself was a thirty-third degree Mason of The Supreme Council of The Republic of France. Count Laurent had lived and had many activities in the United States, South America, and Mexico, and was most knowledgeable in Freemasonry.

The first recorded Supreme Council meeting was held on December 10, 1854, and David Leary presided as Sovereign Grand Commander.

Documentation: The Supreme Council (Caucasian or White) Minute Book of The First Colored Thirty-Third Degree Mason.

◊ ◊ ◊

JOSEPH G. LE COUNT
(1887–1981)
Lawyer

Most Worshipful Grand Master Of Prince Hall Masons Of Rhode Island.

Thirty-Third Degree, Ancient and Accepted Scottish Rite of Freemasonry, Northern Jurisdiction, Prince Hall Affiliation, United States of America.

President, New England Regional Conference of N.A.A.C.P. Branches.

Attorney for Rhode Island State Milk Commission, and Special Awardee, Rhode Island Bar Association.

Chairman of Providence N.A.A.C.P. Legal and Educational Defense Committee.

Past Master, King Solomon Lodge #5, and Past Potentate of The Shrine.

Documentation: United Supreme Council, The Winter Bulletin, Northern Jurisdiction, March 1983.

◊ ◊ ◊

B. ROBERT LEWIS
(1931–1979)
State Senator of Minnesota
Doctor of Veterinary Medicine

Chairman of Minnesota Senate Finance, Health, Welfare and Corrections, Sub-Committee.

Senator Lewis was responsible for legislation that provided

funding for all Health, Welfare, and Vocational Rehabilitation Services for State Hospitals and Correctional Institutional Services.

1960 Graduate of Kansas State University, Doctor of Veterinary Medicine.

Thirty-Second Degree, Prince Hall Freemason, Kansas Consistory.

Private Papers, Minnesota State Historical Society.

Documentation: Dr. John C. Schlotthauser, D.V.M., Researcher at the University of Minnesota, Department of Veterinary Pathobiology.

◊ ◊ ◊

JOHN G. LEWIS, JR.
(1903–1979)
Most Worshipful Grand Master of the State of Louisiana, Fellow of the Phylaxis Society and Past Sovereign Grand Commander, United Supreme Council, Thirty-Third Degree, Ancient Accepted Scottish Rite, Southern Jurisdiction

JOHN G. LEWIS was born in Natchitoches, Louisiana, December 9, 1903.

Member of the Board of Directors: Flint-Goodridge Hospital; Prince Hall Youth Foundation of Louisiana; Southern University Foundation; American Society of Christians and Jews; Legal and Educational Fund, N.A.A.C.P.

Awards and honors too numerous to mention; however, Most Worshipful, Grand Master John G. Lewis, Jr., has been called the greatest Prince Hall Mason to live since the passing of "The Master," Prince Hall, himself.

JOHN G. LEWIS, SR.
Worshipful Grand Master of Masons in the State of Louisiana and Jurisdictions

JOHN G. LEWIS, SR., was Grand Master for twenty-eight years. He established a Charity Bureau or Foundation, which has served Masons of the State of Louisiana for fifty years. Grand Master Lewis laid the foundation for the perpetuity of the Craft, when he insisted upon the quality and not quantity of the membership.

◊ ◊ ◊

SCOTT A. LEWIS
Worshipful Grand Master of Masons in the State of Louisiana and Its Jurisdictions

SCOTT A. LEWIS, Worshipful Grand Master of the State of Louisiana, guided the Craft safely through the years of the Great Depression and established a system of operation which is the foundation of the present success of today's Grand Lodge.

Masonic Oddity
Louisiana believes it is the only Masonic Jurisdiction anywhere to be presided over by a father and his two sons for a period of fifty years.

Masonic Documentation: Worshipful Grand Master Earle L. Bradford, Grand Master of Louisiana.

◊ ◊ ◊

EDWARD HART LIPSCOMBE
Poet and Minister
Professor, Rhetoric and Moral Philosophy
Editor, *The Mountain Gleaner*
President, Western Union Institute

EDWARD HART LIPSCOMBE was born in Orange County near Durham, North Carolina, on September 29, 1858.

Education
Shaw Collegiate Institute, later named Shaw University

While a student at Shaw Institute, Lipscombe formed an association with Dr. H. M. Tupper and Professor N. F. Roberts in the founding and the editing of *The African Expositor*, a newspaper.

In 1879 he was elected the Professor of Mathematics and Languages at Shaw University.

In 1882 he was appointed by the North Carolina Baptist State Convention, as one of the editors of *The Baptist Standard*, official newspaper of the Convention.

1883—He became an ordained minister.

1884—Chairman of the Committee of Prominent Colored Men of the South to address the Republican National Convention.

Poet: Lipscombe's poetry was published in *The African Expositor*.

Founder and Editor-in-Chief of *The Lighthouse*.

1886—Editor and part owner of *The Mountain Gleaner*.
Founder and first President of Western Union Institute.

Educational Advisor, North Carolina State Teacher's Convention and Teacher's Association.

Masonic Documentation: New York State Grand Lodge Library, F. & A.M.

◇ ◇ ◇

CHARLES LONG
Government Employee (Ret.)
Grand Trustee of The Most Worshipful Prince Hall
Grand Lodge of The State of New York
and Jurisdiction

Past Master, Celestial Lodge #3.

Past Potentate, Medina Temple #19.

Grand Patron Eureka Grand Chapter of the Order of Eastern Star (Prince Hall).

Honor Graduate of American Academy of Embalming.

Thirty-Third Degree, Ancient and Accepted Scottish Rite of Freemasonry, Northern Jurisdiction, Prince Hall Affiliation, United States of America.

Documentation: Who's Who Among Black Americans, 1980–1981.

◇ ◇ ◇

TOUSSAINT L' OUVERTURE
(1743–1803)
Governor General of Haiti and Military
and Political Genius

TOUSSAINT L' OUVERTURE, was born a slave on Bredi plantation in Saint Dominique, which is indisputable evidence and unshakable testimony of the black men's capacity for self-government and leadership in the Parliament of Mankind.

Governor General Touissant L' Ouverture was acclaimed for his wisdom, moderation and honesty. His impact on both world freedom and world history remain unmeasured. His remarkable letter to Napoleon, which began: "From the first of the blacks to the first of the whites," documents both the immediate demand and acceptable conditions for freedom before he called the slaves to arms in the name of liberty, freedom and equality.

Masonic Membership: The Grand Lodge of Haiti.

Books on and about General Ouverture: *The Black Napoleon* by Percy Waxman. *Black Liberator* by Stephen Alexis, New York, N.Y., 1931. *Contribution of General Toussaint L' Ouverture To The Independence of The American Republic* by Mary A. Healy.

Documentation: Bibliotheque Nationale, Paris, France. Archives of the Museum and Library of The Grand Orient of Haiti.

◊ ◊ ◊

ROY DALLAS LOWE, SR.
Editor

Treasurer and Past Master of Charlotte Lodge #146, Keysville, Virginia

Past District Deputy Grand Master of the Fourteenth District of Virginia and Jurisdiction.

Thirty-Second Degree, Ancient and Accepted Scottish Rite of Freemasonry, Prince Hall Affiliation, Northern Jurisdiction of the United States of America.

Member of King David Consistory, Number Three, Valley of New York.

Editor of *The Bee Hive Magazine* of the Most Worshipful Grand Lodge of Prince Hall Masons of Virginia, Free and Accepted Masons, Incorporated.

Masonic Documentation: One Hundredth Anniversary King David Journal.

◊ ◊ ◊

JUDSON WHITLOCKS LYONS
(1860–1924)
Attorney at Law

Register of The United States Treasury (1898–1906).

Attorney Lyons was the first black man to practice law in Augusta, Georgia.

Graduated Howard University Law School in 1884.

President, Haines Institute, Augusta, Georgia.

Executive Committee Member of the Republican Party of Georgia.

Member: Aurora Lodge #54, Waynesboro, Georgia. Bannaker Lodge #3, Augusta, Georgia.

Documentation: Georgia Masonic Research Center.

◊ ◊ ◊

LEO MANNING, SR.

District Deputy Grand Master and Lecturer of Michigan State Prince Hall Grand Lodge.

Reporter, *The Michigan Voice of Prince Hall*.

Past Master of Hiram Lodge, Number One, of Detroit, Michigan.

Quality Control Analyst at Chrysler Corporation.

Executive Board Member of the United Automobile Workers Union.

Masonic Documentation: Michigan Masonic Voice.

◊ ◊ ◊

JOHN MARRANT
Minister
Chaplain of African Lodge #459
of Boston, Massachusetts, of which
Prince Hall was the Most Worshipful Master

REVERENT MARRANT was the first person to carry Christianity to the American Indians along with John Stewart. This was documented by Grand Secretary Arthur A. Schomburg in *The Journal of History,* 1936, Washington, D.C., entitled, "Two Missionaries to American Indians."

Brother John Marrant was born in New York, New York on June 15, 1775 and was mostly self-educated. He preached memorable sermons to black Freemasons of Boston, Massachusetts, on "Self-Worth and Black Dignity," at the Celebration Feast of Saint John the Baptist.

The *Narrative of the Life of John Marrant,* would be printed nineteen times forty years after his death. He had traveled to Nova Scotia and other Provinces in Canada, preaching the word of God.

Masonic Documentation: Black Presence in Era of the American Revolution, 1770-1800, Kaplan.

◊ ◊ ◊

THURGOOD MARSHALL
Associate Justice of the United States Supreme Court

JUDGE MARSHALL was born on July 2, 1908, in Baltimore, Maryland.

Thirty-Third Degree, Ancient and Accepted Scottish Rite of Freemasonry, Prince Hall Affiliation, Northern Jurisdiction of the United States of America.

Member of Coal Creek Lodge #88, Prince Hall Masons; member of Medine Temple #19.

Education
Lincoln University, B.A.
Howard University Law School, LL.B.

Former Chief Counsel for the National Association for the Advancement of Colored People (N.A.A.C.P.).

Argued the case of *Brown vs. Board of Education,* before the United States Supreme Court, resulting in the 1954 School Integration Decision.

United States Solicitor General, United States Judge for the Second Circuit Appellate Court.

Honors: Recipient of the Spingarn Medal, N.A.A.C.P. and the Living History Award.

Member of the American Bar Association, former member of the Constitutional Conference for the Independence of Kenya, held in London, England.

Masonic Documentation: Prince Hall Lodge for Research of New York.

◊ ◊ ◊

CHARLES EDWARD MARTIN
Executive

Youth Director, Y.M.C.A., South Bend Indiana.

Teacher-Coach, South Bend School Corporation.

Chairman, C.E.T.A., Advisory Council.

Chairman, Board of Directors, Urban League of Saint Joseph County.

Member of The Phylaxis Society.

Commander, Imperial Legion of Honor.

Community Service Award, 1975, Urban League.

Prince Hall Freedom Award, Most Worshipful Prince Hall Grand Lodge of Indiana and Jurisdiction.

Documentation: Who's Who Among Black Americans, 1980–81.

◊ ◊ ◊

GILBERT RUTLEDGE MASON
Physician

Medical Director, Harrison County Head Start Unit, 1969.

Fellow, American Academy of Family Physicians.

Member, The American Medical Association and The National Medical Association.

President, N.A.A.C.P., Biloxi Branch, 1960.

Member of the Advisory Committee of the United States Civil Rights Commission (1965).

Governor's Emergency Council, Division of Health Planning.

President of Biloxi Civil League (1960–69).

Thirty-Second Degree, Ancient and Accepted Scottish Rite of Freemasonry. Prince Hall Affiliation.

Documentation: Who's Who Among Black Americans, 1980–81.

◊ ◊ ◊

J. BRUCE MASSEY
Physician and Surgeon

Member: World Medical Association

Biography in *International Blue Book of World Notables, American Medical Association, Who Is Important in Medicine,* and *Who's Who Among Black Americans.*

Thirty-Third Degree, Ancient and Accepted Scottish Rite of Freemasonry, Prince Hall Affiliation, Southern Jurisdiction, United States of America.

Invented and Patented five GYN Surgeon Instruments.

Invented and Patented (American and French) Safety Automatic Sun-Visor.

Former Resident Physician and Surgeon at Beth Israel Hospital and Roosevelt Hospital, Newark, New Jersey.

Documentation: Who's Who Among Black Americans, 1980–81.

◊ ◊ ◊

EMANUEL F. MATHIS 33°
Grand Master of New Mexico and Jurisdictions

Chairman, Four Corners Region Conference of Prince Hall Grand Masters.

Member, The Phylaxis Society.

Documentation: The Phylaxis, Vol. XI, No. 4, Fourth Quarter 1985.

◊ ◊ ◊

J. T. MAXEY
Most Worshipful Grand Master of the Grand Lodge of Prince Hall Masons of the State of Texas and Jurisdictions and Sovereign Grand Inspector General, Thirty-Third and Last Degree of Scottish Rite Masonry, the United States of America Master of Amity Lodge, Number Four (4), Galveston, Texas

J. T. MAXEY served as Chairman of Foreign Correspondence and Deputy Grand Master of the State of Texas. He travels fifteen thousand miles in Texas and many thousands of miles in other states.

In the Supreme Council of Grand Masters, Grand Master J. T. Maxey is a member of the Committee on Recognition.

Masonic Documentation: Prince Hall Masonic Digest.

◊ ◊ ◊

BENJAMIN E. MAYS
(1895–1984)
College President, Educator, School Administrator

Consultant to the Ford Foundation, New York, N.Y.

Former Dean of The School of Religion at Howard University, Washington, D.C.

Professor, State College of South Carolina, Orangeburg, South Carolina.

Pastor, Shiloh Baptist Church in the State of Georgia.

President of Morehouse College, in Atlanta, Georgia.

President of The Board of Education of Atlanta, Georgia.

BENJAMIN E. MAYS, was born in Ellworth, South Carolina in 1895, and earned his Doctorate of Philosophy Degree at the University of Chicago. He wrote *Born to Rebel,* an autobiography.

Awarded: The sixty-seventh (67th) Spingarn Medal, of the National Association for the Advancement of Colored People, at the National Convention in Boston, Massachusetts, July 1982.

Thirty-Third Degree, Ancient and Accepted Scottish Rite of Freemasonry, Southern Jurisdiction, Prince Hall Affiliation, United States of America.

Documentation: Born to Rebel, by Benjamin E. Mays. The Crisis, Official Organ, National Association for the Advancement of Colored People.

◊ ◊ ◊

WILLIE HOWARD MAYS, JR.
Baseball Great
Baseball Hall of Fame, Elected 1979
City of Hope, Hall of Fame, Elected 1978

Male Athlete of The Year, Associated Press, 1954.

Golden Plate Award, 1975.

Named the National League's Most Valuable Player (New York Giants).

Mason Mays began his baseball career with The Birmingham Black Barons, of the Black Professional Baseball League.

Author: *Willie Mays—My Life in and out of Baseball.*

Thirty-Third Degree, Ancient and Accepted Scottish Rite of Freemasonry, Southern Jurisdiction, Prince Hall Affiliation, United States of America.

Documentation: New York State Grand Lodge Library & Museum (F. & A.M.). (Paul Brenner, Black Stars).

◊ ◊ ◊

WADE H. McCREE, JR.
Judge

Judge, United States Court of Appeals (Sixth Circuit).

Judge, Formerly, Wayne County Circuit Court.

Judge, Formerly, United States District Court.

Commissioner, Workman's Compensation Commission.

Education
B.A., Fisk University, Phi Beta Kappa
LL.B., Harvard University Law School

Editorial Advisory Board, American Bar Association.

Thirty-Third Degree, Ancient and Accepted Scottish Rite of Freemasonry, Southern Jurisdiction, Prince Hall Affiliation, United States of America.

Documentation: Who's Who Among Colored (Black) Americans, 1980–81.

◊ ◊ ◊

JAMES. H. McGEE
Mayor of the City of Dayton, Ohio and Attorney at Law

Thirty-Third Degree, Ancient and Accepted Scottish Rite of Freemasonry, Prince Hall Affiliation, Northern Jurisdiction of the United States of America.

Education
Wilberforce University
Ohio State University Law School

Membership in the American Bar Association.

Member, Board of Directors, Dayton Art Institute.

Masonic Documentation: Ebony and the Schomburg Library.

◊ ◊ ◊

ROBERT EUGENE McGREGOR
Industrialist

Director, Progressive Mutual Building Society of Jamaica.

Director, Eastwood Park Development Company, Limited.

Member, Imperial Service Masonic Lodge of The Republic of Jamaica.

Documentation: Who's Who in Jamaica, 1972.

◊ ◊ ◊

GEORGE WELDON McMURRAY
Minister

Pastor, Mother African Methodist Episcopal Zion Church. (The oldest church in New York to have been built by free black Americans. Organized in 1796.)

Former Pastor of the Metropolitan African Methodist Zion Church, Birmingham, Alabama.

Leader in the Civil Rights Struggle of the 60's, and won the unqualified respect of both white and black people of the South.

Education
Livingston College, North Carolina.
Gammon Theological Seminary, Georgia.

Masonic: Thirty-Second Degree, Prince Hall Freemasonry, King David Consistory #3, Prince Hall Affiliation. Shriner, The Ancient Mystic Shrine, Prince Hall Affiliation.

Citation: Community Leader of America Award.

Trustee: Lomax-Hannon Junior College, Greenville, Alabama. Clinton Junior College, Rock Hill, South Carolina.

Member of The Board of Directors, Harlem Urban Development Center.

Built the The James Varick Community Center.

The A.M.E. Zion Church maintains a Senior Citizens Program and an After School Tutorial Program for Community youth.

Documentation: Personal interview and reviewed numerous documents.

◊ ◊ ◊

DR. LADDIE L. MELTON, 33°
Beaumont, Texas
23rd Imperial Potentate
Ancient Egyptian Arabic Order Nobles Mystic Shrine
1976-1978

DR. L.L. MELTON, practicing dentist, masonic leader, civic leader, was born September 23, 1900 in Abbeyville, Louisiana.

Education
Public schools of Abbeyville, La.
Strait College, New Orleans
Tuskegee Institute, Alabama
Howard University, College of Dentistry

First set up dental practice in New Orleans, Louisiana, and served as dean of men, head of the athletic department and football coach at Strait College.

Member of Alpha Phi Alpha Fraternity.

Chairman, public housing project of Plymouth Village, Beaumont, and Prince Hall Village, housing project, Port Arthur, Texas.

Past president, Southeast Texas Medical, Dental and Pharmaceutical Society.

Past president, Gulf States Dental Association of Texas.

Masonic membership: Past Master, Pride of Beaumont Lodge #291, F. & A.M. Member, Juniper Chapter #260, OES. Past Commander-in-Chief, St. George Consistory #101, AASR. Past Potentate, Nafud Temple #80, AEAONMS.

Masonic Documentation: Georgia Masonic Research Center.

◊ ◊ ◊

RALPH H. METCALFE
Congressman and Olympic Champion

Born in Atlanta, Georgia, May 30, 1910.

Education
Marquette University
University of Southern California

Illinois's first black State Athletic Commissioner.

Member of the Chicago Commission on Human Rights.

Alderman, Chicago City Council.

Thirty-Third Degree Prince Hall Freemason.

Member, Board of Directors, DuSable Museum on Afro-American History and Mahalia Jackson Scholarship Foundation.

Biography, *Who's Who Among Black Americans*.

Congressman Ralph H. Metcalfe was a Grand Inspector General of the Thirty-Third Degree of the Ancient and Accepted Scottish Rite of Freemasonry, Prince Hall Affiliation, Western Jurisdiction of the United States of America.

Masonic Documentation: Grand Lodge Library, F. & A.M., State of New York, Allan Boudreau, Ph.D., Librarian and Curator.

◊ ◊ ◊

GEORGE MIDDLETON
Third Grand Master of African Lodge #459 of Philadelphia, Pennsylvania
Black Commander of a Revolutionary Army Company
Violinist and Horse-Breaker

GRAND MASTER GEORGE MIDDLETON was the black commander of a Revolutionary Army company commonly called the "Bucks of America." John Hancock presented a banner bearing the initials of "G. M." in recognition of, and a tribute to, the company for courage and devotion throughout independence's struggle. Hancock had also earlier observed the soldiers were neatly dressed and most precise in their maneuvers and at their best with arms when under fire.

The Bucks of America, under the command of George Middleton, were victorious at Red Bank, Point Bridge and at Yorktown.

Masonic Documentation: Harry A. Williamson Collection of Black Masonry.

◊ ◊ ◊

JAMES A. MINGO

Honorary Fellow of the Phylaxis Society and awardee of John G. Lewis Medal for Excellence by the Phylaxis Society, a society of Prince Hall Freemasons who seek more light and have light to offer.

Secretary General, United Supreme Council, Thirty-Third Degree, Ancient and Accepted Scottish Rite of Freemasonry, Prince Hall Affiliation, Southern Jurisdiction of the United States of America.

Thirty-Third Degree, Ancient and Accepted Scottish Rite of

Freemasonry, Prince Hall Affiliation, Southern Jurisdiction of the United States of America.

Masonic Documentation: Southern Masonic News Quarterly.

◊ ◊ ◊

RICHARD E. MOORE
Grand Master of Prince Hall Grand Lodge of Illinois and Member and Historian of Hiram Lodge #14, Chicago, Illinois

GRAND MASTER RICHARD E. MOORE compiled and published the *History of Hiram Lodge* #14 of Chicago, Illinois.

Masonic Documentation: Williamson Collection on Black Masonry and the Schomburg Collection of Black History and Culture.

◊ ◊ ◊

VICTOR O. MORRIS
Most Worshipful Grand Historian of the Prince Hall Grand Lodge of the State of New York
Grand Orator of the Most Worshipful Prince Hall Grand Lodge of the State of New York

Editor-in-Chief—Prince Hall Sentinel. Most Worshipful Grand Master of Ceremonies of The Most Worshipful Prince Hall Grand Lodge of New York State. The first Worshipful Master of Nimrod Lodge #96.

Masonic Documentation: Historian Morris's Private Papers

◊ ◊ ◊

JOHN H. MURPHY
(1840–1922)
Publisher and Editor

Publisher & Editor, *The Afro-American Weekly Newspaper* (1892–1922).

Lecturer, National Negro Business League (1900).

President, The Negro Press Association.

Imperial Potentate of The Shrine of Baltimore (Prince Hall).

A "Noted Singer," who led The Bethel A.M.E. Church Choir for fifteen years.

Member of The Board of Managers of Provident Hospital.

When President Abraham Lincoln issued the call for Colored Troops, in the Civil War, John H. Murphy was twenty-four years old, and he enlisted in Company "G" of the thirtieth Regiment (Infantry) United States Colored Troops, Maryland Volunteers, and during his service advanced to the rank of First Sergeant.

Philosophy: "I have faith in myself, in the ability of my people to succeed in this civilization, and in the ultimate practice of which will secure them full citizenship."

Thirty-Third Degree, Ancient and Accepted Scottish Rite of Freemasonry, Southern Jurisdiction, Prince Hall Affiliation, United States of America.

Documentation: Georgia State Masonic Research Center.

◊ ◊ ◊

X.L NEAL
**Worshipful Grand Master of Prince Hall Masons,
State of Georgia
Grand Minister of State
United Supreme Council Scottish Rite Freemasonary
Thirty-Third Degree, Southern Jurisdiction
Past Potentate, Past Imperial Potentate (Honorary)
Ancient Arabic Order of the Mystic Shrine
Knight Grand Commander of the Liberian Hummane
Order of African Redemption by His Excellency
the late President Tubman
of the Republic of Liberia, 1970.**

Worshipful Grand Master, X.L. Neal, of the Most Worshipful Prince Hall Grand Lodge, of the State of Georgia, was born in Okmulgee, Oklahoma, and completed his Elementary and Secondary Schooling in the State of Oklahoma.

Education
Morehouse College, Atlanta, Georgia.
Atlanta University, Atlanta, Georgia.
Meharry Medical College, Department of Pharmacy.
Nashville, Tennessee.

Honors
Mason of the year, Gold Medal Achievement Award, by
The United Supreme Council, 1975.
Made Honorary African Chief, 1975.

Positions
Instructor in Chemistry at Morehouse College.
Instructor in Chemistry at Spelman College.
President's Committee on Equal Opportunity, 1961.

◊ ◊ ◊

ALEXANDER HERRITAGE NEWTON
Thirty-Third Degree of Ancient and
Accepted Scottish Rite of Freemasonry
Prince Hall Affiliation
United States of America
Grand Chaplain of the Prince Hall
Grand Lodge of New Jersey
Chairman of the Grand Committee
on Charity
Chairman of the Grand Committee on Memorials
Grand Treasurer of the Supreme Council
Member of the Rising Sun Lodge, Number One
Camden, New Jersery

ALEXANDER HERRITAGE NEWTON, was born in New Bern, North Carolina in 1837. His father was a slave, and his mother a free woman.

Brother Newton's middle name was "Herritage," which was selected for the naming of the Military Lodge, instituted at Camp Kilmer, in New Brunswick, New Jersey on March 8, 1949.

Alexander Herritage Newton was Commissory Sergeant, of the twenty-nineth Regiment Connecticut Volunteers.

Masonic Documentation: Black Square and Compass. Two Hundred Years of Prince Hall Freemasonry. By, Joseph A. Walkes, Jr.

◊ ◊ ◊

KWANE NKRUMAH
(1909–1972)
President
President of the Republic of Ghana, 1960–1966

Co-President of The Republic of Guinea, 1967.

Prime Minister of The Gold Coast, 1952–1957.

One of the Founders of the Organization for African Unity.

The first Statesman to lead an African Colony from Colonialism to Independence after World War II. He was President and Founder of the People's Convention Party that demanded self-government for the Gold Coast.

Books written and published:
Ghana: An Autobiography.
I Speak For Freedom.
Africa Must Unite.
Conscioncism.

Masonic Membership: United Grand Lodge of England.

PRESIDENT NKRUMAH was overthrown by a military coup while en route to Viet-Nam to attempt to establish peace. He became an exile in the Republic of Guinea and was made co-President by President Toure, where he resided until death. While President of Ghana one of his monumental accomplishments was the Aswan Dam, providing hydro-electric power to Ghana.

Employed Dr. W.E.B. DuBois, Scholar and Mason, as Editor-in-Chief of The Africanna Encyclopedia.

Masonic Documentation: Archives of The University of Ghana.

◊ ◊ ◊

JORDAN B. NOBLE
Founding Member of Richmond Lodge Number One
Later, A Member of Berry Lodge Number Two
Teenage Drummer of the
Seventh Regiment Army Unit

BROTHER NOBLE, was a drummer who executed many of the signals and calls during battle. During the war of Independence, he beat his drum through thick fog and smoke, which came from bombs and rockets. His inspiring slogan was forever forward until the British are defeated.

Brother Noble served in three wars with distinction. The Battle of New Orleans (1815) The Seminole War, in Florida (1836) and the War with Mexico, (1846)

Brother Noble's drum is on exhibit at The Cadido Louisiana State Museum.

Masonic Documentation: The Williamson Collection, The Schomburg Library of Black History and Culture.

◊ ◊ ◊

HERBERT C. NORRIS
Grandmaster of The Most Worshipful Prince Hall
Grand Lodge of
Free and Accepted Masons of Deleware.
Retired—Wilmington, Delaware
School Administratior
Thirty-Third Degree, Ancient and
Accepted Scottish Rite of Freemasonry
Prince Hall Affiliation
Northern Jurisdiction
United States of America

Education
Lincoln University—A.B. 1939.
Atlanta University—M.A. Degree in Social Work.
University of Pennsylvania—Graduate Study.

United States Army—First Lieutenant—92nd Division.
Member of the Board of Directors, Deleware Technical and Community College.
Member of Omega Psi Phi Fraternity.
Grandmaster Norris, is an Elder in the Community Presbyterian Church.

◊ ◊ ◊

LESLIE C. NORRIS 33°
Chairman of the Board of Trustees
of the Most Worshipful Prince Hall
Grand Lodge of Free and Accepted Masons of the
State of New York and Jurisdictions

Worshipful Master of Boyer Lodge, #1 (1964–65). Thirty-Third Degree, King David Consistory, #3, A.A.S.R. Past Potentate and Temple Director, Medina Temple #19, A.E.A.N.O.M.S.

Chairman of the Grand Lodge Convention, 1967–68.

Honorary Member, Olive Branch Lodge #5, Hot Springs, Arkansas. Progressive Lodge #64, Mount Vernon, New York.

Deputy Grand Marshall, 1966–67.

Committeeman, Boy Scouts of America, Bronx, New York.

Musician, Graduate of The Bronx Conservatory of Music, Bronx, N.Y. Performer of Music in Colleges and Private Clubs.

Member, The Nocamba Theatre Talent Booking Agency.

Shareholder, The Barrow Music and Publishing Company.

Projectionist, The Borough of Manhattan Housing Center.

Documentation: Who's Who Among Black Americans and a personal letter.

◊ ◊ ◊

E. THOMAS OLIVER
(Accountant)

President, First Masonic District, Prince Hall Freemasonry, State of New York.

Trustee—Antioch Lodge #66, Prince Hall Freemasonry.

PAST MASTER

Antioch Lodge #66, under the Jurisdiction of The Prince Hall Grand Lodge of the State of New York.

PROGRAM DIRECTOR

Great Black Men of Masonry—Qualitative Black Achievers Who Were Freemasons Project.

Education
B.A., Accounting, City University of New York.
M.A., Accounting, City University of New York.

Employment
Accountant in the Office of the Controller.
Board of Higher Education, City of New York.

◊ ◊ ◊

HONORABLE MR. JUSTICE NII AMAA OLLENNU
Assistant District Grand Master
of the District Grand Lodges (Forty-four)
of The Republic of Ghana

Past Senior Grand Deacon, 1978.

Justice of The Court of The Republic of Ghana.

Documentation: The Masonic Year Book For 1981–82. United Grand Lodge of England.

◊ ◊ ◊

ANTHONY OVERTON
Judge, Corporate Executive, Manufacturer

Judge of The Municipal Court of Topeka (Shawnee County) Kansas.

President, Victory Life Insurance Company.

President and Founder, Douglass National Bank.

President and Founder, Overton Hygienic Manufacturing Company.

Education
B.A., Washburn College, Kansas.
LL.B., University of Kansas Law School

Author: *The Successful Salesman.*

Awarded: The Springarn Medal by The N.A.A.C.P.

Recipient: The Harmon Award for Excellence in Business.

The Anthony Overton Elementary School, in Chicago, Illinois, named in his Honor and Memory.

Thirty-Third Degree, Ancient and Accepted Scottish Rite of Freemasonry, Prince Hall Affiliation, Northern Jurisdiction, United States of America.

Documentation: The Chicago Negro Almanac and Reference Book, edited by Ernest R. Rather.

◊ ◊ ◊

L. JOSEPH OVERTON
Administrative Consultant in Labor and Management
Thirty-Third Degree, Ancient and Accepted Scottish Rite of Freemason
Prince Hall Affiliation
Northern Jurisdiction
United States of America

Past Imperial Potentate, Ancient Arabic Order, Noble of The Mystic Shrine. Past Illustrious Potentate, Medina Temple #19. Former Business Agent, Local 338 Retail, Wholesale and Chain Store

Food Employees Union. (AFL-CIO.)
Former Executive Director, Negro Labor Committee.
President, HARYOU-ACT Community Corporation.
Past President, New York Branch, N.A.A.C.P.
Member, National Board of Directors, N.A.A.C.P.
Past President, Community School Board, District Five.
Founding Member, The National Urban League's Labor Committee.
Chairman, Board of Directors, Youth Development Agency of Central Harlem.

Education
Cornell University, School of Labor Relations.

Present Employment
Circulation Manager—Amsterdam News
and
Coordinator of Display Advertising and Promotion.

Masonic Documentation: Personal resume from Brother L. Joseph Overton.

◊ ◊ ◊

HENRY PARKER
Treasurer, State of Connecticut

Thirty-Third Degree, Ancient And Accepted Scottish Rite of Freemasonry, Prince Hall Affiliation, Northern Jurisdiction—United States of America.

Masonic Documentation: The Bulletin, Official Organ of the United Supreme Council, Ancient and Accepted Scottish Rite of Freemasonry, Prince Hall Affiliation, Northern Jurisdiction, United States of America.

◊ ◊ ◊

WILLIAM CARTER PARKER, JR. 33°
Greensboro, North Carolina
President, Shepargob Foods, Inc.
Deputy Grand Master
M. W. Prince Hall Grand Lodge of North Carolina
Imperial Director of Talent and Scholarship
Ancient Egyptian Arabic Order Nobles Mystic Shrine

WILLIAM CARTER PARKER, JR., was born in Mt. Gilead, North Carolina.

Education
B.S., M.S., North Carolina A. & T. State University
M. Ed., University of North Carolina
Ph.D., Indiana University

He is a member of Omega Psi Phi Fraternity.

Noble Parker serves on the Board of Directors of L. Richardson Memorial Hospital, the Greensboro Chamber of Commerce, Vice President of the Board of Directors of United Way, the Better Business Bureau of Greater Greensboro, the Greensboro Board of Realtors, and the Advisory Board of the *Carolina Peacemaker Newspaper.*

Parker is past president of Head Start and Child Abuse Prevention Services and the Greensboro Minority Business League, and is a member of the Merchants Association of Greater Greensboro.

Professionally, Parker has served as an Agriculture Extension Agent and teacher of Vocational Agriculture. He also served as Counselor, Associate Professor of Education, Director of the North Carolina Fellows Program and Dean of Student Affairs at North Carolina A. and T. State University.

Achievements
Burger King Franchises in Greensboro and
Winston Salem, N.C.
Owner, Gate City Barber Shops

Owner, Piedmont Realty Company
President, Piedmont Development Corporation
President, Wilpar Development Corporation
President, Wilpar Construction Company
Developer, Parker Brothers Restaurant

Honors
James T. Isler Family and Children Service Award
Worshipful Master of the Year, 16th Masonic District-1964
Shriner of the Year, Imperial Council, AEAONMS, 1973
Honorary 33rd Degree, John "Pop" Freeman Class of 1973
Businessman of the Year, Greensboro Minority Business League-1979

Masonic membership: Past Master, Invincible Lodge #251, F. & A.M. Member, Greensboro Consistory #106, AASR. Past Potentate, Khalia Temple #144, AEAONMS.

Documentation: Georgia Masonic Research Center.

◊ ◊ ◊

CHARLES HENRY PARRISH
Pastor
Professor of Greek
Secretary and Treasurer of the
State University of Kentucky

CHARLES HENRY PARRISH, was born in Lexington, Fayette County, Kentucky, on April 18, 1859. His parents were slaves. He was sent to Public School, directly after Emancipation. His parents were poor, and he was compelled to leave school, to support himself, and also to help his parents. He found employment in John O. Hodges Dry Good Store. But his spare moments were devoted to reading and studying.

At the age of twelve, Charles joined the Baptist Church. In 1872, after many years of training in the Sabbath School, he was made secretary. This position he held for eight years, at the same time, filling in as a teacher.

In 1880, Parrish was appointed Pastor of the First Baptist Church. Later, he received a student call from the State University at Louisville, Kentucky to begin his course of studies. Graduating with highest honors, the University's Gold medal. Charles Henry Parrish, was immediately appointed, Professor of Greek, a position he ably held.

In retrospect, another black qualitative achiever who was a Freemason—From Janitor to Secretary and Treasurer of the State University of Kentucky—from firemaker to a Professor of Greek—from dire poverty to honor among faculty and students—During his eighteen months as a Pastor, his church's membership doubled.

Masonic Documentation: New York State Grand Library for Research. (F. & A.M.)

◊ ◊ ◊

CHARLES RICH PATTERSON
Slave—Blacksmith—Carriage-Maker.
Worshipful Master of Cedar Grove Lodge #17, Greenfield, Ohio
Served as Lodge Secretary, Junior Warden and Senior Warden.

Determined men can conquer anything. Charles Rich Patterson, was a determined man. As a slave he was assigned to his Master's blacksmith shop and he mastered the trade. He later escaped by hiking over the Allegheny Mountains and thereafter swimming across the Ohio River, into the State of Ohio, just before the Civil War.

Charles Rich Patterson, arrived in Greenfield, Ohio and soon went to work in the local blacksmith shop, and within a few years he bought the business and founded C.R. Patterson Carriage Company. He married and had four children, and built a reputation of honesty and fairness, and was considered the county's finest blacksmith. Nevertheless, he had higher goals, to build a factory that would manufacture buggies, backboard, rockaways and surreys, the eras most popular wagon.

Masonic Documentation: From Slave to Automobile Manufacturer: The Black Man Who Built Cars. (Wards Auto World, Volume 17, Number 4, Published by Ward's Communication, Inc. Detroit, Michigan 48226. By Reginald R. Larrie. Proceedings of the Prince Hall Grand Lodge of Ohio, 1915, Page 97. "An Official History of the Most Worshipful Grand Lodge Free and Accepted Masons, for the State of Ohio." William Hartwell Parhem and Jeremiah Arthur Brown (1906) Page 65.

◊ ◊ ◊

FRED D. PATTERSON
Manufacturer of the Patterson-Greenfield Automobile. Worshipful Master of Cedar Grove Lodge #17, Greenfield, Ohio

FRED D. PATTERSON was the son of Charles Rich Patterson, who after graduating from Greenfield High School, entered Ohio State University, but returned home when his father became ill. When his father died, Fred with other members of the family operated the company.

While on a business trip, Fred began to see more and more horseless carriages. He talked his family into producing the horseless carriages. He strove to manufacutre an automobile with better fuel economy than those currently on the market.

On September 23, 1915, Fred idea came to fruition when the first Patterson-Greenfield came off the assembly line, with a four cylinder engine of thirty horsepower. The price was less than one thousand dollars. When Patterson-Greenfield ceased production in 1918, because of lack of investors, Fred began producing School Bus Bodies to meet the rising demand. The company closed its doors for the last time in 1939.

Masonic Documentation: Ward's Automobile World, Volume 17, Number 4. Wards Communication, Inc. Detroit, Michigan 48226. "Proceeding of Prince Hall Grand Lodge of Ohio, 1915, Page 97.

◊ ◊ ◊

CLYDE F. PAYNE
Masonic Leader

Right Worshipful Grand Lecturer, Most Worshipful Prince Hall Grand Lodge.

Worshipful Master of Tuscan Lodge #58, Prince Hall Affiliation.

Associate Editor: *The Prince Hall Sentinel.*

Member, The Phylaxis Society.

Member, Prince Hall Grand Lodge Committee on Jurisprudence, Works and Lectures.

Graduate: Refrigeration and Technological Institute of Great Britain.

Refrigeration Specialist at the British Naval Station at Benbow.

Founder of The Pioneer Credit Union of Barbados and Trinidad, and The Everett School and Sports Club.

Masonic Documentation: The Phylaxis, Fourth Quarter, 1984.

◊ ◊ ◊

WILLIAM H. PERRY, JR.
Masonic Officer and Educator

Grand Secretary, Prince Hall Freemasons of The Most Worshipful Grand Lodge of Kentucky (F. & A.M.) and Deputy from Kentucky to The United Supreme Council.

Principal, William H. Perry Senior Elementary School, Louisville, Kentucky.

Principal, Russell Junior High School of Louisville, Kentucky.

Secretary-Treasurer, Kentucky Black Educator's Association.

Appointed by Governor Willis as Trustee of Lincoln Institute in Kentucky.

Thirty-Third Degree, Scottish Rite of Freemasonry, Southern Jurisdiction, Prince Hall Affiliation, United States of America.

◊ ◊ ◊

JOHN PETERSON
Educator, Minister, Masonic Leader

The First Black Schoolmaster in the City of New York, he was assigned to the Public School for Colored Children, Number One, Located on Mulberry Street.

Minister of The Abyssinia Church of The Lord.

Masonic membership and leadership: Goyer Lodge, #1 of New York City, N.Y. Grand Chaplain, Grand Lodge of The State of New York (1855–1858). Grand Secretary, Grand Lodge of the State of New York (1859). Grand Treasurer, Grand Lodge of The State of New York (1860–1869).

◊ ◊ ◊

PINCKNEY BENTON STEWART PINCHBACK
Governor of the State of Louisiana
1872–1873
Lawyer—Congressman
United States Senator—Lieutenant-Governor
and
Wealthy Gentleman

Member Berry Masonic Lodge, Number Two, New Orleans, Louisiana. Brother Pinchback was born in Holmes County, Mississippi, May 10, 1837.

Education
Gilmore High School, in Cincinnati, Ohio.
Law School of Mississippi State University.
Passed the "Mississippi State Bar Examination",
on April 10, 1886.

In 1887, Pinchback joined and assisted in the reorganization of the Fourth Ward Republican Club, and afterward won enduring honor for his extraordinary work. Later considerable political patronage came to him.

He was appointed:
Inspector of Customs.
School Director, State Board of Education for the
City of New Orleans.

Thereafter, he was elected United States Congressman, and later, United States Senator, and was elected Delegate to the State Convention, where he introduced thirteen articles, which were adopted.

Senator Pinchback served six years in the United States Senate before becoming Lieutenant Governor. When the State of Louisiana impeached Governor Warmouth, Lieutenant Governor Pinchback was sworn in as Governor and served until January 13, 1873. Louisiana State records reveals that he displayed administrative ability of high order.

Governor Pinchback, was a delegate to another Constitutional Convention of the State of Louisiana, and again displayed rare talent and unusual ability. He was a seasoned master of argumentation and logic. Some delegates considered "Governor Pinchback", a spellbinder.

During the Constitutional Convention, "Governor Pinchback", was appointed to the, "Board of Trustees", of Southern University.

Masonic Documentation: Williamson Masonic Collection, The Schomburg Library.

◊ ◊ ◊

LYNDEN OSCAR PINDLING
The Right Honorable, Lynden Oscar Pindling, P.C., M.P.,
Prime Minister of the Commonwealth of the Bahamas.
Thirty-Third Degree, Ancient and Accepted Scottish Rite of Freemasonry,
Prince Hall Affiliation, Northern Jurisdiction, United States of America

LYNDEN OSCAR PINDLING, was born in Nassau, on March 22, 1930, and attended the Government High School in Nassau. During which time he became junior sprint champion of The Bahamas. After graduation he left The Bahamas to attend the University of London, where he earned his Bachelor of Law degree. Thereafter, he was called to the English Bar, Middle Temple, as a Barrister-at-Law. He also passed The Bahamas Bar Examination.

As Prime Minister, Lynden Oscar Pindling, has achieved many of his major goals. His principal object was Sovereignty for The Bahamas, and in 1973, this became a reality. Another milestone was his acceptance of United Nation's Membership. He said: "The Bahamas hold a unique position in the Western World. In no other part of the hemisphere, do all the social, economic, political and security considerations merge into one focal point, as do The Bahamas, thereby making it a pivotal point in hemispheric relations."

The Prime Minister has received numerous doctorates, including Howard University, and Bethune Cookman College.

Masonic Documentation: Public Relations Officer, The Bahamas.

◊ ◊ ◊

JOHN PINE
(1690–1756)
Noted Black Engraver, Grand Masonic Lodge of England

JOHN PINE (1690–1756) was born in London, England. He was a distinguished engraver and close friend of the great artist and painter, Hogarth, and achieved lasting fame as a member of the Masonic fraternity by engraving the frontispiece to Dr. James Anderson's Constitution of 1723. The same engraving was used again in 1738, the revised edition of Anderson's Constitutions. Brother Pine was a black Mason and engraver.

Pine was a member in 1725 of the Masonic Lodge at Globe Taver, Moorgate (his name was spelled "Pyne"). He also engraved a quaint list of lodges from about 1725 to 1741.

The Book of Constitutions came about when the Grand Lodge, organized in London in 1717, was ordered by the Right Reverend James Anderson, Doctor of Divinity, in 1721 to digest the old Gothic Constitutions in and with a new and better method. A committee of fourteen learned brethren examined the results of his work and, after a few changes, it was printed for the benefit of the lodges in 1723.

Keith Arrington, Assistant Librarian of Iowa Masonic Library, stated his library has two copies of the original 1723 edition, as well as the 1738 edition of *The Book of Constitutions,* that John Pine engraved.

Brother Pine served as Marshall of the Processions on January 29, 1730, when Lord Kingston, Grand Master, escorted the Duke of Norfolk, Grand Master-elect, from the Duke's House in Saint James Square (London) to Merchant Taylor's Hall.

Hogarth painted his friend, John Pine, twice. The portrait, with a written article was painted by Hogarth in 1735 in the style of Rembrandt. Later, Hogarth included Pine in a satirical painting called, "The Gate of Calais," in which he depicted Pine as a monk. From this painting, Pine acquired the nickname, "Friar Pine."

Brother Pine was trained as a silversmith's engraver and he surpassed Hogarth in heraldic and decorative engraving. Probably, because of Pine's superb heraldic work, he was made, "Bluemantle Pursuiyant," in the College of Heralds in 1743, and he took up residence there.

A monumental work was the exquisite edition of *Horace,* in which the whole text was engraved and illustrated with ancient bas-reliefs and representative gems. This was known as *Pine's Horace,* was published in two volumes in 1733 and 1737, and is now a collector's item of considerable value.

The *Dictionary of National Biography,* whose approximately seventy volumes list the most important Britsh personages through the years, devoted about two full columns to John Pine and almost as much space to his son, Robert Edge Pine, who was also an artist. Robert migrated to America after the signing of the Declaration of Independence, with intentions of painting important persons who were involved in the American Revolution as well as scenes of interest. He spent three weeks at Mount Vernon, painting George Washington and his family.

Brother Pine was described as being dark, fat and jovial. Other than Masonic engravings, he produced an unbelievable quantity of quality art chiefly in the form of book illustrations.

JOSEPH I. PLEASANT, JR.
(Thirty-Third Degree)

Past Master of Ceremonies, King David Consistory Number Three, Ancient and Accepted Scottish Rites, Prince Hall Affiliation, Northern Jurisdiction of the United States of America and Past Grand High Priest, R.A.M., State of New York.

The Record: Past Master, Prince Hall Lodge Number Thirty-Eight.
Past Treasurer, Prince Hall Lodge Number Thirty-Eight.
Past High Priest, Eureka Chapter, Prince Hall Lodge Number Thirty-Eight, 7 R.A.M.
Past M.E. Commander, St. John's Commandery Number Four, Knights Templar.
Treasurer, M.E. Prince Hall Grand Chapter, R.A.M., State of New York.
Past Illustrious Potentate, Medina Temper Number Nineteen.

Past Deputy of the Oasis, New York, A.E.A.O.N.M.S.
Past Treasurer, Zabud Council Number Seven, Royal and Select Masters.
Past Treasurer, V.I.R.F., First Masonic District.

◊ ◊ ◊

WILLIAM C. PONDER
Most Worshipful Prince Hall Grand Master of The State of Wisconsin and Jurisdiction

Thirty-Third Degree, Ancient and Accepted Scottish Rite of Freemasonry, Northern Jurisdiction, Prince Hall Affiliation, United States of America.

Documentation: The United Supreme Council, Northern Jurisdiction, Prince Hall Affiliation, United States of America.

PRESTON L. POPE

Most Worshipful Preston Pope, Grand Master of the Prince Hall Grand Lodge of Connecticut and Jurisdiction.

Thirty-Third Degree, Ancient and Accepted Scottish Rite of Freemasonry, Prince Hall Affiliation, Northern Jurisdiction of the United States of America.

Masonic Documentation: The Bulletin, official organ of the United Supreme Council.

◊ ◊ ◊

ADAM CLAYTON POWELL, JR.
Congressman, Political Leader and Baptist Minister

Born: New Haven, Conn., November 29, 1908. Died: Miami, Florida, April 4, 1972. Minister: Abyssinian Baptist Church, New York City, N.Y.

Education
Colgate University, B.A. 1930.
Columbia University, M.A. 1932.
Shaw University, D.D. 1935.

Founder
The People's Voice, Weekly Newspaper.

Elected to Congress with nominations from:
The Democratic Party, The Republican Party
and The American Labor Party.

Elected:
Chairman of the Education and
Labor Committee of The House of Representatives.

Mobilized the masses of New York City blacks against discrimination in employment, housing and social services, including but not limited to Harlem Hospital.

Influential in the passage of President Johnson's AntiPoverty and The Great Society Programs.

Books Authored: "Is This A White Man's War?" (1942). "Marching Blacks" (1945).

Listed: Encyclopedia of American Biography.

◊ ◊ ◊

HON. S. A. J. PRATT
Barrister

Former Minister of State of The Republic of Sierra Leone.

Deputy District Grand Master of The Republic of Sierra Leone and The Gambia Jurisdiction of The United Grand Lodge of England.

Documentation: Masonic Year Book (1981–1982), The United Grand Lodge of England, and Brother Isaac Christian During of The Republic of Sierra Leone.

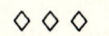

◊ ◊ ◊

JAMES PRICE, JR.
**Thirty-Third Degree, Scottish Rite of Freemasonry, Prince Hall, Affiliate, Northern Jurisdiction, United States of America.
Microbiologist, Bureau of Laboratories Pennsylvania Department of Health.**

Past Master, Campbell Washington Joppa Lodge #37, F.A. & M. Past Chairman, Education Committee First Masonic District of The Most Worshipful Prince Hall Grand Lodge of Pennsylvania. Former District Deputy Grand Master of the First Masonic District. Most Worshipful Prince Hall Grand Lodge of Pennsylvania. Chairman, Historical Research Committee— Pennsylvania Council of Deliberation. Cathedral Librarian, United Supreme Council, Northern Jurisdiction Prince Hall Affiliate.

Author and Co-Author of Scientific Papers for Journals of the United States Department Housing, Education and Welfare's Public Health Reports American Society of Microbiology's Journal of Clinical Microbiology of The Public Health Laboratory.

Masonic Documentation: Thomas Gilchrist, Past Commander-in-Chief, King David Consistory #3.

◊ ◊ ◊

SAMUEL DEWITT PROCTOR
Clergyman and Educator

Senior Minister, Abyssinian Baptist Church of New York.

Professor of Education, Graduate School of Education, Rutgers University in New Brunswick, New Jersey.

Former Professor, Religion and Ethics, Virginia Union University.

Trustee, Overseas Development Conference on Religion and International Affairs.

Trustee, United Negro College Fund and Meharry Medical College.

Doctorate in Theology (Ph.D.), Boston University.

Honorary Doctorates: Ottawa University, Stillman College, Coe College, Virginia Union University, Atlanta University.

Thirty-Third Degree, Ancient and Accepted Scottish Rite of Freemasonry, Southern Jurisdiction, Prince Hall Affiliation, United States of America.

◊ ◊ ◊

MATTHEW W. PROPHET
Educator

Superintendent of Public Schools of the City of Portland, Oregon.

Former Superintendent of Public Schools of Lansing, Michigan.

Military Career: Advanced from Army Private to Lieutenant Colonel.

Member of The Phylaxis Society.

Prince Hall Freemason, Member of Most Worshipful Stringer Grand Lodge of Mississippi.

Documentation: The Phylaxis Newsletter, Vol. VI, No. 1 (July 1983).

◊ ◊ ◊

CHESTER C. PRYOR
Medical Doctor

Director of Medical Services of The United Supreme Council of Ancient and Accepted Scottish Rite of Freemasonry, Northern Jurisdiction, Prince Hall Affiliation, United States of America.

Dr. Pryor initiated an extensive preventive medical educational program.

Thirty-Third Degree, Ancient and Accepted Scottish Rite of Freemasonry, Prince Hall Affiliation, United States of America.

Masonic Documentation: The Bulletin, Official Organ, The United Supreme Council.

◊ ◊ ◊

RICHARD PRYOR
Member
Henry Brown Masonic Lodge #22, of Peoria, Illinois.
Member
The Consistory and A Shriner.

RICHARD FRANKLIN LENNOX THOMAS PRYOR, III, was born in Peoria, Illinois, on December 1, 1940. He accepted his first show business challenge at the early age of seven years, when he sat in as a drummer with the House Orchestra at Peoria's Famous Door Cabaret. This was followed with his bebut as a dramatic actor, in Rumpelstiltskin, at the age of twelve.

During 1981, Brother Pryor, who is a Comedian, Actor and Musician sent his check for fifty thousand dollars to Henry Brown Prince Hall Masonic Lodge #22, of Peoria, Illinois and advised Past Master Ronal Brown, to use and distribute the money as he chooses.

Masonic Documentation: The Phylaxis, Vol Seven, Third Quarter. Johnson Publication, The Jet, October 3, 1981.

◊ ◊ ◊

CHARLES B. PURVIS
(A.M.-M.D.)
First Lieutenant
Professor of Obstetrics and Disease
Surgeon-in-Charge of Freedman Hospital.

CHARLES B. PURVIS, was born in Philadelphia, Pennsylvania.

Education
Quaker Schools, of Philadelphia, Penna.,
Oberlin College, Oberlin, Ohio,
Western Reserve Medical College
of Western Reserve University
in Cleveland, Ohio. M.D.
Degree, in 1885.

Two months after graduation with highest honors, he was offered and accepted a Commission in the United States Army, as Acting Assistant Surgeon, with the rank of First Lieutenant, and assigned to duty in Washington, D.C.

Later he accepted the position of Assistant Surgeon at Freedman Hospital.

Thereafter, Dr. Purvis, was appointed Professor of Medical Jurisprudence, at Howard University Medical School. And thereafter, Chairman of Obstetrics and Disease of Women and Children.

The last appointment for Dr. Charles B. Purvis, was Surgeon in Charge of the Surgical Department of Freedman Hospital.

Masonic Documentation: Williamson Masonic Collection, Schomburg Library of Black History and Culture.

ALEXANDER PUSHKIN
(1799-1837)
Poet, Novelist and Playwright
Member of the Russian Grand Masonic Lodge

ALEXANDER PUSHKIN, son of an Abyssinian Prince who was kidnapped, and sold to the Sultan of Turkey, then abducted by the Russian Ambassador and sent to Russia as a gift to Peter the Great. He was born in Moscow, Russia, on May 26, 1799, and began writing at the age of thirteen, and his work was published when he was the same age.

Education
Tsarskoye Selo Lycee, Graduated with top Honors.

Books published
The Queen of Spades, The Black Shawl, The Bronze Horseman, The Negro of Peter The Great, Eugene Onegin, The Caucasian Captive, Imitation of the Koran, Mozart and Salieri, The Captain's Daughter, The Tales of The Late Ivan Petrovich Belkin and Napoleon—Narrative poem.

Alexander Pushkin was killed in a duel in 1837. He believed that a poet should aim to appeal to man's conscience.

Dostoevsky, great Russian writer summed up Pushkin's influence in two sentences in his address on June 8, 1880, on the occasion of the unveiling of Pushkin Memorial in Moscow: "It can be said positively that if Alexander Pushkin hadn't existed, there would have been no talented writers to follow him. At least, they wouldn't have appeared with such force, and with such clarity, in spite of their great gifts, as they succeed in expressing themselves later in our own times."

Valery Bryusov, eminent poet and Pushkin scholar, wrote: "Alexander Pushkin became the father of the whole Russian Literature. When genius is combined with great intelligence, eager for knowledge, and with indefatigable industry, we get a Titan of Literature, like Pushkin. Till now, our literature has not outlived Pushkin; till now in all directions when it tries to break through, it meets landmarks, put down by Pushkin to indicate that he knew and saw the path."

Alexander Tvardovsky said on the occasion of the one hundred twenty-fifth anniversary of Pushkin's death in 1962: "Our Pushkin is a living, active force, a mighty factor in Soviet Literature and Art, and in our multi-national socialist culture. His poetry is a treasured heritage that belongs to the entire Soviet People.

We Soviet Poets and Writers regard Pushkin as our teacher, the highest model of artistic values, the founder of our aesthetic code, and in him we find support in our quest and aspirations."

Masonic Documentation: Mille Volti Di Massoni di Giordano Gamberini 1975.

◊ ◊ ◊

A. PHILIP RANDOLPH
(1889–1979)
Founder and International President of the Brotherhood of Sleeping Car Porters, Vice President of the American Federation of Labor and the Congress of Industrial Organization (A.F.L. & C.I.O.) and Member of Joppa Lodge #55, Prince Hall Masonic Lodge of New York

Organized the "March on Washington" Movement for Jobs and Freedom.

Founder and Editor of *The Messenger Magazine.*

Awarded the Spingarn Medal (N.A.A.C.P.) and the Medal for Freedom.

Education
Bethune-Cookman College
City College of New York

Organized the Shakespearean Society while a student at the City College of New York.

Thirty-Third Degree, Ancient and Accepted Scottish Rite of Freemasonry, Prince Hall Affiliation, Northern Jursidiction of the United States of America.

◊ ◊ ◊

CHARLES B. RANGEL
Lawyer and Congressman

Born in New York City, June 11, 1930.

Education
New York University, B.S., Business Administration (1957)
St. John's University Law School, LL.B. (1960)

Positions
Assistant District Attorney, Southern District of New York
Assemblyman, New York State Assembly, 1966–1970
Congressman, U.S. Congress, 1970–1980

Member of the law firm of Weaver, Evans, Wingate & Wright, Harlem Lawyers Association, Martin Luther King, Jr., Democratic Club, Fordham University Council, and Prince Hall Masons.

Masonic Documentation: Schomburg Library of Black History and Culture.

◊ ◊ ◊

DR. W. L. RANSOME
Editor-in-Chief, *The Bee Hive*, Official Publication, Most Worshipful Prince Hall Grand Lodge of the State of Virginia, Free and Accepted Masons, Inc. and Past Grand Master of the Most Worshipful Prince Hall Grand Lodge of the State of Virginia

Dr. W. L. Ransome, Past Grand Master and Editor-in-Chief, has made *The Bee Hive*, a non-partisan and non-sectarian publication devoted to the Grand Lodge and printing news of interest to Masons as well as news of general interest, and it is distributed through second class mail.

Masonic Documentation: Southern Masonic News.

◊ ◊ ◊

PETER W. RAY
Medical Doctor

Past Worshipful Grandmaster, New York State and Jurisdiction, Prince Hall Freemasons (1868).

The first black medical official of King's County Medical Society (1868).

Commander-in-Chief, Supreme Council of Scottish Rite Freemasons.

Brother Peter W. Ray was a well-known physician in the Williamsburg section of Old Brooklyn, New York. He was the first black medical officer of King's County Medical Society.

Commander-in-Chief of Scottish Rite Supreme Council of Freemasonry.

Masonic Documentation: The Phylaxis Society.

CHARLES L. REASON
Poet and Educator
Member of African Lodge #459
of Philadelphia, Pennsylvania

CHARLES L. REASON was born of parents who fled from battle during the revolution of 1793. He attended the African Free School and was considered a good scholar. He earned extra money helping other students.

In 1844 Reason was appointed Professor of Belles Lettres at New York Central College, in McGrawville, New York. After serving for a few years, he resigned to accept an appointment as Director of the Institute for Colored Youth in Philadelphia. Among his many contributions to the institute, he also broadened the curriculum by adding an appreciation of culture.

Charles Reason wrote remarkable poetry. His immortal poem entitled, "Free," was hailed by literary critics as the best "Anti-Bellum poem written by a Black man." He also wrote another great poem entitled, "The Spirit Voice or Liberty Call to the Disfranchised."

Masonic Documentation: The Williamson Collection, the Schomburg Collection, the New York State Grand Lodge Library and Museum.

◊ ◊ ◊

KING SOLOMON REED
Thirty-Third Degree

Retired Master Sergeant, thirty-five years of service.

Grand Inspector General, Bison Consistory Number Twenty-Nine, Buffalo, New York, Ancient and Accepted Scottish Rites, Prince Hall Affiliate, Northern Jurisdiction of the United States of America.

Past Master, Mount Sinai Lodge Number Fifty-Six, Jamestown, New York.

Past District Deputy Grand Master, 7B District.

Past Commander-in-Chief, Bison Consistory Number Twenty-Nine, Buffalo, New York.

Noble, Hadji Temple Number Sixty-One, Buffalo, New York.

Past Most Wise and Perfect Master, Erie Chapter of Rose Croix, Buffalo, New York.

◊ ◊ ◊

HIRAM R. REVELS
United States Senator, Secretary of the State of Mississippi and Minister of the African Methodist Episcopal Church

Hiram R. Revels was born in Fayetteville, North Carolina, on September 1, 1822. He was the first black man elected to the United States Senate from the State of Mississippi (February 25, 1870).

Education
Quaker Seminary, Ordained Minister
Knox College, Galesburg, Illinois, B.A.

Former school teacher in St. Louis, Missouri; President, Alcorn University; active in Masonic affairs.

Masonic Documentation: Williamson Masonic Collection, Schomburg Library.

◊ ◊ ◊

GRANT REYNOLDS
Attorney

Deputy Regulations Administrator United States Department of Housing and Urban Development.

Treasurer, Northside Center for Child Development.

Chief Counsel and Contract Negotiator for The Police Benevolent Association of Greenburg, New York.

Member: American Bar Association, National Bar Association, American Trial Lawyers Association.

Thirty-Second Degree, Prince Hall Freemasonry and Imperial Shrine.

Former Trustee, Cleveland Urban League and Past President of the Cleveland Branch, N.A.A.C.P.

President, Westchester Clubman, Inc.

Documentation: Who's Who Among Black Americans.

◊ ◊ ◊

HOBSON R. REYNOLDS
Organizational Leader

Past Worshipful Grand Master of Prince Hall Grand Lodge of the State of Pennsylvania and Jurisdictions.

Thirty-Third Degree, Ancient and Accepted Scottish Rite of Freemasonry, Northern Jurisdiction, Prince Hall Affiliation, United States of America.

Grand Exalted Ruler of Improved Benevolent Protective Order of Elks of The World, 1960.

Chairman of The Board of Trustees, Cheyney State College, Pennsylvania.

Representative of Pennsylvania General Assembly.

Ebony Magazine voted Hobson Reynolds one of the most influential Black men in the United States.

Documentation: *Who's Who Among Black Americans, 1976–1977.*

◊ ◊ ◊

WILLIAM J. RICHARDSON
Past Grand Master of Prince Hall Mason of the Grand Lodge of the State of New York and Jurisdictions and Sovereign Grand Inspector General, Thirty-Third and Last Degree, Scottish Rite of Free and Accepted Masonry, United States of America

PAST GRAND MASTER WILLIAM J. RICHARDSON became a Freemason in 1958 by joining Joppa Lodge Number Fifty-Five (55) in New York City.

Member of King David Consistory Number Three, Ancient and Accepted Scottish Rite of Freemasonry. He also served as Worshipful Master of Joppa Lodge Number Fifty-Five (55).

Member of Medina Temple Number Nineteen (19), Nobles of the Mystic Shrine.

Besides being a member of the Urban League and the N.A.A.C.P., Past Grand Master Richardson is honorary member of eleven lodges of Delaware and Illinois.

Masonic Documentation: Prince Hall Sentinel.

RONALD DEL RINSLAND
Educator and University Official

Earned his Educational Doctorate at Columbia University in 1954.

Assistant Dean of Student Affairs, Columbia University 1960–66.

Registrar and Director of the Office of Doctoral Studies at Teacher's College, Columbia University, 1972.

Director of Philosophy Degrees in Education, at Columbia University.

Life Member, The National Education Association.

Thirty-Second Degree, Ancient and Accepted Scottish Rite of Freemasonry, Prince Hall Affiliation, Northern Jurisdiction, United States of America.

Biography in *Dictionary of International Biography*.

Documentation: Who's Who Among Black Americans, 1980–81.

◊ ◊ ◊

JOSEPH JENKINS ROBERTS
(1809–1876)
First President of the Republic of Liberia, Father of Prince Hall Freemasonry in the Republic of Liberia, and Second Grand Master of Liberia's Prince Hall Freemasonry (1869–1872)

JOSEPH JENKINS ROBERTS was born in Norfolk, Virginia on March 15, 1809. He was well educated and self-confident.

While a youth, his family moved to Petersburg, Virginia, and at the time of his father's death, had accumulated a substantial amount of wealth for a free black man of his day. Thereafter, he went to Africa to seek fame and fortune.

In June 1978, the people of Petersburg, Virginia, dedicated and unveiled a marble monument in sacred memory of its native son, His Excellency, Joseph Jenkins Roberts, First President of the Republic of Liberia and a Prince Hall Freemason.

There is a marble monument of his full stature in the center of the City of Monrovia and his picture appears on numerous Liberian Postage Stamps of the Republic of Liberia (1848, 1850, 1876, 1961 and 1966).

Masonic Documentation: The Phylaxis Society Magazine and a personal visit to Monrovia, Liberia.

◊ ◊ ◊

PAUL ROBESON
(1898–1976)
Lawyer, Actor and Concert Artist
Made a Prince Hall Mason on Sight

PAUL ROBESON, the youngest of seven children, was born in a parsonage in Princeton, New Jersey, on April 9, 1898. His father, Reverend W. D. Robeson, reared Paul in a Christian home with cultured surroundings.

Education
Rutgers University, B.A., 1919, Phi Beta Kappa
Four-year scholarship and fifteen letters in
four major sports in four years (football,
basketball, baseball and track).
All-American end, Walter Kemp's selection.
Columbia University Law School, LL.B., 1923.

Elected to The Order of Coit, distinguished legal fraternity. Paul passed the New York Bar examination and was admitted to the practice of law. After securing employment in a Wall Street law firm, Robeson resigned after encountering racial discrimination. He then turned his attention to his interest in the theatre and acting.

After a short time playing minor roles and parts, including a brief appearance on the English stage, Robeson turned his attention to the Provincetown Theatre in Massachusetts, where he made a powerful impression in two plays by Eugene O'Neill. *All God's Chilun Got Wings,* and *The Emperor Jones.* Thereafter, Paul Robeson, the tall, handsome and powerful black man with a dynamic presence was soon to be regarded as an actor with major promise.

In 1928 Robeson sang "Old Man River," a song to be identified with him throughout his life. It was the hit from his performance in the musical, *Show Boat,* in which he starred in London, England. Another outstanding stage performance for which Robeson will be remembered was Shakespeare's *Othello,* in which he was Othello. He opened playing the lead thirteen years later on New York's Broadway.

In 1933 Robeson went to Hollywood to make his first American film, the screen version of *Emperor Jones.* He subsequently made several more including, *Sanders of the River, Show Boat,* and *King Solomon's Mine.*

He was author of a book entitled, *Here I Stand.*

Statement
"The artist must elect to fight for freedom or for slavery. I have made my choice. I had no alternative."

Honors
The Spingarn Medal, N.A.A.C.P.

Biography
Who's Who in America
International Who's Who
International Biographical Dictionary

Masonic Documentation: Williamson Masonic Collection, the Schomburg Library of Black History and Culture.

◊ ◊ ◊

SUGAR RAY ROBINSON
World's Middleweight Boxing Champion,
World's Light Heavy Boxing Champion and
Member of Joppa Lodge #55,
New York City Prince Hall Freemasonry

RAY ROBINSON, born in Detroit, Michigan was a Golden Gloves boxing champion. After turning to professional boxing, he won both the Middleweight and the Light Heavy Weight boxing championships of the world. He was a successful New York City businessman and a member of Joppa Lodge #55, Prince Hall Masons of New York City.

Masonic Documentation: Ten Thousand Famous Freemasons by William R. Denlow.

◊ ◊ ◊

EBENEEZER A. SACKEY
Doctor

District Grand Master of The Republic of Ghana, and The Forty-Four Lodges in Ghana.

Awarded, The Order of The British Empire, 1968.

Documentation: Masonic Year Book For 1981–82, United Grand Lodge of England.

◊ ◊ ◊

PRINCE SAUNDERS

PRINCE SAUNDERS, a Teacher in the African School, in Boston, Massachusetts, and a Prince Hall Freemason. He was initiated into the African Lodge in the year of 1809, and became Secretary of the Lodge, two years later. He studied at Dartmouth College, and became a man of remarkable attainments and versatility. Later he became a member of the Prince Hall African Lodge of Philadelphia, Pennsylvania.

Saunders was the founder and an active member of the "Belles Lettres Society", a literary group of young white men of Boston. He won the friendship and esteem of numerous prominent white brother masons, including but not limited to William Ellery Channing, William S. Shaw and William Wilberforce.

When Saunders visited England as a delegate of the Masonic Lodge of Africans, who held a charter from England, he bacame acquainted with England's Royal Duke, who was head of the craft, was liked, and was immediately introduced into the highest circles. The nobility walked arm and arm with Prince Saunders through the streets of London, England.

"The Life of Prince Saunders," appears in the autobiography of William Bentley Fowle.

While in England William Wilberfore, persuaded Prince Saunders to visit Haiti and meet Emperor Christophe. Thereafter, he organized an educational system in Haiti on the English Lancastrian plan. In 1816, he introduced vacination to the Island of Haiti. And Emperor Christophe made him his Special Envoy to England. In England, Prince Saunders published, "The Haitian Paper.

Returning to the United States of America, Prince Saunders became a reader in "Saint Thomas Episcopal Church", founded by Rev. Absolom Jones, a fellow Freemason. Also he took an active part in the "American Anti-Slavery Convention.

Prince Saunders returned to Haiti, after the overthrow of Emperor Christophe. President Boyer made him, the Attorney General for the Republic of Haiti. Brother Saunders died in Port Au Prince, Haiti in 1839.

Masonic Documentation: Williamson Prince Hall Masonry, The Schomburg Collection of Black History and Culture.

◊ ◊ ◊

RUBEN SEBESTIAN SCHOFIELD
Attorney at Law

Partner, Chance and Schofield.

Director, Newark Housing Development and Rehabilitation Corporation, and Community Development Administration of Newark, New Jersey.

Former Attorney, Charles E. Smith Management Corporation.

Former Attorney, Law firm of Chance, Mitchell & McFadden.

Administrator, Newark Legal Services.

Attorney, Office of The Mayor of The City of New York. (Model City Program.)

Adjunct Lecturer in Criminal Law and Procedure, Bronx Community College of The City of New York.

Education
B.A., Clark College, Atlanta, Georgia.
LL.B., Howard University School of Law, Washington, D.C.
Rutgers University, Graduate School of Business
(Graduate Seminar)

Masonic Affiliations: Joppa Lodge #55, F. & A.M., Prince Hall Affiliations. Legal Redress Staff Member of Prince Hall Grand Lodge.

Member: The American Bar Association, The Harlem Lawyers Association, and The Association of the Bar of The City of New York.

Documentation: Personal Interview and Prince Hall Grand Lodge.

◊ ◊ ◊

ARTHUR ALFONSO SCHOMBURG
(1874-1938)
Grand Secretary Prince Hall Masons State of New York

ARTHUR ALFONSO SCHOMBURG, born in San Juan, Puerto Rico on January 24, 1874. Curator at the Fisk University Library, Writer of hundreds of articles, letters, and made numerous speeches on and about the black experience. He was also the Grand Secretary of Prince Hall Masons in the State of New York. An awardee of the Springarn Medal by the National Association for the Advancement of Colored People, for his distinguished service and monumental contribution to raqcial equality and educational advancement.

Schomburg spent most of his life collecting books and material, that would establish the greatness, past and present of African and American black people. He collected over five thousand volumes of books, three thousand manuscripts, two thousand etchings and portraits, along with thousands of pamphlets, which the New York Public Library purchased in 1926, and established the Schomburg Collection of the Library Division of Black Literature, History and Prints, elevating the collection to a level unmatched in America.

Masonic Truths, A Letter and a Document—written by Arthur A. Schomburg, while he served as Grand Secretary of Prince Hall Masons of New York. However, Brother Schomburg's legacy to future generations is irreplaceable, considering the rare and current books, manuscripts, etchings and portraits, along with thousands of pamphlets, in The Schomburg Center for Research in Black Culture.

◊ ◊ ◊

ROBERT M. SEARLES
Grand Inspector General, Thirty-Third Degree of the Ancient and Accepted Scottish Rite of Freemasonry, Prince Hall Affiliation, Northern Jurisdiction, of The United States of America and Keeper of the Archives

ROBERT M. SEARLES, a member of Tuscan Morning Star Lodge, number forty-eight (48) of Philadelphia, Pennsylvania, and DeMolay Consistory, Number one of Philadelphia, Pa. He served as "Most Wise and Perfect Master of Adoniran Chapter, number One, Knights of Rose Croix. A member of Pyramid Temple, #1, (One.) A.E.A.O.N.M.S.

Illustrious Robert M. Searles, was elevated to the Thirty-Third Degree, in May 1975, and thereafter elected, "Keeper of the Archives."

◊ ◊ ◊

JOHN HERMAN HENRY SENGSTACKE
Publisher

President, Robert S. Abbot Publishing Company, Inc.

President, Sengstacke Publications.

President, Amalgamated Publishers, Inc.

Board Member: Illinois Federal Savings and Loan Association, Golden State Mutual Life Insurance Company, Bethune Cookman College, and Washington Park Y.M.C.A.

Member of the Board of Trustees: Hampton Institute and Allen University.

Awards: Commander of The Stars of Africa by President William V. S. Tubman and Distinguished Service Award by President Paul Magloire of Haiti.

Thirty-Third Degree, Ancient and Accepted Scottish Rite of Freemasonry, Prince Hall Affiliation, Northern Jurisdiction, United States of America.

Documentation: The Chicago Negro Almanac and Reference Book.

◊ ◊ ◊

HERBERT BELL SHAW
Paster Master of James E. Shepard Lodge of Free
and Accepted Masons
Prince Hall Masonic Grand Lodge of
North Carolina
Past Grand Master of Prince Hall Masons
of The Worshipful Grand Lodge of
Prince Hall Masons of North Carolina and Jurisdiction
Presiding Bishop of the First Episcopal District
of the African Methodist Episcopal Zion Church
which includes New York State, New England,
Bahama Islands, Trinidad-Tabago, Jamaica,
West Indies, and London-Birmingham, England Conferences.

BISHOP HERBERT BELL SHAW, was born February 9, 1908, in Wilmington, North Carolina.

Education
St. Emma Prepartory School, Rock Castle, Virginia. Fisk University, BA. Nashville, Tennessee. Howard University, MA. Washington, D.C. Livingston College, Doctorate of Divinity. Salisbury, North Carolina.

Achievements
Pastor, (1929-1937) African Methodist Episcopal Church. Secretary-Treasurer, Department of Home Missions. Second Vice President of the National Council of Churches of Christ in the United States of America. Presidium member of the World Council of Churches. Member, General Commission of Army and Navy Chaplains. Chairman of the Bi-Centennial Celebration of Methodist in America.

Biographical sketch of Bishop Herbert Bell Shaw.

Achievements
Delegate—8th World Methodist Conference, Oxford University 1950). Delegate—9th World Methodist Conference, Lake Junaluska, (1956). Delegate—10th World Methodist Conference, Oslow, Norway (1961). Chairman of the Board of Trustees, Livingston College Salisbury, North Carolina. Trustee, Clinton Junior College, Rock Hill, South Carolina. Trustee, Lomax-Hamon College, Greenville, Alabama. Trustee, Jackson Memorial Institute, Batesville, Mississippi. Ebony Magazine, twice elected Bishop Herbert Bell Shaw, as one of the one hundred most influential black persons in America. He was a Philanthropist, Humanitarian, Church-Expansionist, Champion of Freedom and Friend of Mankind.

◊ ◊ ◊

ROBERT A. SIMMONS
Masonic Official
Second Vice-President of The Phylaxis Society
Chairman of The Committee on Bogus Masonry, The Phylaxis Society

Chairman of the Credential Committee of The Most Worshipful Prince Hall Grand Lodge of the State of New York.

Master Mason, Mount Moriah Lodge #107, Prince Hall.

Thirty-Second Degree, King David Consistory #3, A.A.S.R., Prince Hall.

Documentation: Tenth Anniversary Journal of The Phylaxis Society.

◊ ◊ ◊

WILLIAM JOSEPH SIMPKINS
Army Officer

Director of Personnel & Community Activity, Walter Reed Medical Center.

Executive Officer, United States Army Medical Command, Korea, 1978–79.

Chief of Personnel & Division of Troop Command, Eisenhower Medical Center, Fort Gordon, Georgia.

Executive Officer, McDonald Army Hospital, Fort Eustis, Virginia.

Thirty-Second Degree, Keystone Consistory #85, Free and Accepted Masons.

Awarded: Legion of Merit, Office of the Surgeon General, and the Meritiorious Service Medal, Fort Gordon, Georgia.

Born in Edgefield, South Carolina.

Documentation: Who's Who Among Black Americans, 1980–1981.

◊ ◊ ◊

NORVELL J. SIMPSON
Property Control, Control Manager, and Executive Director

Executive Director, Pikes Peak Community Action Progress, Inc. (1972–74).

Production Coordinator, T.R.W., 1971–72.

Master Sgt., United States Army Air Force, 1975.

First Black Person elected to District eleven (11) School Board, Colorado Springs, Colorado.

Commissioner, Colorado Springs Human Relations Commission.

Advisory Board, Pikes Peak Mental Health & Family Relations.

Thirty-Second Degree, Pikes Peak Consistory #81. (F. & A.M.)

Potentate, Shrine Temple, Colorado Springs, Colorado.

Member, National Urban League and N.A.A.C.P.

◊ ◊ ◊

NOBLE SISSLE
(1889–1975)
Lieutenant—U.S. Army—Drum Major—Violinist
Song-Writer
Lyricist and Orchestra Leader

Awardee of the, "Ellington Medal," presented at Yale University, and called "The Conservatory Without Walls."

Member
Medina Lodge #19, F. & A.M., Prince Hall Freemasonry.

Noble Sissle, was a breaker of racial barriers. He and his Orchestra were the first black orchestra leader with orchestra to play at the Ritz Carlton, in New York, according to Actress and Singer, Lena Horne. Sissle's musical, "Shuffle Along," created a partnership with Eubie Blake, and opened doors for black writers, musicians and entertainers.

After graduating from High School at the age of twenty-one, in 1911, Sissle entered DePauw University, in Greencastle, Indiana, but after one year transferred to Butler University in Indianapolis, where he attended college and worked.

Sissle helped to write and produce the pageant, "O' Sing A New Song," which in 1934, was staged in Chicago's Soldier Field. Thereafter, The Sissle Orchestra played a long term engagement at Billy Rose's Diamond Horseshoe 1938–1942.

Documentation: New York City Lodge for Research. (Prince Hall.)

◊ ◊ ◊

F. HERBERT SKEETE
Bishop

Bishop, The African Methodist Churches of Philadelphia and Pennsylvania Jurisdiction.

Former Senior Minister, Salem United Church of New York. (Developed Community Program, Outreach Program and Senior Citizens Program.)

Masonic Affiliations: Beacon Light Lodge #76, New York, N.Y.

Documentation: Beacon Light Lodge #76, New York, N.Y.

◊ ◊ ◊

HERMAN LAWSON SLAUGHTER, SR.
**Director of Masonic Education
of the Most Worshipful Prince Hall
Grand Lodge of Indiana and Jurisdiction
Thirty-Third Degree, Ancient
and Accepted Scottish Rite of Freemasonry
Prince Hall Affiliation, Western Jurisdiction
United States of America**

Organized and was first worshipful master of the Lawson E. Slaughter Lodge of Research, under the administration of Most Worshipful Edgar J. Davis, Grandmaster.

Organized the Temple Builder's Study Club 1952—Established a Masonic Library.

Founder and the First Dean of the Central District Masonic School. Mason of the Year of the Central District.

Draftman in the United States Army, with rank of Technical Sgt. Past Master of Central Lodge, Number One. (1957)

Served
Thrice Potent Master of Henry Rogan Lodge of Perfection. First Lieutenant in the Consistory.

Member
Oriental Band of Persia, Temple #46.

The Lawson E. Slaughter Lodge of Research is now a Phylaxis Society Chapter, A Society of Prince hall Freemasons who seek more light and have light to impart.

◊ ◊ ◊

ROBERT SMALLS
Pilot and Captain of the Steamer Planter
Congressman
Prince Hall Freemason
United States Senator

ROBERT SMALLS, born on April 5, 1839, at Beaufort, South Carolina. Being born a slave limited his opportunities for gaining book knowledge; but he was one of many men, who can be no more bound than the waves of the ocean, and despite all opposition he learned to read and write. Where there's a will, there's a way.

In 1851, Robert Smalls, moved to Charleston, South Carolina, where he worked as a "rigger," thus becoming familiar with ships, and the life of a sailor, by actual experience. Later, he became connected with the Planter, a steamer plying plying the harbor of Charleston as a transport in 1861.

The report in the House of Representatives, Forty-seventh Congress, Second session, 1887. The Document was a Bill, authorizing the President of the United States to place Robert Smalls, on the retired list of the U.S. Navy. It stated that Robert Smalls was Pilot and Captain on board "The Planter," and "The Crusader," between Charleston and Beaufort, South Carolina.

On January 23, 1888, recommended to the Committee on Naval Affairs and ordered to be printed Bill House Resolution #7059. The bill didn't pass as there was no grounds, nor precedent for placing a civilian on the United States Naval Retired List.

However, after the Planter was put out of Commission in 1866, Captain Smalls, was elected a member of the State Constitution Convention. He was the idol of both the delegates, and the people, whose faith in him was unbounded. He is popular to this day.

1868, Captain Robert Smalls, was elected to the United States Congress, where he introduced the Homestead Act, and secured passage of the Civil Rights Bill.

1870, Captain Smalls, was elected to fill the unexpired term of Senator Wright, who was appointed Associated Justice of the United States Supreme Court.

1872, Elected United States Senator defeating General W. J. Whipper. His record in the Senate was brilliant, consistent, and indeed he led in all the most prominent measures. Senator Smalls was acknowledged to be a powerful and superior debater. Member of the Committee on Finance. Chairman, Committee on Public Printing.

Delegate: The Republican National Convention. Senator Smalls, nominated Grand and Wilson, for President and Vice-President of the Republican Party. At the next convention, he nominated Hayes and Wheeler, for President and Vice-President.

Masonic Documentation: New York City Lodge for Research. (Prince Hall.)

◊ ◊ ◊

CHARLES R. SMITH
Watchmaker

President of the North Carolina Watchmakers Association.

Member of The Phylaxis Society.

Thirty-Third Degree, Ancient and Accepted Scottish Rite of Freemasonry, Southern Jurisdiction, Prince Hall Affiliation, United States of America.

Documentation: *The Phylaxis Newsletter, Vol. VI, No. 2, July 1983.*

◊ ◊ ◊

HARRY E. SMITH, 33°
Toledo, Ohio
25th Imperial Potentate
Ancient Egyptian Arabic Order Nobles Mystic Shrine
1980–1982

HARRY E. SMITH was born in Toledo, Ohio.

Education
Liberty High School, Toledo
Paul Quinn College, Waco, Texas
University of Toledo

Retired superintendent for Champion Spark Plugs.

First Black to serve on the Champion Spark Plug Credit Union Board of Directors.

First Black to serve on the Toledo Civil Service Commission.

First Black president of the Toledo Chapter of the National Management Association.

Served 31 months in the United States Air Force with 9 months service in the Philippine Islands as Battalion Sergeant Major.

Masonic membership: Past Master, Amazon Lodge #4, F. & A.M. Past Commander-in-Chief, St. Matthews Consistory #24, AASR. Past Potentate, Mecca Temple #43, AEAONMS.

Masonic Documentation: Georgia Masonic Research Center.

◊ ◊ ◊

J. J. SMITH
Past Grand Master of The Prince Hall Grand Lodge of Massachusetts (F. & A.M.)

Member, African Lodge #459 (1846).

Past Grand Master J. J. Smith conducted the dedication service in 1895, when Prince Hall Masons throughout the United States dedicated a monument to Prince Hall in Boston, Massachusetts.

Documentation: New York Prince Hall Lodge for Research. History of Freemasonry Among Negroes In America, by Harry E. Davis.

◊ ◊ ◊

JOSCELYN E. SMITH
Judge

Judge, Civil Court, City of New York.

Former Assistant, Corporation Counsel of New York City.

Former Counsel for the Borough of the County of Queens.

Former Counsel for the Joint Legislative Committee on Interstate Cooperation of New York State.

Adjunct Professor, Queens College, Flushing, New York.

Past Master, African Lodge #63.

Chairman, Education & Scholarship Committee of the Prince Hall Grand Lodge of New York State.

Thirty-Third Degree of Scottish Rite Freemasonry, Northern Jurisdiction, Prince Hall Affiliation, United States of America.

Education
Julliard School of Music
Howard University
Long Island University
Brooklyn Law School

Lieutenant Colonel (Ret.), Judge Advocate General's Office, United States Army.

Documentation: The Prince Hall Sentinal, Fall 1985, Grand East, State of New York.

◊ ◊ ◊

JOSHUA BOWEN SMITH
1813–1879
Legislator and Caterer

Representative in Massachusetts Legislature from the City of Cambridge.

Renowned Caterer in Boston and Cambridge, Massachusetts.

Member: Saint Andrews Masonic Lodge of Cambridge, Massachusetts, and Royal Arch Mason in Saint Andrews Royal Arch Chapter in South Boston, Massachusetts.

Knighted in Saint Omar Commandery, K.T., South Boston, Mass., 1869.

There's an extended memorial of Brother Smith in the Lodge of Perfection and references in Boston newspapers of December 1, 1867, and in The Lodge of Saint Andrews and Massachusetts Grand Lodge records of 1870.

Masonic Documentation: Negro Freemasons In White Lodges After 1870, by Harold Van Buren Voorhis.

◊ ◊ ◊

GUSTAVE M. SOLOMON
Electrical Engineer

Electrical Engineer, New England Power and Construction Company. Supervising Electrical Engineer, Bethlehem Steel Corporation.

Education
Massachusetts Institute of Technology (Engineering degree)

"The Gustave M. Solomon Transportation Career Center," in The Cambridge School in Massachusetts, was dedicated in 1977.

Thirty-Third Degree, Ancient and Accepted Scottish Rite of Freemasonry, Prince Hall Affiliation, Northern Jurisdiction, United States of America.

Deputy for The State of Massachusetts on behalf of The United Supreme Council.

◊ ◊ ◊

JAMES J. SPELLMAN
Special Correspondent The New York Tribune
Justice of the Peace
Baptist Layman
State Senator, Alderman
Official of Freemasonry, State of Mississippi

JAMES J. SPELLMAN was born in Norwich, Connecticut on January 118, 1841. He attended the schools of Connecticut. In 1855, he moved to New York, N.Y.

In 1859, Spellman engaged in newspaper work, serving as carrier. Later he advanced to Dealer, then Editor, Publisher and finally Proprietor. He was a regular contributor to, "The Angelo African," in New York.

When President Abraham Lincoln called for troops after the Civil War was declared, Spellman was among the first to assemble at the Metropolitan Designation point in New York City. He and the other black men were dispersed by the New York City Police, on the theory that "the tender of colored men to the government would exasperate the South."

In 1868, Spellman went to Mississippi under the auspices of the Freedman's Bureau, and engaged actively in educational work.

In 1869, he was appointed "Justice of the Peace," and "Alderman," for the City of Canton, by General A. Ames, Military Commander. Thereafter, he was elected to the "Mississippi State Senate, from Madison County, and was appointed Chairman of the Committee on Corporations. Also serving on the, "Board of Trustees of Alcorn University, and was elected Secretary of the Board.

1872, Delegate to the Republican National Convention, at Philadelphia, and was chosen President elector. 1876, Rules Committee member.

◊ ◊ ◊

JAMES ROBERT SPURGEON
Thirty-Third Degree
Past Master, Carthaginian Lodge #47
Member of the Grand Lodge of Liberia.
Grand Senior Warden of Liberia.
Member: United States Legation at Monrovia, Liberia.

JAMES ROBERT SPURGEON, while in the position of Grand Senior Warden of Liberia, delivered an Address to The Grand Lodge of Liberia, on December 27, 1899, under the title, "The Lost Word," comprising twenty pages and it was printed in Liberia in 1900, as it contained pictures of prominent Liberians, who were both members of the craft, and officials of Government.

Masonic Documentation: President V. Tubman's private papers. Late Liberian President.

◊ ◊ ◊

VINCENT STACKHOUSE
Past Master of Mount Zion Lodge #90
New York City

Imperial Deputy of The Oasis of Brooklyn, New York, Alu Bekr Temple #91.

Documentation: The Prince Hall Sentinel, Vol. 36, No. 2, Summer 1986.

◊ ◊ ◊

JOSEPH I. STATION
Grand Inspector General, Thirty-Third Degree,
Ancient and Accepted Scottish Rite of Freemasonry,
Prince Hall Affiliation, Western Jurisdiction,
United States of America
Past Worshipful Grand Master of the Prince Hall
Grand Lodge of Freemasonry of the
State of Washington
Past Commander-in-Chief, Prince Hall Consistory
Number Sixty-Seven (67)
Past Master Hercules Lodge Number Seventeen (17)

JOSEPH I. STATION, was educated in the State of Washington and graduated from the University of Washington, School of Journalism.

Thereafter, he was a reporter and feature writer for The Northwest Herald News. Theatre Manager of The Washington Repetory Theatre. As a tradesman, he was an accomplished carpenter.

◊ ◊ ◊

HARRY STEPHENS, JR.
Grand Secretary of the Most Worshipful Prince Hall Grand Lodge
State of New York, and Jurisdictions
Retired Civil Servant, City of New York

HARRY STEPHENS, was born in New York, New York in 1916.

Positions in Freemasonry: Past Master, Crispus Attuck Lodge, #60. Rising Sun, Number 4, R.A.M. Medina Temple, Number 19.

King David Consistory, #3, of the Ancient and Accepted Scottish Rite, Affiliated with Prince Hall Freemasonry, Northern Jurisdictions, Thrity-Second Degree.

◊ ◊ ◊

HOPE STEVENS
Attorney and Corporate Director
Senior Law Partner: Stevens, Hinds, Jackson & White

President, United Mutual Life Insurance. (1956–1960). Former Chairman and Director, Harlem Urban Development Corporation. Former Chairman and Director, The Carver Federal Saving and Loan Association. Former President, The Uptown Chamber of Commerce of New York City. (Presently serves as General Counsel.) Co-Founder of Allied Federal Saving and Loan Association of Queens, New York. Founding Member of The World Association of Lawyers. National Co-Chairman of The National Conference of Black Lawyers. (Elected October 1975.) Former Member of the Executive Committee of The Association of the Bar, of the City of New York. Member, Alpha Lodge #116, Free and Accepted Masons of New Jersey. Member, Allied Lodge #1170, Free and Accepted Masons of New York. Former Member of the Committee on Character and Fitness of the Appellate Division of the Supreme Court, First Department, State of New York.

Education
City College of the City of New York,
B.A. 1933.
Brooklyn Law School of St. Lawrence University.
(Degrees LL.B. and LL.M., 1937.)

Masonic Documentation: Attorney Hope Stevens personal file of biographical notes.

◇ ◇ ◇

LEON H. STEWART
Recipient of Copley First Citizen Award by The Springfield State Journal and Registered in the Hall of Fame.

Owner and Manager, Stewart Service Station. Former President of The Springfield Urban League. Former President, The Frontier International. Former President, The Springfield Council of Churches. Awarded The Webster Plaque, by the National Association for the Advancement of Colored People for Meritious Community Service.

Scoutmaster and Director, Springfield Unit of The Boy Scouts of America.

Thirty-Third Degree, of Ancient and Accepte Scottish Rite of Freemasonry, Prince Hall Affiliation, United States of America.

Masonic Documentation: The Bulletin, Official Organ, United Supreme Council.

◇ ◇ ◇

308

CARL B. STOKES
Former Mayor of Cleveland, Ohio
News Reporter Nationalwide News

CARL B. STOKES, the first black elected Mayor, of Cleveland, Ohio, a major city in the United States was raised to Master Mason, by the Most Worshipful Herbert R. Bracken, Grandmaster, of the Most Worshipful Grand Lodge of Ohio, before more than three hundred members at the Cleveland Symbolic Blue Lodge, at The Prince Hall Temple.

Masonic Documentation: The Schomburg Library of Research in Black History and Culture.

◊ ◊ ◊

LOUIS STOKES
Congressman and Attorney at Law
Member of Pythagoes Lodge #9
Prince Hall Masonic Order

CONGRESSMAN LOUIS STOKES was born in Cleveland, Ohio, on February 23, 1925.

Education
Western Reserve University.
Cleveland Marshall Law School.

Board of Trustees: Martin Luther King Center for Social Change. Cleveland State University. Saint Paul A.M.E. Church. Forest City Hospital.

◊ ◊ ◊

CLIFFORD J. STORY
Thirty-Third Degree
Past Potentate, Medina Temple, Number Nineteen
Past Commander-in-Chief, Kind David Consistory,
Number Three,
Ancient Accepted Scottish Rite,
Affiliation Prince Hall Freemasonry
Thirty-Third Degree, Northern Jurisdiction
United States of America.

Past Master, Lewis Hayden Lodge, Number Sixty-Nine. Past High Priest, Widows Sons, Number One. Past Potentate, Medina Temple, Number Nineteen. Pst Thrice Illustrious Master, Alpha Council, Number One.

◇ ◇ ◇

THOMAS W. STRINGER
Worshipful Grand Master of the Grand Lodge
of the State of Mississippi and its Jurisdictions
1866–1893
District Deputy Grand Master for Masons in the
State of Pennsylvania and its Jurisdictions.
Worshipful Grand Master of the Grand Lodge of the
State of Ohio, and its Jurisdictions.

GRAND MASTER THOMAS W. STRINGER, was the organizer of Richmond Lodge, number four (4.) in the City of New Orleans, on March 5, 1849. Later, he secured a place for Richmond Lodge, number four (4.) on the Roster of the Grand Lodge of Ohio.

Masonic Documentation: Worshipful Grand Master, Earle L. Bradford, Grand Master of Prince Hall Masons of Louisiana and its Jurisdictions.

◇ ◇ ◇

FRANK M. SUMMERS, 33°, Active
East St. Louis, Illinois
Sovereign Grand Commander
United Supreme Council, AASR, N.J.
1973–1977

FRANK M. SUMMERS, attorney-at-law, Masonic and civic leader, was born August 13, 1893, in Marion, Illinois.

Education
Indiana University
Harvard Law School
Chicago Kent Law School

Past Grand Polemarch, Kappa Alpha Psi Fraternity.

Made survey of public housing and public health in Mexico City, Mexico.

Served four years as Commissioner of Illinois Court of Claims.

Senior law partner of former law firm of Summers and Orr.

Was first Illustrious Deputy-Orient of Wisconsin, AASR, in 1950.

Masonic membership: Raised in North Star Lodge #1 (1922) Chicago. Past Master, Joppa Lodge #79, F. & A.M. Past Commander-in-Chief, Tyree Consistory #64, AASR. Past Imperial Potentate, Aahmes Temple #132, AEAONMS. Honorary Past Grand Master of Illinois. Past Deputy for Illinois, AASR.

Masonic Documentation: Georgia Masonic Research Center.

◊ ◊ ◊

GEORGE BENJAMIN SWANSTON
Secretary of Prince Hall Military Lodge #140
Frankfurt, Germany
District Deputy Grand Master of the
Eighth Masonic District of Western Europe
Commander in Chief of Prince Hall
Military Consistory #304.
First Imperial Deputy of the Desert of Western Europe
(A.E.A.O.N.M.S.)
Illustrious Potentate 1966.
Deputy of the Year at the Eighty-First
Imperial Council Session.
(Philadelphia, Pennsylvania.)
Staff Member of the Controller Division,
United States Army, Frankfort, Germany
Thirty-Third Degree, Ancient and
Accepted Scottish Rite of Freemasonry
Prince Hall Affiliation, Southern Jurisdiction
United States of America
Jurisdiction Oklahoma.
Tenor Singer with the Metropolitian Opera
Home Boy's Choir.
(At age fourteen years.)

GEORGE BENJAMIN SWANSTON, was born in New York City, New York on December 8, 1911. He was a graduate of the City College of New York, with a major in accounting.

The George Benjamin Swanston Masonic Lodge, and a charity foundation is named in his honor with the purpose to perpetuate his memory and to continue his monumental work.

Masonic Documentation: Brother Michael A. Delgado, of the George Benjamin Swanston Memorial Medallion.

◊ ◊ ◊

GARDNER CALVIN TAYLOR
Educator and Minister
Member: Consistory #179, Ancient and Accepted Scottish Rites of Freemasonry, Prince Hall Affiliation, Northern Jurisdiction, United States of America
Former Member of the Board of Education of New York City.

GARDNER CALVIN TAYLOR, was born in Baton Rouge, Louisiana, on June 18, 1918.

Education
Leland College (A.B., 1937)
Oberlin Graduate School of Theology (B.D., 1940)

Pastorate
The Concord Baptist Church of Christ (1948 to Present.) Eight thousand and four hundred members added since 1948. Church was destroyed by fire in October 1952, New Structure completed April 1, 1956, at cost of One million seven hundred thousand dollars. ($1,700,000.00) The church operates a fully accredited Elementary School designed to give children at the earliest scholastic levels the disciplines that train for leadership roles in society.

Past President, Council of Churches, City of New York. Past Vice President, The Urban League of New York City. Lecturer on Preaching: Harvard Divinity School (1970-1975.) Lyman Beecher Lecturer, Yale Divinity School 1975.

Former member—General Council, American Baptist Convention. Author: "How Shall They Preach," 1976 Lyman Beecher Lectures. Yale University. International Honors: Knight Commander, Order of African Redemption conferred by President William V.S. Tubman, and the Republic of Liberia, Spring 1969. Order of the Star of Africa, conferred by President Willialm R. Tolbert, Jr., and the Republic of Liberia., in 1973.

Contributor to Publications
Anthology: "Why I Believe There Is A God."

"The Best Sermons of 1959."
"The Cry of Freedom."
Former member of the Board of Education of The City of New York.

◊ ◊ ◊

ROSWELL A. TAYLOR, SR., MPS, 33°
Alexandria, Virginia
26th Imperial Potentate
Ancient Egyptian Arabic Order Nobles Mystic Shrine
1982–1984
Past Grand Master
M. W. Prince Hall Grand Lodge of Virginia

ROSWELL A. TAYLOR was born in Culpepper County, Virginia. He is a printer by trade and retired from the federal government in 1966.

Masonic membership: Past Master, Acacia Lodge #32. Past High Priest, Eureka Chapter #3, RAM. Past Commander-in-Chief, Shadrack Jackson Consistory #156. Past Potentate, Magnus Temple #3, AEAONMS.

Masonic Documentation: Georgia Masonic Research Center.

◊ ◊ ◊

SAMUEL COLERIDGE TAYLOR
(1875–1912)
The First Modern Black To Achieve World Fame As A Composer.
Member of The Grand Masonic Lodge of England.

BROTHER SAMUEL COLERIDGE TAYLOR was recognized as one of the great composers. The wide sweeps of his creations proved that he was universal in sympathy land feeling; and like other "Titans of the Arts," he was of all times, and of all people.

Brother Samuel Taylor's (Coleridge) visit to America was a triumph. President Theodore Roosevelt entertained him at the White House, and American Society, both white and black, lionized him.

Note: His father Dr. Daniel Hughes Taylor, Physician and Surgeon, and an African by birth was unusually able, a brilliant doctor, and an extraordinary surgeon, who at the age of twenty-two, was elected to the "Royal Academy of Physicians and Surgeons." But the English color prejudice encountered in daily life was too much for his sensitive nature. He abandoned his family and his medical practice and returned to Africa.

Masonic Documentation: W. C. B. Sayers, "Samuel Coleridge Taylor" Cassell Publishers, London 1915.

◊ ◊ ◊

WALTER C. TAYLOR
Most Worshipful Grand Master of Prince Hall Masons, The Grand Lodge of Free and Accepted Masons, State of California and Jurisdictions. Member: West Gate Lodge, Number Thirty-Six, at Oakland, California

Most Worshipful Grand Master Walter C. Taylor, of the Grand Lodge of Prince Hall Masons is best expressed in his statement as it appeared in "The Prince Hall Masonic Digest": "Let the yardstick with which we measure the fruitful labors of Prince Hall Masons, and the Grand Lodge, and its jurisdictions be based upon our collective contribution, and our active participation in all phases, of all programs, working together as Prince Hall Masons, should and will."

Prince Hall Masonic Digest.

WALTER E. TAYLOR

Trainmaster, New York City Transit Authority.

Former Transit Supervisor, New York City Transit Authority.

Worshipful Master of Antioch Lodge #66, in 1979.

Dean of the School of Instructions, Antioch Lodge #66.

Education
Brooklyn College, Brooklyn, New York
Columbia University, New York, N.Y.

President of The Charity Club of Antioch Lodge #66, F. & A.M.

Served in the United States Foreign Services and the United States Army.

◊ ◊ ◊

GEORGE J. THOMAS, THE THIRD
Orthopedic Surgeon

President and Chairman of The Board, T. S. Mining Company.

Fellow of The American College of Surgeons.

Staff Orthopedic Surgeon, United States Naval Hospital.

Orthopedic Surgeon, Granada Hills Community Hospital.

Thirty-Second Degree, Prince Hall Freemason.

Noble, Ancient Egyptian Order Mystic Shrine.

Member: National Medical Association, Naval Institute, N.A.A.C.P., Urban League, and Amnesty International.

Publication: "Compartment Compression Syndromes of the Leg."

Award: Los Angeles Urban League Award.

◊ ◊ ◊

ROBERT THREATT
President
Morris Brown College
(Atlanta, Georgia)

President of Muscogee Teachers and Education Association.

President of Georgia Teachers and Education Association.

President of the College and University Administrators, Higher Education National Association.

Doctorate in Education, from the University of Oklahoma.

Member of Frederick Douglass Lodge #143, Fort Valley, Georgia.

Documentation: Georgia Masonic Research Center.

◊ ◊ ◊

FRANK E. TOLBERT
Senator and Grand Master

Senator, The Senate of The Republic of Liberia, Monrovia, Liberia. (1967.)

The Most Worshipful Grand Master of Grand Lodge of Masons of The Republic of Liberia, 1967.

Commissioner, The Special Commission for the Sesquicentennial Celebration.

Documentation: Private Papers, William R. Tolbert, President, The Republic of Liberia.

◊ ◊ ◊

WILLIAM R. TOLBERT, JR.
(1913–1980)
**Former President of the Republic of Liberia.
Former President of the Organization of African Unity.
Past Worshipful Grandmaster of the
Most Worshipful Prince
Hall Grand Lodge of Liberia**

WILLIAM R. TOLBERT, JR., born in Liberia, in 1913, was the son of a South Carolina slave, who migrated to Africa in 1880, and became a prosperous rice and coffee grower.

Tolbert began his career as a typist with the National Treasury in 1935, and within one year advanced to the post of Government Disbursing Officer, a position he held until elected to the House of Representatives. And in 1951, he became Liberia's youngest Vice-President. On the death of President Tubman, Vice-President Tolbert became the President of Liberia.

As the President Tolbert maintained close ties with the United States, as well as with Firestone Tire and Rubber Company. He established diplomatic relations with the Soviet Union, and Czechoslovakia, while charting an independent course in Foreign policy.

When elected Chairman of the Organization of African Unity, and thereafter President Tolbert worked and concentrated on both African Unity, and on focusing world attention on racial inequalities in the Union of South Africa, while attempting to cement African Unity throughout the Continent.

Masonic Documentation: President William R. Tolbert's Collected Papers.

◇ ◇ ◇

E. REGINALD TOWNSEND
Grand Treasurer of Prince Hall Freemasonry of The Republic of Liberia.

Minister of State for Presidential Affairs.

Thirty-Second Degree, Ancient and accepted Scottish Rite of Freemasons, Valley of Mesurado Consistory #237 of Liberia.

Documentation: Presidential Papers, President William R. Tolbert, Jr. Grand Master of the Republic of Liberia

◇ ◇ ◇

LEVI TOWNSEND, 33° Active
Seattle, Washington
Ill. Deputy for Washington State
Ancient Accepted Scottish Rite, Northern Jurisdiction

LEVI TOWNSEND was born September 28, 1917, in Madison County, Alabama. He is a retired expeditor, Building Property Department of the First National Bank of Seattle.

Education
Alabama A & M College

Life member, Veterans of Foreign Wars, and serves on the Board of Directors-Central Board of Mental Health.

Masonic membership: Past Master, M. L. King, Jr. Lodge #65, F. & A.M. Past Commander-in-Chief, Prince Hall Consistory #67, AASR. Past Potentate, Beni Hassan Temple #64, AEANOMS.

Masonic Documentation: Georgia Masonic Research Center.

◊ ◊ ◊

WILLIAM VACANARAT SHADRACK TUBMAN (1895–1971)
President of the Republic of Liberia, West Africa
Worshiful Grand Master of the Republic of Liberia.
Past Grand Patron of the Order of the Eastern Star.

Sponsor
The first meeting of the Organization of African Unity Monrovia, Liberia., where the Constitution was adopted.

Born: Harper, Maryland, United States of America. 29 November 1895. An arresting personality. Sreved seven terms as President. Founder of "The True Whig Party.

Grand Master Mason of Liberia and Brother in the Mesurado Valley Consistory Number #237, and the Royal Arch Chapter of Masonry. These were instituted by President Tubman. Also, The William V.S. Tubman Lodge, numbers fifteen and sixteen, in Lofa, and Nimba Counties respectively.

The Liberia Official Gazette, reported before the thirty day, National Mourning Period began: "President Tubman, carried his heart in his hands like a palm branch, turning discord into peace, disunity into unity, and chaos into order.

Masonic Documentation: President Tubman's Collected Papers and Letters.

◊ ◊ ◊

HON. JAMES CAMERON TUDOR
**Member of Parliment and Leader of the House.
Minister of State for the Caribbean and Latin America
Master Mason, Freemasonry in Barbados.**

Minister of Education (1961–1967)

Education
Harrison College
Keble College, Oxford University.

Minister Tudor studied the United States Educational Institutions with United States State Department Grant.

Masonic Documentation: International Guide To Who's Who In The West Indies.

◊ ◊ ◊

GEORGE N. TUNNELL
Grand Inspector General, Thirty-Third Degree,
Ancient and Accepted Scottish Rite of Freemasonry,
Prince Hall, Affiliation, Northern Jurisdiction,
United States of America
Pennsylvania State Director of Public Relations
The Most Worshipful Prince Hall Grand Lodge of the
State of Pennsylvania.
Member: De Molay Consistory, Number One,
of Philadelphia, Penna.

GEORGE N. TUNNELL, internationally known as, "Bon-Bon," from his days on National Radio, with Jan Savitt's Band. In 1932, as a member of "The Keys," he toured London, England, and met the Prince of Wales, who later became the King of England, Kind Edward, the Eighth. During the absence of a drummer due to illness, Prince Edward of Wales played the drums in the orchestra for the missing drummer.

George N. Tunnell's hit songs:
"I don't want to set the world on fire."
"Seven twenty, In the Book."
"It's a wonder world."

◊ ◊ ◊

THOMAS RUDOLPH VICKERS, 33°, MPS
Portland, Oregon
M. W. Grand Master
M. W. Prince Hall Grand Lodge of Oregon
1976–78
Imperial Deputy For Oregon
Ancient Egyptian Arabic Order Nobles Mystic Shrine
President
Rose City Chapter, The Phylaxis Society

THOMAS R. VICKERS was born June 22, 1917 at West Palm Beach, Florida, and is a member of Kappa Alpha Psi Fraternity.

Education
Tuskegee Institute High School
Morehouse College
North Carolina A & T
Bethune-Cookman College
University of Portland, B.A.
Portland State University, M.S.
Stanford University
University of Oregon

Vickers served four years in the United States Army, and saw foreign service in North Africa, Italy, and Sicily. He moved to Portland after discharge in 1941.

The Frater has taught in the public schools of Portland, and worked as a career education counselor. He retired December 31, 1982 after more than 29 years.

Noble Vickers has served as president of the Portland Branch-NAACP, and has been Education Director of the Urban League.

Masonic membership: Past Master, Beaver Lodge #3. Past C-in-C, Williamette Consistory #23, AASR. Past Potentate, Mina Temple #68, AEAONMS.

Documentation: Georgia Masonic Research Center.

◊ ◊ ◊

F. R. VINCINAZA

Third District Grand Principal of The District Grand Chapter of The Republic of Nigeria. (Comprised of Thirteen Masonic Chapters.)

Documentation: The Masonic Year book For 1981–82, United Grand Lodge of England.

◊ ◊ ◊

PETER VOGELSANG
Founder and Member—First Prince Hall Masonic Military Lodge
First Lieutenant—Quartermaster Officer
Black Abolitionist and Apostle of Freedom

BROTHER PETER VOGELSANG was born August 21, 1815, in New York City, and he died on April 4, 1887, in New York, New York. He was a Founder and Member of the thirty-five member Chartered Military Prince Hall Lodge. The charter was from Boston, Massachusetts.

Brother Peter Vogelsang advanced from Sergeant to Second Lieutenant, and weeks later, to First Lieutenant. The date June 20, 1863.

Remarkable feats mentioned
"Apostle of Freedom" By Brother Charles H. Wesley.
"Black Abolitionist" By Benjamin Quarles.
"Life and Public Service of Martin R. Delany."
By Benjamin Quarles.

Masonic Documentation: "Black Square and Compass" Two Hundred Years of Prince Hall Freemasonry. By Joseph A. Walkes. "The Schomburg Collection on Black History and Culture."

◊ ◊ ◊

DAVID WALKER
Author and Lecturer

DAVID WALKER, Author and Lecturer, born in approximately 1780. The decade that saw the achievement of American Independence, and the writing of the United States Constitution.

In 1825, after considerable travel throughout the Nation, Walker moved to Boston and set up a used clothing business, which he managed with moderate success the remainder of his life. He was a six footer, slim and powerfully built man who emerged as the leading intellectual in Boston, Massachusetts. He addressed numerous meetings on "Black Unity" and pleaded for an end of complacency.

Walker's early writing and speaking lead to the publication of his only lengthy work, "Walker's Appeal." The book was considered wide-ranging, fiercely lmilitant and unequival in tone, it represented both the rupture, and the advance in the abolitionist writings of the day:

> Bretheren, arise, arise! Strike for your lives, and
> for your liberties. Now, is the day, and the hour.

In 1830, when "Walker's Appeal," was in its third printing, each issue becoming more militant, and enjoying brisk sales, Walker's sudden death caused some conjecture that he had been kidnapped and murdered.

Masonic Documentation: Williamson Colelction on Black Freemasonry.

◊ ◊ ◊

McCLINTON OLYN WALKER
Physician

Medical Officer of The Most Worshipful Prince Hall Grand Lodge of Texas.

Consultant, United States Army Medical Command for Europe.

Chief of Thoracic Cardiovascular Surgery, Second General Hospital, Germany (1977).

Chief of Surgery at the twenty-seventh Surgical Hospital.

Resident Physician at Homer G. Phillips Hospital.

Bronze Star Medal and Meritorious Service Medal, U.S. Army Medical Corp.

Documentation: Who's Who among Black Americans, 1977–1978.

◊ ◊ ◊

PATRICK H. WALKER, JR.
Educator

Vice-President, Cheyney State College, Cheyney, Pennsylvania.

Former Assistant Dean of Men at Morgan State College.

Educator Walker was the first Black Principal of an integrated High School in the State of Delaware, De La Warr High School, Wilmington, Delaware.

Masonic membership: Temple Lodge #8, Milford, Delaware.

Documentation: Georgia Masonic Research Center.

◊ ◊ ◊

WYATT TEE WALKER
Member: Boyer Lodge #1, Prince Hall Masonry.

WYATT TEE WALKER, Minister and former Chief of Staff to Dr. Martin Luther King, Jr., with the Southern Christian Leadership Conference.

Born: Brockton, Massachusetts, August 16, 1929.

Education
Virginia Union University, B.S. Richmond, Va.
Magna cum laude 1950.
Colgate-Rochester, School of Divinity,
Masters of Divinity 1953.
Colgate-Rochester, School of Divinity,
Doctorate of Human Letters, 1967.
Black Christ Studies.

Minister
Canaan Baptist Church of Christ, New York, N.Y.

Rev. Dr. Walker, was the key figure in organizing the International Freedom Mobilization to dramatize the plight of victims of the South African Apartheid, in the Union of South Africa. He was also an invited delegate to the meeting of the Organization of African Unity (O.A.U.) held in Monrovia, Liberia, in July 1979. This was a conference of all the African Heads of State. Dr. Walker served as "Special Assistant to the Governor of New York on Urban Affairs. And Special Assistant to the National Progressive Baptist Convention, and is a member of the "Board of Directors," of Freedom National Bank. He is also one of the principals of the "Black Gospel Collection," an assemblage of the world's greatest gospel music and gospel recording artist.

The author: "Somebody's Calling My Name."

Co-Author: "The Black Church Looks at The Bicentennial."

◊ ◊ ◊

JOSEPH A. WALKES, JR.
Author—Writer—Administrative Assistant
United States Penitentiary, Leavenworth, Kansas.
Thirty-Third Degree, Ancient and Accepted Scottish Rite of Freemasonry, Southern Jurisdiction, Prince Hall Affiliation, United States of America
President, The Phylaxis Society

Member of The Cecil A. Ellis, Sr. Lodge #110., Karlsuhe, Germany Jurisdiction Prince Hall Grand Lodge of Maryland.

Reporter—United Supreme Council—Northern and Southern Jurisdiction—Thirty-Third Degree, Ancient and Accepted Degree of Scottish Rite of Freemasonry—Prince Hall Affiliation, United States of America.

Editor—Masonic Light 1968–1973.

Special District Deputy Grand Master at Large (Military.) Assisted in the formation of the Canal Zone Military Lodge #174, as well as Pythagoras Lodge #175, Athens, Greece.

Worshipful Master, King Solomon Lodge #15, Fort Leonard Woods, Missouri, of the Most Worshipful Prince Hall Grand Lodge of Missouri. Founder and First President, The Phylaxis Society. (1973.) Elected Fellowship in The Phylaxis Society (March 1976.) Awarded the Certificate of Literature, March 1979. Awarded the John G. Lewis, Jr., Medal of Excellence. (1980.) Joseph A. Walkes, Jr., was born in New York City, New York., on November 12, 1933.

Books Published: The Documentary History of King Solomon Lodge, Number 15, (1971.) Black Square and Compass: Two Hundred Years of Prince Hall Freemasonry. (1979.) John G. Lewis, Jr., End of an Era: History of the Most Worshipful Prince hall Grand Lodge of Louisiana. (1849–1979.)

Masonic Documentation: Joseph A. Walkes, Jr., and The Phylaxis Society.

◊ ◊ ◊

SOLOMON WALLACE 33°
Most Worshipful Grand Master of Prince Hall
Grand Lodge of New York State and Jurisdiction

Thirty-Third Degree, Ancient and Accepted Scottish Rite of Freemasonry, Northern Jurisdiction, Prince Hall Affiliation, United States of America.

Documentation: United Supreme Council, Northern Jurisdiction, U.S.A. Inc.

◊ ◊ ◊

JOSIAH T. WALLS
(1842–1905)

JOSIAH T. WALLS, Farmer, Representative in Florida State Legislature, and Congressman from the State of Florida. Born free in Winchester, Virginia, on December 20, 1842. Attended primary schools and later became a successful farmer.

During the Civil War, he was drafted into the Confederat Army, and served in an Artillery Battery, until he was captured by Union forces, at Yorktown. Walls, then attended school in Harrisburg, Pennsylvania. Thereafter joined the Union Army, as a Private, and rose to the rank of Sergeant Major. Later, he became an instructor with the Artillery.

When the War was over he returned to Florida and entered State Politics, and was elected to the Florida House of Representatives, and thereafter to the United States Congress.

Masonic Documentation: Prince Hall Lodge for Research of New York.

◊ ◊ ◊

HENRY GEORGE WALTON
Assistant Treasurer and Member of the
Executive Board of Local #802,
American Federation of Musicians—
Associated Musicians of New York
Past Master of Hiram Lodge Number Four (4)
Past Grand Treasurer of Prince Hall Grand Lodge,
State of New York and Jurisdiction

Past Grand Trustee of Prince Hall Grand Lodge, State of New York and Jurisdiction.

Past Grand Commander of New York State.

Organizer of the Prince Hall Masonic Musical Association, State of New York (1941).

Thirty-Third Degree, Ancient and Accepted Scottish Rite of Freemasonry, Prince Hall Affiliation, Northern Jurisdiction, United States of America.

Past Commander-in-Chief and Life Member of
King David Consistory #3.
Past Potentate and Life Member—Medina Temple #19
AEAONMS.
Past Imperial Potentate—Imperial Council, AEAONMS.
Grand Inspector General—United Supreme Council
AASR—Masonry.
United States Military Service—Rank—Major.

Education
New York University, B.A., Major in Mathematics, N.Y.C.
Ecole Normale de Music, Degree in Music, Paris, France.

Concerts and recordings throughout the United States and Europe. Recorder with: The Musical Spillers, W. C. Handy Group, Eubie Blake Group, The National Five, W. O. R. Radio, New York Concert Orchestra.

Past Imperial Director—Finance and Budget
Imperial Council.

Past Imperial Advisor—Imperial Court, Daughters of Isis.
Past Worthy Patron—Omega Chapter #25, O.E.S.
Member of the Alpha Council #1, Royal and Select Master.

◊ ◊ ◊

BOOKER T. WASHINGTON
(1859-1915)
Founder and President of Tuskegee Institute in Alabama

Owner of *The New York Age,* a leading weekly newspaper.

Autobiography: *Up From Slavery.*

Made a Freemason on sight by the Most Worshipful Grand Master of the State of Massachusetts, although a resident of Alabama.

Historians consider Booker T. Washington, one of the greatest men born in the South, and among the twelve greatest born in the United States of America.

Biographies: *Booker T. Washington: Builder of Civilization,* by Emmett Scott and Lyman Beecher Stowe. *Life and Times of Booker T. Washington,* (1916), by Benjamin F. Riley.

◊ ◊ ◊

GENOA S. WASHINGTON
Attorney at Law

Assistant Attorney General of the State of Illinois.

Delegate to the General Assembly of the United Nations.

First Vice-President of the Cook County Bar Association.

President, The Chicago Branch, N.A.A.C.P.

Former Captain, United States Army.

Past Master, Richard E. Moore Lodge. (F. & A.M.)

Earned a Doctorate of Laws, Northwestern University.

Thirty-Third Degree, Ancient and Accepted Scottish Rite of Freemasonry, Prince Hall Affiliation, Northern Jurisdiction, United States of America.

Documentation: The Chicago Negro Almanac and Reference Book. Edited by Ernest R. Rather.

◇ ◇ ◇

HAROLD WASHINGTON
Mayor

Mayor of the City of Chicago, Illinois.

Former United States Congressman of Chicago.

Masonic Membership: Harmony Lodge, #88, of Chicago, Illinois. Ancient Accepted Scottish Rite, Western Consistory #28. Shrine, Arabic Temple #44.

Among the distinguished witnesses, The Most Worshipful Melvin Frierson, Grand Master of the State of Illinois and Jurisdiction.

Documentation: The Phylaxis, Vol. XII, No. 3, Third Quarter, 1986, by R. W. Joseph Mason Andrew Cox, Grand Historian of New York State and Jurisdiction.

◇ ◇ ◇

JAMES W. WASHINGTON, JR.
Sculptor

JAMES W. WASHINGTON, JR.'s sculpture in stone represents and embodies spiritual ideas and qualities in physical form. His philosophy: "All art expresses varying degrees and states of consciousness, and he uses his art as conscious communion with the Absolute." He is a mystic, somewhat akin to Scientist and Educator George Washington Carver, who expressed himself through communion with peanuts and flowers.

Thirty-Third Degree, Ancient and Accepted Scottish Rite of Freemasonry, Northern Jurisdiction, Prince Hall Affiliation, United States of America.

Documentation: The Winter Bulletin, Official Organ of the United Supreme Council, Prince Hall Affiliation, Northern Jurisdiction, March 1983.

◊ ◊ ◊

WALTER EDWARD WASHINGTON
Chairman, New York City Housing Authority
Commissioner of Washington, District of Columbia
Mayor of Washington, District of Columbia

WALTER EDWARD WASHINGTON, was appointed Commissioner of the District of Columbia, by President Lyndon Baines Johnson, and became the first black chief executive of a major American city.

Washington, the grandson of a slave, was born in Dawson, Georgia, on April 15, 1915, the only child of William L. Washington, a factory worker.

Education
Howard University, B.A., 1938
American University, M.A.
Howard University, LL.B., 1948

He was admitted to practice law in the District of Columbia. He was sworn in as Chairman of the New York City Housing Authority by Mayor John V. Lindsay, on November 22, 1966.

Walter Edward Washington received the Distinguished Achievement Award of the Howard University Alumni Association.

Masonic Documentation: Schomburg Collection on Black Freemasonry.

◊ ◊ ◊

LEVI WATKINS
Educator
President, Alabama State University

Thirty-Third Degree, Ancient and Accepted Scottish Rite of Freemasonry, Prince Hall Affiliation, Southern Jurisdiction, United States of America.

Masonic Documentation: Masonic News Quarterly, Southern Jurisdiction.

◊ ◊ ◊

JAMES L. WATSON
Attorney at Law
Judge of United States Custom Court in New York

Formerly
New York State Senator
New York Civil Court Judge

Thirty-Second Degree Freemason of Prince Hall Affiliation of the Northern Jurisdiction of the United States of America.

Judge Watson was born in New York, New York on May 21, 1922.

Education
New York University, B.A., 1947
Brooklyn Law School, LL.B., 1950

Masonic Documentation: New York State Masonic Library and Museum.

◊ ◊ ◊

FRANCIS EDWARD WATT
Building Contractor

Director of Watt & McDermott Company, Limited.

Director of The National Building Society of The Republic of Jamaica.

Served Building apprenticeship with Jamaica Government Railway.

Master Mason, Arch E. Mark Lodge of Montego Bay.

Served the Government of Jamaica as Senior Inspector and Resident Engineer.

Documentation: Personalities in the Caribbean.

◊ ◊ ◊

JOSEPH D. WEAVER
Physician

Physician and Owner, Weaver Clinic, of Winston, North Carolina.

Chief of Staff, Rosnoke Chowan Hospital.

Medical Examiner, Hertford Company.

Treasurer, Eastern North Carolina Medical, Dental and Pharmacy Association.

Member of The Airplane Owners and Licensed Pilots Association.

Thirty-Second Degree, Ancient and Accepted Rite of Freemasonry. (Prince Hall)

Certificate of Merit, Scottish Rite Freemasons.

◊ ◊ ◊

MARTIN O. WEDDINGTON
Most Worshipful Grandmaster of the Most Worshipful Prince Hall Grand Lodge of Minnesota and Thirty-Third Degree, Ancient and Accepted Scottish Rite of Freemasonry, Prince Hall Affiliation, Northern Jurisdiction, U.S.A.
President—The Thomas H. Lyles Chapter of the Phylaxis Society
Trustee—Prince Hall Building Corporation, District One, St. Paul, Minnesota

Past Master—Ashlar Lodge #4
Commander-in-Chief of the North Star Consistory #14
Vice-Commander, Fourth District American Legion, Ramsey County
Delegate to the American Legion National Convention
President—Twin City Reel and Trigger Club

Member—Urban League—N.A.A.C.P.
Phi-Beta-Sigma Fraternity
Committeeman—Boy Scouts of America
Pilgrim Baptist Church

Masonic Documentation: Personal notes from the file of Brother Weddington.

◊ ◊ ◊

AARON O. WELLS 33°
Medical Doctor

Medical Director for Grants and Credentials, Cancer Control.

Masonic Membership: Prince Hall Lodge #38. King David Consistory AASR. Medina Temple #19 AEANOMS.

Imperial Medical Director.

DR. CHARLES H. WESLEY 33°
Educator, Historian, College President, Fraternal Leader and Religious Leader

President, Central State University, 1947–1965.

President, The Ohio Association of College Presidents and Deans.

President, The Association for the Study of Afro-American Life and History.

Author: *Prince Hall: Life and Legacy*. The History of Prince Hall Grand Lodge of Ohio.

◊ ◊ ◊

JAMES T. WHITE
State Representative—State Senator
Commissioner of Public Works—Minister

JAMES T. WHITE was born August 25, 1837 in New Providence, Clark County, Indiana.

White had a Common School education. However, he professed a belief and a hope in Christ at the age of seventeen, and he became a minister four years later. The year was 1858.

In the spring of 1865, Reverend White was elected a delegate from his church to the Consolidated American Baptist Convention, which met in the City of St. Louis, Missouri. While attending the convention, he received a call and an assignment to a church in Helena, Arkansas.

On his arrival in Arkansas, he found widespread confusion, as would be expected just after the close of the Civil War. The battles fought between Federal and Confederate forces left a defeated and angry Southern group. Nevertheless, Reverend White converted and baptized almost two thousand people with his own hands.

In 1868, Reconstruction of the Southern states took place under the direction of Congress. Reverend White was induced to canvass for Reconstruction and, in the fall of 1868, was elected to the State Convention to frame a Constitution for Arkansas. He assisted the canvass for ratification at the Convention and was elected to the Arkansas House of Representatives, then to the State Senate. Later, the Governor appointed Senator White Commissioner of Public Works and Internal Improvement for the State of Arkansas.

◊ ◊ ◊

REUBEN WHITE, MPS, 33°
Lamarque, Texas
M. W. Grand Master
M. W. Prince Hall Grand Lodge of Texas
1981–Present

REUBEN WHITE was born September 25, 1917, in Shreveport, Louisiana.

Education
Central High School, Galveston, Texas
Texas Southern University

He retired from the United States Air Force as a Master Sergeant and was employed as a heavy equipment operator for American Oil Company.

Former President of the Lamarque Chapter of the NAACP.

Vice-President, Chamber of Commerce.

The only Black to serve on the board of directors of the American Oil Company Federal Credit Union.

Member, The Phylaxis Society.

Masonic membership: Past Master, Lamarque Lodge #373, F. & A.M. Past Patron, Silver Circle Chapter #101, OES. Past Joshua, Sweet Esther Court #327, H of J. Member, Royal Arch Chapter #25. Member,Wynn Consistory #234, AASR. Member, El Kappa Temple #85, AEAONMS.

Masonic Documentation: Georgia Masonic Research Center.

◊ ◊ ◊

JAMES L. WILDER, SR.
District Deputy Grand Master Emeritus

Thirty-Third Degree, Ancient and Accepted Scottish Rite of Freemasonry, Prince Hall Affiliation, Northern Jurisdiction, United States of America.

Worshipful Master, Boyer Lodge, Number One (1936–37).

Secretary, Boyer Lodge, Number One (1938–48).

Past High Priest, Rising Sun Chapter Number Four.

Member of King David Consistory #3.

Past Potentate, Medina Temple #19.

Treasurer, Alpha Council #1, Royal Select Masters.

Documentation: Heritage Antioch Lodge #66, F. & A.M., Prince Hall Affiliation.

◊ ◊ ◊

ARTHUR C. WILLIAMS
Most Worshipful Grand Master of Prince Hall Masons of The State of Alaska and Jurisdictions

Lodge: North Pole, Alaska.

Thirty-Third Degree, Ancient and Accepted Scottish Rite of Freemasonry, Northern Jurisdiction, Prince Hall Affiliation, United States of America.

Documentation: The United Supreme Council, Northern Jurisdiction, Prince Hall Affiliation, United States of America.

◊ ◊ ◊

CHARLES F. WILLIAMS
Grand Master

Most Worshipful Grand Master of Prince Hall Masons of The State of Tennessee.

Thirty-Third Degree, Ancient and Accepted Scottish Rite of Freemasonry, Southern Jurisdiction, Prince Hall Affiliation, United States of America.

Active Member of The United Supreme Council of the Southern Jurisdiction.

Documentation: One Hundredth Anniversary Journal, United Supreme Council, Prince Hall Affiliation, Northern Jurisdiction.

◊ ◊ ◊

NORRELL L. WILLIAMS
Publisher

Publisher and Owner, Midtown Instant Printers.

Publisher and Distributor, *The Phylaxis Magazine.*

Masonic Membership: Blue Valley Lodge #64, Kansas City, Kansas.

Member, The Phylaxis Society.

Documentation: The Phylaxis, Vol. XII, No. 1, First Quarter 1986.

◊ ◊ ◊

PAUL REVERE WILLIAMS
Architect
Thirty-Third Degree Ancient and
Accepted Scottish Rite of Freemasonry,
Prince Hall Affiliation,
Southern Jurisdiction
United States of America

PAUL REVERE WILLIAMS was born in 1896 in Los Angeles, California.

Educated
Howard University and Lincoln University

President
Paul R. Williams Associates

Distinguished Architecture
Los Angeles Airport
United States Federal Custom House
W. J. Sloan and Huggerty, Beverly Hills, California
University of California Campus Building

Books Published
Small Homes for Tomorrow
New Homes for Today

Masonic Documentation: Who's Who Among Black Americans, Schomburg Library, Williamson Masonic Collection.

◊ ◊ ◊

DR. PEYTON WILLIAMS, JR., 33°
Atlanta, Georgia
Associate State Superintendent of Schools
Georgia Department of Education
Chartered First Lieutenant Commander
Lamar Carter Consistory No. 321, AASR
Sylvania, Georgia

DR. PEYTON WILLIAMS, JR. was born April 10, 1942, at Cochran, Georgia. He is a member of Omega Psi Phi Fraternity.

Education
B.S., Fort Valley State College
M. Ed., Tuskegee Institute
Ed. S., University of Georgia
Ph. D., Georgia State University

When the schools in Screven County, Georgia, were desegregated in 1970, Williams was appointed by the Board of Education as principal of Central Middle School, the largest school in the county, with an enrollment of 1,100 students in grades six through nine. Because of its model and innovative approaches in dealing with discipline problems of middle school students, Williams' school was featured in the *Christian Science Monitor*.

He served as organist, choir director, and deacon of St. Paul Baptist Church in Sylvania from 1966 through 1976.

The Frater was the first Black in Screven County to be appointed to the Selective Service Board.

First Black to be named to the Screven County Board of Family and Children Services.

In June of 1977, the Georgia State Board of Education appointed Williams Assistant State Superintendent of Schools. At age 33, he became the first Black in the history of the state of Georgia to serve in this capacity.

He was promoted to Associate State Superintendent of Schools in July of 1978. Dr. Williams is in charge of state-operated schools and special services. He manages a state budget in excess of $12 million with a staff of more than 650 employees.

Honors: 1976: Outstanding Citizens Award, Screven County NAACP; Distinguished Service Award, Lamar Carter Consistory No. 321, AASR; Man of the Year, Georgia Council of Deliberation, AASR. 1977: Meritorious Service Award, Screven County Board of Education. 1978: Administrator of the Year, West Georgia Chapter of Phi Delta Kappa.

First Black educator in Screven County to be named, "Educator of the Year," by the Sylvania-Screven Optimist Club.

Masonic membership: Pearl Juvenile Chapter. Raised, Jeremiah Lodge #182, Cochran. Demitted, Mystic Tie Lodge #39, Sylvania. Member, Lamar Carter Consistory #321, AASR.

Documentation: Georgia Masonic Research Center.

◇ ◇ ◇

WINSTON OSCAR WILLIAMS, 33°, Active
Philadelphia, Pennsylvania
Cathedral Secretary
Editor-The Bulletin
United Supreme Council, AASR, North Jurisdiction

WINSTON OSCAR WILLIAMS was born December 6, 1916, in Panama City, Republic of Panama. His father, a native of Barbados, worked on the Panama Canal. After the official opening of the canal in 1920, the Williams family immigrated to the United States and settled in Philadelphia.

Education
Public schools of Philadelphia
University of Florence, Italy, 1945
Temple University, 1955

Past Master Williams is an Elder of Reeve Memorial United Presbyterian Church. He is a member of the National Council of United Presbyterian Churches. He serves as president of the Synod of the Trinity Council, an organization of 187,000 men in Ohio, Pennsylvania, and West Virginia.

The Frater served in the Army Air Corps during World War II, and in the United States Army during the Korean Conflict.

Noble Williams is a professional class musician who plays symphonic, jazz, and military type music on the bass violin.

Honorary Fellow, The Phylaxis Society.

He served as Chairman, Centennial Anniversary Commemorative Souvenir Journal.

Masonic membership: Past Master, John S. Watson Lodge #23, F. & A.M. Past High Priest, William Cooper Chapter #6, RAM. Past Commander-in-Chief, De Molay Consistory #1, AASR. Past Imperial Potentate, Pyramid Temple #1, AEANOMS.

Masonic Documentation: Georgia Masonic Research Center.

FREDERICK C. WILLIAMSON
State Official

Director of The Department of Community Affairs, State of Rhode Island.

Chairman of The Committee Planning the Thirtieth Anniversary Observance of the National Conference of Christians and Jews, and a member of the National Committee of the Conference of Christians and Jews.

Honoree of The National Committee of Christians and Jews, Brotherhood Award.

Thirty-Third Degree, Ancient and Accepted Scottish Rite of Freemasonry, Northern Jurisdiction, Prince Hall Affiliation, United States of America.

Documentation: United Supreme Council, One Hundredth Anniversary Journal, Philadelphia, Pennsylvania.

◊ ◊ ◊

HARRY A. WILLIAMSON
Author—Lecturer—Researcher
Historian—Man of Letters

HARRY A. WILLIAMSON, founder of the Harry A. Williamson Collection on Black Masonry at the Schomburg Collection of the New York Public Library. Born in New York in 1875.

Masonic Record
Initiated, passed and raised in Mount Olive Lodge Number Two in New York, New York, on March 5, 1904.

Senior Warden—Carthaginian Lodge, U.D., Brooklyn, N.Y., October 18, 1904.

1910—Deputy Grand Lecturer, Second Masonic District of New York
1911—Grand Secretary (served two terms)
1915—Senior Grand Warden (served three terms)
1918—Deputy Grand Master (served three terms)
1920—Chairman of the Diamond Jubilee Celebration.
1911-1924—Grand Historian for thirteen years. During that period he wrote a history of Masonry in New York, covering the years 1812-1910, which was adopted by the Grand Lodge.
1925-1926—Grand Lecturer.

Author
Negroes in Freemasonry
Prince Hall Primer
History of Freemasonry Among Negroes

Membership
Manchester Association for Masonic Research
Manchester, England
Dorsett Master's Lodge #3366, Poole, England
National Masonic Research Society of U.S.A.

◊ ◊ ◊

ALBERT WILSON
Most Worshipful Grand Secretary of the Most Worshipful Prince Hall Grand Lodge of New York State and Jurisdictions and Secretary of Downshire Lodge or Progressive Lodge Number Twelve of New York City, N.Y.

ALBERT WILSON, a black American who was a member and Secretary of Downshire Lodge or Progressive Lodge Number Twelve, a Lodge composed entirely of Hebrews of German extraction, with the exception of Secretary Wilson, working under the Authority of the Most Worshipful Prince Hall Grand Lodge. Brother Wilson was also Most Worshipful Grand Secretary of the Most Worshipful Prince Hall Grand Lodge. This is one of the most interesting facts in American Masonic history.

After Wilson's death, Downshire Lodge or Progressive Lodge Number Twelve changed to Shakespeare Lodge Number Seven Hundred Fifty under the Jurisdiction of New York Grand Lodge (Caucasian Lodge).

Masonic Documentation: A History of Freemasonry Among Negroes in America, by Harry E. Davis; A Chronological History of Prince Hall Masonry—1784–1932, by Harry A. Williamson; and Black Square and Compass—Two Hundred Years of Prince Hall Freemasonry, by Joseph A. Walkes, Jr.

◇ ◇ ◇

CARL LYNWOOD WILSON 33°
Architect

CARL L. LYNWOOD was born on December 24, 1921, in Warren, Ohio. He is a member of the Waymon A.M.E. Church, Dayton, Ohio.

Secretary General H.E. from 1975 to 1983.

Education
Ohio State University, Columbus, Ohio

Masonic membership: Progress Lodge #85, Sandusky, Ohio. L. D. Easton Consistory #21, Columbus, Ohio. Past Master, Progress Lodge #85. Past Grand Master, Grand Lodge of Ohio. Member, Johnson Chapter #3, Columbus, Ohio. Member, Boone Commandery, Lawton, Ohio.

Masonic leadership: Past Commander-in-chief, L. D. Easton #21, Columbus, Ohio. Grand Inspector-General, Supreme Council. Past Potentate, Alla Baba Temple #53, Columbus, Ohio. Past Potentate, Imperial Council.

Created Thirty-Third Degree in May 1957 and crowned in 1975.

◇ ◇ ◇

PAUL LAWRENCE WILSON
Past Master, Doric Lodge
Chairman, Board of Trustees, Doric Lodge
Past Grand Master of Prince Hall Masons
in the State of Iowa
President of A. G. Clark Chapter
of the Phylaxis Society—A Society
for Prince Hall Freemasons Who Seek More
Light and Have Light to Impart

PAUL LAWRENCE WILSON was born in Buxton, Iowa, and is a product of Doric Lodge Number Thirty (30). He has been a Prince Hall Mason for more than thirty years. He is also a member of William Frank Powell Consistory Number Forty-Six (46).

◊ ◊ ◊

ANDREW A. WOMACK
Clergyman

Pastor, Mount Haven Baptist Church of Virginia.

President, Black Minister's Conference (1950–1951).

President, Interracial Minister's Conference.

Chairman, Foreign Missionary Division of the Baptist Conference.

President of Virginia N.A.A.C.P.

Thirty-Third Degree, Ancient and Accepted Scottish Rite of Freemasonry, Prince Hall Affiliation, Southern Jurisdiction, United States of America.

◊ ◊ ◊

GRANVILLE T. WOODS
(1856–1910)
Freemason — Inventor — Engineer

GRANVILLE T. WOODS attended school until he was ten years of age. Thereafter, he worked in a machine shop on the Missouri railroad. However, his education and training was supplemented with mechanical engineering training and study at an Eastern College in 1876. Two years later he became an engineer on "The Ironsides," a British Steamer. In 1880, Woods operated a steam locomotive on the D&S Railroad. Thereafter, Woods started his own company, The Woods Railway Telegraph Company in Cincinnati, Ohio.

Woods obtained United States Government Patents for the following:
>Steam Boiler, 1884
>Incubator, 1900
>Automobile Air Brakes, 1902

He held many inventions for American Bell Telephone and the General Electric Company. Westinghouse Air Brake Company bought his air brake patent. Later, Woods invented the Induction Telegraph, a system for communicating to and from moving trains.

The prolific fertility of Granville T. Woods, mechanical genius, is evidenced by and in more than thirty-five patents that he secured from the United States Patent Office.

Masonic Documentation: Masonic Grand Lodge of New York, F. & A.M., Library.

◊ ◊ ◊

JOSHUA WOODLIN
Minister
Member of the African Grand Lodge of Pennsylvania
Member of Hiram Grand Lodge of Pennsylvania

JOSHUA WOODLIN was a minister and an important black Masonic writer and author.

Books Authored
The Masonic National Union
A History of the Origin of Ancient Freemasonry Among Colored Citizens of the United States of America

Masonic Documentation: Prince Hall Lodge for Research of New York.

◊ ◊ ◊

CLEO W. WOOTEN
(1903–1982)
Historian
Prince Hall Grand Lodge of the State of Massachusetts

Thirty-Third Degree, Ancient and Accepted Scottish Rite of Freemasonry, Prince Hall Affiliation, Northern Jurisdiction, United States of America.

Member: Castle Williams Lodge, #11, the Syria Temple Shrine, The Phylaxis Society, and the N.A.A.C.P.

Documentation: The Bulletin, United Supreme Council, Northern Jurisdiction, Prince Hall Affiliation, United States of America.

◊ ◊ ◊

ALBERT WALTER WRIGHT, JR.
Certified Public Accountant and Educator

Professor of Accounting at California State University.

Former Professor of Business at Texas Southern University.

Educational Achievement Award, National Association of Black Accountants.

Member: Prince Hall Masonic Lodge #19. American Accountants Association. National Association of Black Accountants. Beta Gamma Sigma Honor Society.

Publications: "Net Income and Extraordinary Changes and Credits." "Maintaining Balance in Financial Position."

Documentation: Who's Who Among Black Americans, 1977-78.

◊ ◊ ◊

JONATHAN J. WRIGHT
(1840-1885)
Lawyer—State Senator—Associate Justice of the Supreme Court of the State of South Carolina

From 1866 to 1868, Attorney Jonathan J. Wright was employed by the Freedman's Bureau to give legal aid to emancipated slaves. Later, he attended the South Carolina Constitutional Convention and was elected State Senator from Beaufort, South Carolina.

In 1870, Senator Wright was elected Associate Justice of the Supreme Court of South Carolina to fill the unexpired term of Justice Solomon L. Hoge, who resigned to be a Congressional candidate. During his term of office, Justice Jonathan J. Wright wrote eighty-seven opinions for the Supreme Court of South Carolina.

Masonic Documentation: The Grand Lodge Library of New York State, F. & A.M.

◊ ◊ ◊

C. T. ENUS WRIGHT
President
Cheyeny State College

Member of the Commission for College and University Presidents.

Former Vice-President for Academic Affairs at Talladega College, Talladega, Alabama.

Member: Tuscan Lodge #38, Monroe, Georgia. Atlanta Consistory #24, Atlanta, Georgia. Sakkara Temple #196, Spokane, Washington.

Documentation: Georgia Masonic Research Center.

◊ ◊ ◊

LEONARD STANFORD WRIGHT
Jeweller

Managing Director, Wright's Jewellery Limited of Jamaica.

Master Mason—Lodge of Imperial Service #978, S.C.

Membership
Kensington Cricket Club

Watchword
"Do unto others as you would have done unto you."

Masonic Documentation: International Guide to Who's Who in the West Indies.

◊ ◊ ◊

LOUIS TOMKINS WRIGHT
Medical Doctor and Surgeon
Thirty-Third Degree, Ancient and
Accepted Scottish Rite of Freemasonry,
Prince Hall Affiliation, Northern Jurisdiction
United States of America
Chairman of the Board of Directors
of the National Association for the
Advancement of Colored People

DR. WRIGHT was the first black doctor appointed to a New York City municipal hospital (1919). He served for more than thirty years.

Captain in the United States Army Medical Corps.

Chief of Surgery at New York's Harlem Hospital.

Dr. Wright invented an intradermal vaccination against smallpox, and, under his supervision, the first tests on aureomycin were performed on humans.

Dr. Wright graduated from Harvard Medical College in 1915 at the age of twenty-four. While a student at Harvard College Medical School, he was not allowed to deliver babies at Boston-Lying-In-Hospital because he was black. He fought the issue and threatened to take the matter to court if necessary. The issue was resolved in his favor and all color barriers were removed. Thereafter, black medical students were treated like all other students.

Masonic Documentation: New York State Masonic Library and Museum, Williamson Masonic Collection, the Schomburg Library.

◊ ◊ ◊

RICHARD ROBERT WRIGHT, SR.
(1855–1945)
Businessman and Educator

Grand Inspector General—Thirty-Third Degree, Ancient and Accepted Scottish Rite of Freemasonry, Prince Hall Affiliation, Southern Jurisdiction, United States of America.

Graduated from Atlanta University.

Founder of Savannah State College, 1891, Savannah, Georgia.

In 1921, Brother Wright moved to Chicago, Illinois, where he founded the Citizens and Southern Bank and Trust Company.

Masonic Documentation: Afro-American Encyclopedia, the Phylaxis Society, the Williamson Collection, Schomburg Library.

◊ ◊ ◊

ANDREW YOUNG
Mayor of Atlanta, Georgia, 1982

Thirty-Third Degree, Scottish Rite of Freemasonry, Prince Hall Affiliation, Southern Jurisdiction, United States of America.

Former United States Congressman, Fifth District of Georgia.

Former United States Ambassador to the United Nations.

Born in New Orleans, Louisiana, March 2, 1932.

Education
Dilliard University and Howard University
Hartford Theological Seminary

Mayor Young was associated with the late Dr. Martin Luther King, Jr., in the Civil Rights Movement and organized the Citizens Education and Voter's Right Committees.

Officer
Southern Christian Leadership Conference

Biography
Dictionary of International Biography
Who's Who in America
Who's Who in Colored America

Mayor Young is the first black Congressman to represent the State of Georgia since Congressman Jefferson Long (1870–1871).

Member of the Board of Directors
World Council of Churches
Americans for Democratic Action
Martin Luther King, Jr., Center for Social Change

Masonic Documentation: Most Worshipful Grand Lodge of Georgia.

◊ ◊ ◊

COLEMAN A. YOUNG
Mayor
The City of Detroit, Michigan

National Democratic Committeeman.

Military Service: Second Lieutenant United States Army Air Force.

Masonic Affiliations: Abiff Lodge #21, F. & A.M. Wolverine Consistory #6.

Thirty-Third Degree, Ancient and Accepted Scottish Rite of Freemasonry, Northern Jurisdiction, Prince Hall Affiliation, United States of America.

◇ ◇ ◇

WHITNEY MOORE YOUNG
(1921-1971)
Executive Director—National Urban League
Dean of Nebraska School of Social Work (1954-1961)
Member of Prince Hall Rescue Lodge #4, Omaha, Nebraska

BROTHER WHITNEY MOORE YOUNG, an American educator, social work administrator and civil rights leader, was born in Lincoln Ridge, Kentucky, on July 31, 1921.

Education
Kentucky State College, B.A., 1941
University of Minnesota, M.A., 1947

Record
In his ten years as National Urban League Administrator, Brother Young helped 54,000 blacks find jobs and raised forty-five million dollars for practical programs such as Street

Academies for high school drop outs and also established job training facilities in over one hundred cities.

Brother Whitney Moore Young was a credit to Masonry and humanity.

◊ ◊ ◊

PROFOUND APPRECIATION FOR INVALUABLE ASSISTANCE:

1. Joseph A. Walkes, Jr.
   President and Fellow of the Phylaxis Society.
   A Society of Prince Hall Freemasons who seek more light and have light to impart.

2. The staff of the Williamson Prince Hall Masonic Collection of the Schomburg Center for Research in Black History and Culture.

3. Allen Boudreau, Ph.D., Librarian and Curator, the Grand Lodge Library (Free and Accepted Masons), State of New York.

4. Ira S. Holder, Sr.
   Fellow of the Phylaxis Society
   Past Grand Historian, Most Worshipful Prince Hall Grand Lodge of the State of New York.

5. Past Master E. Thomas Oliver.
   Antioch Lodge #66, Free and Accepted Masons, Prince Hall Affiliation.

6. Records and papers from the Prince Hall Lodge for Research of New York.

7. Most Worshipful Paul J. Cooper, Past Grandmaster of the Most Worshipful Prince Hall Grand Lodge of New York State and Jurisdiction.

8. Wylton James, Art Director, Scholastic Magazine.

MOST WORSHIPFUL PRINCE HALL, GRANDMASTER

Grandmaster Prince Hall envisioned love, freedom and brotherhood
Although his days were arrested by darkness at noon,
Nights transfigured and measureless
And the American Nation oblivious to its mountainous paradox,
Countless termites inherent in its ideological contradictions,
The fantasy of unenvisioned love, freedom and brotherhood.
Yet, racism, inequality, fear and doubt were household dogs.
Proudly, the American Nation proclaimed equality for all men,
Nevertheless, the legitimacy of slavery in almost the same breath,
As the Brotherhood rescuers moved from reality to fantasy.
Grandmaster Prince Hall's message was loud and clear, Brotherhood!
Brotherhood for economic, political, social freedom, and more.
Dark days and transfigured nights dictated the mode of adjustment,
And the Anatomy of Minority Survival under Majority Domination,
Place the Gold Square, Silver Compass, and the Holy Book, at the closed metal guarded door.
Grandmaster Prince Hall's legacy of Love, Equality and Brotherhood,
Should be interpreted to mean never allow the limitation of Time,
Nor the erosion of memories to deaden the heart's longing, in its
Morning demand for Love, Freedom and Brotherhood.

Joseph Mason Andrew Cox
Historian
Antioch Lodge #66,
Prince Hall, F. & A.M.

REFERENCES

News Quarterly, United Supreme Council, 33° Ancient and Accepted Scottish Rite of Freemasonry, Southern Jurisdiction, Prince Hall Affiliation, U.S.A.
The Bulletin, Official Organ of the United Supreme Council, Ancient and Accepted Scottish Rite of Freemasonry, Prince Hall Affiliation, Northern Jurisdiction, U.S.A.
History of Freemasonry Among Whites and Negroes in America, Melvin M. Johnson.
Black Square and Compass—Two Hundred Years of Prince Hall Freemasonry, Joseph A. Walkes.
Ten Thousand Famous Freemasons, William R. Denslow.
The Afro-American Encyclopedia, Educational Book Publishers.
Encyclopedia Britannica.
Americanna Encyclopedia.
The Beginning of Freemasonry in America, Melvin M. Johnson.
Who's Who in America.
The International Who's Who.
The Beginning of Black Nationalism, Martin R. Delaney.
Victor Ullman, Beacon Press.
Masonic Truths—A Letter and a Document, Arthur Schomburg.
History of Freemasonry Among Colored People in America, William H. Grimshaw.
Encyclopedia of American Biography, John A. Garraty.
Prince Hall—Life and Legacy, Charles Wesley, Ph.D.
The Crisis, Official Magazine of the N.A.A.C.P.
The Harry A. Williamson Collection of Black Masonry, Harry A. Williamson.
The Phylaxis, Official Organ of the Phylaxis Society.
The Making of a Mason, George Draffen.
Men of Mark, William Simmons.
The Black Presence in the American Revolution, (1770-1800), Sidney Kaplan.
The Colored Patriots of the American Revolution, with Sketches of Several Distinguished Colored Persons, William Nell.
Conditions and Prospects of Colored Americans, Introduction by Harriet Beecher Stowe.
The Negro in the American Revolution, Benjamin Quarles.
Mille Volti Di Massoni Di Giordano Gamberini, Roma, 1975.

A Chronological History of Prince Hall Freemasonry, 1784–1932.
The Williamson Collection of the Schomburg Library of New York.
Marquis—Who's Who in the World, (1978–1980).

Don King,
Inducted into the Boxing Hall of Fame in 1997. Supporter of several charities, which include NAACP, the United Negro Fund, Martin Luther King, Jr. Foundation, among other charities. Awarded the Black Achievement Award, and named Man of the Year by the Black United Fund and Brother Crusade, recipient of Martin Luther King Jr. Humanitarian Award from Southern Christian Leadership women's Conference membership in 1987. Received honorary doctorate degree from South Shaw University. Don King is a member of the Prince Hall Masonry.

Carter G. Woods,
Education received B.A. in 1907, M.S. in 1908, Ph.D. from Harvard in 1912. Director and Editor of the Journal of Negro History. National Council for the Social Studies established the Carter G. Woods neritous Books award. Carter G. Woods was an educational supervisor in the Philippines. Carter G. Woods was a member of the Prince Hall Masonry.

Asa Philip Randolph,
Trade unionist and civil-rights leader, co-founder of employment agency in 1912. Also co-founded the magazine named Messenger, renamed to The Black Worker in 1929. 1925 founding president of the Brotherhood of Sleeping Car Porters, A. Philip Randolph built the first successful black trade union. Randolph founded the league for Nonviolent Civil Disobedience Against Military Segregation. First president (1960-66) of the Negro American Labor Council, became Vice President of AFL-CIO, he was a director of the March on Washington movement for jobs and Freedom. A. Phillip Randolph formed the A. Philip Randolph Institute for community leaders to study the cause of poverty, also a Spingarn medallist, he received his Doctorate from Columbia University before retirement from the labor movement. Worked for the unification of Prince Hall Masonry.

AUTHORS GUILD BACKINPRINT.COM EDITIONS are fiction and nonfiction works that were originally brought to the reading public by established United States publishers but have fallen out of print. The economics of traditional publishing methods force tens of thousands of works out of print each year, eventually claiming many, if not most, award-winning and one-time best-selling titles. With improvements in print-on-demand technology, authors and their estates, in cooperation with the Authors Guild, are making some of these works available again to readers in quality paperback editions. Authors Guild Backinprint.com Editions may be found at nearly all online bookstores and are also available from traditional booksellers. For further information or to purchase any Backinprint.com title please visit www.backinprint.com.

Except as noted on their copyright pages, Authors Guild Backinprint.com Editions are presented in their original form. Some authors have chosen to revise or update their works with new information. The Authors Guild is not the editor or publisher of these works and is not responsible for any of the content of these editions.

THE AUTHORS GUILD is the nation's largest society of published book authors. Since 1912 it has been the leading writers' advocate for fair compensation, effective copyright protection, and free expression. Further information is available at www.authorsguild.org.

Please direct inquiries about the Authors Guild and Backinprint.com Editions to the Authors Guild offices in New York City, or e-mail staff@backinprint.com.

0-595-22729-5

Printed in the United States
29612LVS00004B/160-162